Something to Declare

Terrace Books, a trade imprint of the University of Wisconsin Press, takes its name from the Memorial Union Terrace, located at the University of Wisconsin–Madison. Since its inception in 1907, the Wisconsin Union has provided a venue for students, faculty, staff, and alumni to debate art, music, politics, and the issues of the day. It is a place where theater, music, drama, literature, dance, outdoor activities, and major speakers are made available to the campus and the community. To learn more about the Union, visit www.union.wisc.edu.

Something to Declare

Good Lesbian Travel Writing

Edited by

GILLIAN KENDALL

———

Terrace Books

A trade imprint of the University of Wisconsin Press

Terrace Books
A trade imprint of the University of Wisconsin Press
1930 Monroe Street, 3rd Floor
Madison, Wisconsin 53711-2059

www.wisc.edu/wisconsinpress/

3 Henrietta Street
London WCE 8LU, England

1   3   5   4   2

Printed in the United States of America

Library of Congress Cataloging-in-Publication Data
Something to declare: good lesbian travel writing / edited by Gillian Kendall.
p.   cm.
ISBN 978-0-299-23354-9 (pbk.: alk. paper)
ISBN 978-0-299-23353-2 (e-book)
1. Lesbian authors—Travel.   2. Lesbians—Travel.
3. Travelers' writings.   I. Kendall, Gillian.
HQ75.25.S66   2009
910.4086'643—dc22
2009010255

"Fruits at the Border" by Lucy Jane Bledsoe originally appeared in *Lodestar Quarterly* 14 (Summer
2005), reprinted by permission of the author; "A Friend in America" by Gillian Kendall originally
appeared in *The Sun* 262 (October 1997), reprinted by permission of the author; "Bashert" by Lesléa
Newman originally appeared in *She Loves Me, She Loves Me Not* (Los Angeles: Alyson Books, 2002),
© 2002 by Lesléa Newman, reprinted by permission of the author; "Postcard: A Story" by Ruthann
Robson originally appeared in *Harrington Lesbian Literary Quarterly* 8.2 (2007): 65–79, reprinted by
permission of the author; "Shopping" by Lauren Sanders originally appeared in *Lodestar Quarterly* 14
(Summer 2005), reprinted by permission of the author; "Outrageous" by Sheila Ortiz Taylor originally
appeared in *OutRageous* (Midway, FL: Spinsters Ink, 2006), © 2006 by Sheila Ortiz Taylor, reprinted
by permission of the author.

Contents

Acknowledgments

First I want to acknowledge all the women who submitted work to this anthology and shared their travel adventures; I wish we'd had more room to include more of the funny, strange, and beautiful stories. Also, I would like to thank my family and friends (and the friends of friends) around the globe who make the world a welcoming place for lesbians and for travelers of all kinds.

Raphael Kadushin, senior acquisitions editor at the University of Wisconsin Press, honored me with the offer of editing this collection, sister to his own two wonderful travel anthologies, *Wonderlands: Good Gay Travel Writing* and the recently published *Big Trips: More Good Gay Travel Writing*. Both he and my editor, Sheila Moermond, have been delightful, diligent, and down-to-earth as we wrestled this collection into place, aided by intern Nicole Kvale and publicist Chris Caldwell. I'm also indebted to Erin Holman for her excellent copyediting.

Something to Declare

Introduction

GILLIAN KENDALL

On this, the first day of autumn in Melbourne, Australia, I woke up to see orange, blue, and yellow hot-air balloons wafting above my house. I'm glad when I get up early enough to see these sunrise flights, even though I haven't yet taken the ride myself. Just watching their bulbous shapes and hearing the whoosh of bellows makes me happy for the people up there, looking down at my neat garden and brick house.

For some reason, I don't get travel envy (to which I'm usually prone) from watching the people in those Wizard-of-Oz baskets, cruising aloft with their binoculars and champagne brunches. In the same way, while putting together this collection, I felt encouraged—not jealous—as I read about other lesbian travelers, even when they'd been to countries I haven't seen. Choosing the best ones to share was as hard as saying which balloon is the prettiest and most alluring.

If you're reading this, you probably already have an opinion about the definition of "lesbian," let alone the word "travel." I was clear on those concepts, too, before I started editing this collection. But I had to wonder exactly What Makes a Lesbian a Lesbian when I got pieces that contained no reference to sexuality or orientation: they were just about places and people. Women. Who were, one assumed, lesbians. But, then, what defines lesbianism? (Yawn.) I didn't care: I just wanted to hear good stories.

But some of those good stories concerned women whom I guessed were transgendered: could a "lesbian" anthology include works by people who were born male? And if it's true that, as the buttons and bumper stickers proclaim, We Are Everywhere, does that include lesbians in heterosexual relationships? I wanted this collection to include the piece by a lesbian who falls for—and sleeps with—a man, when she's far from home: hence "Playing with Fire" by Patty Smith.

Like the redneck trucker disparagingly described by the first-time visitor to Florida in "Outrageous" by Sheila Ortiz Taylor, I began wondering where my responsibilities lay. As editor, did I need to be the heavy arbiter of social mores, policing the definition of "woman" as well as "lesbian"? Fortunately—and, not incidentally, saving myself a lot of work—I decided that my responsibility was not to create exclusive definitions but just find stories with heart.

Besides, it was hard enough just to figure out what constituted "travel writing," anyway. The stories in this collection span the globe, from Japan to Chile to Senegal to Australia, including all the continents but the coldest one. Some of them would obviously be travel stories proper simply by dint of exotic location. The teenage narrator of Hannah Tennant-Moore's "What Happens after This Day" flies back and forth between India and the United States, between the rule-bound stability of an ashram to the committed insanity of first (dysfunctional) love. In "Oaxaca," by Suzanne Parker, flu and disorientation combine to heighten the traveler's perceptions of the city, making her account vivid and feverish.

On the other hand, several of the stories take place in the United States, not only where the book will be first published but also the home country for most of the contributors. For instance, Lori Soderlind, in "Hot Springs, Montana," returns to the land where her family once lived. There, with the help of Native residents and a woman called Wolf Crone, she tracks down old parts of herself in wild, half-familiar landscape.

Some great "travel writing" takes place in areas local to and well known by the author, where women are not exploring new geography so much as navigating "foreign" cultures and ways of being. "Outrageous" dramatizes racial tensions in the Deep South, as seen by two cosmopolitan Californians; and Kate Lynn Hibbard's "Not Viva in Las Vegas" shows that fast-growing, fast-living city through the eyes of a visitor who pretty much loathes it. While the best friends of "Five Days in Palm Springs," by Rebecca Chekouras, enjoy kitsch and controlled substances, they also find lasting love and commitment for two fat Chihuahuas.

Despite the varied landscapes and protagonists, the uniting thread through these stories is that the narrators want to share their most dramatic, beautiful, moving, or dykey experiences—these are the best stories from women who value and appreciate storytelling. Similarly, avid readers appreciate other readers, and fans of lesbian bookstores will see themselves and some of their favorite places in "Bookstore Bound" by Sima Rabinowitz.

I've always thought that lesbians were brave. That's not because same-sex attraction necessarily entails courage or heterosexuality diminishes it, but because in order to define yourself as a lesbian, at some point you have to leave the (straight) road more traveled and find others of your kind. Most of us start out on the journey alone and with bad directions.

Not every one—not even every lesbian—is willing to go down the road of first introspection, and then affirmation, but those who do end up taking some wild trips. Once you've come out to your rigidly Catholic, non-English-speaking great-aunt, once you've worn a buzz-cut to your prom, once you've found the courage (and the girl) for your first lesbian kiss, you're probably going to be a lot less timid about the rest of your life, including vacations. We are not prone to the lure of package tours.

And when we do travel with a group, we're apt to become leaders, as in this excerpt from "You Can Take Me to the Shrine, but You Can't Make Me Pray" by Louise Blum:

> [W]hen my lover, Connie, and I discovered that the tour
> we'd signed onto for the pyramids stopped first at the Shrine

of Guadalupe, we decided to talk our fellow travelers out of it. We tended to approach every situation with the assurance that we could control it. It's almost as if we thought we could hijack the tour bus, subject everybody in it to our own agenda. "You don't really want to go there!" we'd tell them. "Just follow us." And they would, of course, comply.

We are not, on the whole, followers. For one thing, lesbians are used to not depending on a man to read the maps, pay for the meals, warn off predators, and figure out the route. We do it all ourselves, often working out the best plan very shortly after it should have happened.

But unpredictability makes for great storytelling. The dullest travel tales—and the dullest travelers—are those that follow the itinerary. As Jane Churchon finds in "The Gift Shop Is Never *Fermé*," sometimes you can travel a long way, at great expense and with much careful planning, to reach the destination you've wanted to visit for years, only to have the doors slammed in your face.

But from such mistakes and misadventures, we've learned self-sufficiency, which makes us intrepid, and we've learned interdependency, which makes us good at bonding with each other. Perhaps predictably, some of our favorite stories feature relationships formed in foreign settings: Lesléa Newman's "Bashert" describes a young American woman, sent overseas by her parents, failing to find interest in the nice Jewish boys around her but falling instead for a large, loud, lesbian, who is the kibbutz kvetch.

Of course, not all of us go overseas—or even across the road—looking for love. In "Coyote Autumn," city-girl Jourdan Imani Keith says, about moving to Yosemite:

> My intention was to be an employee for just one season, to see the majesty of mountains whose photo had been tacked to the wall, like an unfamiliar prescription, posted in the dinge of the Philadelphia unemployment office. Healing had seemed only footsteps away.

On the other hand, lesbians go nowhere without considerable emotional baggage. Sometimes people have to go away to make changes to relationships back at home. In "Following in Tim's Footsteps," Pearlie McNeill scrambles through the tunnels and boats the river jungles of Vietnam, in an attempt to understand the hell that her veteran brother had experienced decades before. In the only purely fictional story in the collection, "Postcard: A Story," by Ruthann Robson, the narrator has to vacation in the Caribbean to understand the truth about a relationship she thought she'd left a long time ago. My contribution, "A Friend in America," tells about trawling through a tiny Irish village to find a man with no address and inform him that he was father to a nineteen-year-old son in Arkansas. No matter where we go, lesbians seem to put relationships high on the agenda and itinerary.

But nowhere is the famous "lesbian invisibility" more prevalent and more frustrating than when we're away from home. "Wind" by Tzivia Gover captures the struggle and slow rewards of overcoming shyness and monolingualism to "come out" to people whose dictionary has no word for what you are.

My partner and I try to run into other dykes when we travel. In San Francisco or parts of London, of course, this isn't a challenge, especially if we stay at gay-run B&Bs. But sometimes we find "sisters" in unexpected places: on a ferry to the outer islands of Fiji, we spotted "family" who ended up on the same remote, low-budget resort as we did. We befriended them and have since spent time with them in three countries, all because, with their short hair and sensible shoes, their serious meals and easy affection, they were identifiably lesbians—they looked like *us*. This collection obviates games with gaydar and questions of identity. Reading it is like meeting new friends at a good, late-night party, where lesbians have gathered to laugh, eat, flirt, show off, sympathize, and—mostly—tell stories.

Most impressive, maybe, are stories of women who've gone to remote places alone. "Fruits at the Border" by Lucy Jane Bledsoe describes a dangerous and wonderful adventure involving hostile border guards and a red pepper, while Lauren Sanders's "Shopping" describes taking a different kind of risk, starting in the changing room of an Italian boutique. I wanted to go along on most of those trips, especially with the cheerful, bickering group in "Looking for the V," where Sandra Gail Lambert contrasts her single status with that of her coupled-up friends as they kayak through both rapids and still waters.

In selecting the best lesbian travel writing for this book, I gave up on defining "lesbian," quit trying to determine how far one had to go to "travel," and settled instead on choosing the stories that let me know the narrator's heart. I hope the collection takes you, the reader, where you want to go, or at least somewhere you never expected.

Outrageous

SHEILA ORTIZ TAYLOR

A hearse as blue as north Florida sky purrs toward Tallahassee, sun glinting off roof and hood. Out the driver-side window, a woman's small hand gestures to the lyrics of Grace Slick: "One pill makes you larger, and one pill makes you small." Out the passenger-side window, a brown arm lounges, fingers tapping accompaniment, voice rising to agree with the next line, "And the ones that mother gives you, don't do anything at all."

Arden Benbow, unlikely refugee from southern California and equally unlikely new assistant professor of English at Midway College, is approaching employment and the American south with a naiveté that makes falling down a rabbit hole, or, for that matter, passing through the looking glass, seem like child's play. Her friend Topaz Wilson has come along to protect her from he knows not what. Perhaps from southern culture, perhaps from her own fecund imagination. He leans forward and snaps off the radio.

But he cannot hear, much less control, the sounds in her head, the continuing interior monologue describing the new and surprising trajectory of her own sweet life. It is the middle of a delicious April in 1973. She has a job in a new place. Life, which she tends to think of as a novel, or—after the great Henry Fielding—"a comic epic poem in prose," itself sets a fresh chapter before her, a chapter whose opening letters are decorated in all the gay colors of an antique manuscript.

Chapter, the First, in which Arden Benbow, Our Poet Hero, Enters the Jeweled City.

And the prospect does promise jewels. Along either side of the highway, waist-high grass of an improbable green defines each curve, a green she has never known in the seared southern California rolling hills she has always adored, in the land of her mother, and her mother's mother, and her mother's mother's mother's mother. She perhaps feels, despite her *Californio* lineage, her devotion begin to waver, to wander toward this new, lovely one, she who shimmers in moist heat and seductive promise: La Florida.

Arden drums her hands on the steering wheel and looks out at voluptuous grasslands that seem to part before the Cadillac's hood ornament like a healthy head of green hair through which she is driving. She has always thought of states by color. Colorado, of course, was paprika. Washington was slate blue. Idaho, baked potato brown. Maine, cerulean. Florida, on her personal color chart, had always been yellow, but she sees now she has been mistaken, that it is instead rolling shades of yellow-tinged, blue-rooted, purple-tipped green. Has she not all her life been hungry for green, starved for it, like a lost sailor scarcely surviving on a diet of the driest hardtack?

She will drop anchor here, right here in this green field, and live forever. Florida, La Guapa, the handsome woman to whom—at this very minute—she must somehow award the passion flower of her heart. Florida.

She feels faintly adulterous, thinks guiltily of her lover Alice, at this very moment three thousand miles away caring for the six children that Arden herself had given birth to, hears in her mind Alice say, "Oh, Arden, you are so Catholic," and so dismisses the pang, allows herself the innocence of falling in love with a state, a geography, a demography. The simple innocence of it.

And what was innocence, anyway? What, passion?

"She's heating up again," says Topaz, leaning in toward the wheel to read through dazzling glare the gauge on the dash. "Better pull over and let her breathe a while."

"Let's stop for lunch, then. Florida makes me hungry. It looks like a salad."

"What do people eat here, anyway," asks Topaz in a mistrustful tone, "in this Florida?"

"Didn't we have wonderful food in Louisiana?" says Arden in dreamy recollection.

"That was then. Goodbye, Louisiana; hello, Florida."

"Pessimist. I'm going to find us some fine native food. We'll eat whatever it is Floridians eat."

"Chain cuisine. You know that. You can feel it."

"There," says Arden, pointing across her companion at a sign already vanishing. "'Eat at Glenda's!' it says. That's no chain. Glenda is preparing our lunch right now. She rose before daylight. I hear her scrubbing the carrots."

"I don't like to eat at places that tell me to eat there. It sets up a positive resistance. 'Eat here.' The gastronomical imperative, a mood that takes my appetite clean away."

"Nothing takes your appetite away. Besides, you said yourself the engine's overheating."

Topaz turns to make sure the U-Haul is dutifully following the laboring hearse. "I hate that trailer," he says. "I wish the damn thing had fallen into that ravine in Texas."

"No you don't. And here's Glenda's." She slows down. "Look, trucks. Four semis and a pickup."

"What makes people think truck drivers know where to eat? We don't copy anything else they do. We don't like the way they vote. We don't even like the way they drive."

Arden turns into the gravel parking lot and pulls up next to a glittering black Peterbilt that says in red letters, "Grandma's Kuntry Cookin'."

"I hate to say 'I told you so.'"

"On the contrary—you love to say 'I told you so.'"

He laughs in admission, slings his pith helmet into the back seat, and emerges into the heat of early June, where his sunglasses immediately fog up. He stretches out to his full six feet three inches and calls to his friend, who is checking the trailer hitch. "I'm blind, Arden. Just like Bette Davis in *Dark Victory* before she staggered into the garden and died nobly."

"It wasn't the garden," Arden says gently, taking off his shades and slipping them into her breast pocket. "She died at the foot of the spiral staircase."

"I like that even better," says Topaz, taking her arm. They crunch across glittering rock toward the entrance. The dim, frigid interior smells like Gravy Master. A large, handmade sign advises, "Faith should be your steering wheel, not your spare tire. Wait here for hostess." Four truck drivers in separate booths and three teenage girls in another all stare at them, suspending time.

The long silence has its effect: Glenda herself emerges through swinging doors, wiping her hands down the front of an apron that is decorated with the culinary history of the day. She stops dead and takes in the two strangers. "You two together then?" Glenda fumbles for laminated menus. Then she leads them in the direction of an empty dining room, where rows of tables seem to slumber in the half-light.

Arden comes to a sudden halt and says, "We'd rather be in here with the other truck drivers. We're not much on formality."

"Y'all truck drivers then, sure 'nough?" Glenda squints out the weeping, sun-drenched plate glass into the parking lot, searching for clues to their identity.

"In a manner of speaking," Arden says.

"Transportin' a corpse, looks to me like. Land sakes. Haven't seen a hearse like that in twenty years. Chillin' sight. Musta worked up an appetite, though."

Topaz is eyeing the sign that says, "If our waitresses start to act grumpy, please notify management and we'll administer additional medication."

"I wrote that," says Glenda, with pride of authorship. "This here's my place."

"Glenda," says Arden, "it was your sign out on the highway that accounts for us, strangers here, coming to your doorstep. Do you suppose we could see a little of that Southern hospitality which has inspired this enterprise of yours?"

"Yes, ma'am," says Glenda, recovering her manners. "Now y'all just set yourselves down right here by the window, and I'll bring you some nice cold tea."

When Glenda's out of sight, Arden says, "Nobody ever called me that before."

"Called you what?" asks Topaz, studying the menu.

"Ma'am."

Topaz drops his menu. "You been called a lot of things in your time and yet you're complaining about a little ma'aming? The real issue here is the honest-to-god fried baloney sandwich on this menu. And what's a corndog, anyway?"

"What if she called you 'sir'?"

"Not in this lifetime she won't. Culture forbids it. No, Glenda's got another word she's keeping for me. I know about the South." He reaches across the table for his sunglasses.

"You know about *movies* about the South," she says, handing them over.

"Art imitates life." He puts on his glasses and through dark lenses watches Glenda approach with their tea.

"Can I bring y'all the special?" Glenda asks, thunking down perspiring red plastic tumblers before the travelers.

"Yes," says Arden, "we'll both have the special."

"Actually I was interested in your fried bologna sandwich."

"Gone as yesterday. Same for the mullet basket. But I can get you the special if you want, like your . . . friend here is having. Folks around here seem to like it just fine."

Topaz nods and Glenda drifts off toward the kitchen in big, dingy nurse shoes. As soon as she disappears through the double doors, he sinks his head in his hands. "Not the special. I could have had a corndog. Whatever that is."

"Today, Topaz, we're going to eat what Floridians eat. The special."

"We're going to eat what truck drivers eat. Did you see that display up by the cash register? Right there under the sign that says 'Buckle up for Jesus'? They've got the whole trinity up there: Alka Seltzer, Tums, and Pepto-Bismol. Truck drivers live on stomach remedies."

Topaz unrolls his paper napkin, sending knife and fork skittering across the table. In the silence that follows, his eye falls on a truck driver in a faded red cap, holding his barbecued pork sandwich in two enormous hands as if the bun is the steering wheel of his truck. The man's eyes bore across the room trying to fix him in the cross-hairs of his attention.

"Oh, shit," says Topaz, "I was afraid of this. He thinks you're a white woman, and he *knows* I'm a black man, and he assumes that everybody here is heterosexual, despite compelling evidence to the contrary. Now he's wondering exactly where his responsibilities lie."

Just then Glenda bursts through double doors with a heavy plate on each hand, catches the gaze of the truck driver, and gives her bee-hive an almost imperceptible shake, transmitting the ancient coded warning from Southern female to Southern male that means *Now you behave yourself, hear?* Bubba reaches for his check and heaves himself up onto his Red Wings.

Glenda sets down the heavy plates and, avoiding eye contact, observes, "Don't guess you folks are from anywhere around here. You look like you came from a *long* ways off."

Topaz regards his plate, which resembles an aerial photograph of an Arabian desert.

"We're from California," says Arden, lifting her fork.

At the word "California," *everyone* is looking: the man in the red hat waiting at the cash register, the other truckers, the teenagers, and a middle-aged black man who has come out of the kitchen wearing an apron streaked with colors that match up with the aerial photographs of the Arabian Desert.

"But I'm moving to Tallahassee. Well, actually to Midway," Arden corrects herself. "I guess it's practically the same thing."

"Not hardly," says Glenda, fixing her eyes on Topaz, who is directing his fork into the side of a perfect volcano of mashed potatoes, thereby releasing a torrent of brown gravy onto his fried okra, field peas, and summer squash.

"My compliments to the chef," he says, looking up.

"And you're not?" Glenda asks him.

"Not what?"

"Not moving to Midway."

"My dear lady, not for all the tea in Florida."

"That's a 'no'?"

"That's an unequivocal no."

"*I* live in Midway," says Glenda, looking now into Arden's eyes, her expression easing. "Welcome, stranger."

"Is there a motel in Midway you can recommend?" Arden asks, sawing with her dull knife through layers of leathery roast beef suspended on a bed of spongy white bread.

"There's not no motel at all," Glenda says. "Only a IGA grocery and the Unocal gas station. Throw in the food-stamp store, the Baptist church, and Ace Hardware and you've just about got Midway. Oh, and the college, of course. But they keep to theyselves, that bunch. For a hotel, though, you'll have to go on in to Tallahassee. It ain't that far. Twenty minutes, maybe. I'll leave y'all to enjoy your dinner now. Need anything else, just give us a holler."

Topaz sips his drink and grimaces. "I hate sugary iced tea, and I hate Florida even worse."

Arden is thoughtfully crunching up medallions of okra. "It was you who said I should take this job in the first place. You said Florida was not the South, Florida was just Florida. Oranges and Cubans and Disney World. You liked the money too, as I recall."

"That's true; you do need money. Six kids is a lot of kids to have. Okay, keep the job then, Arden. But just be careful, for Christ's sake. Bust your cards, as my Aunt Hazel used to say. Southerners can play rough, and some of them can play subtle." He lifts a flap of meat and looks under it suspiciously.

"Topaz, my way is to march forward, assuming the best."

"Until your ass gets whipped."

"My ass has never been whipped in *your* memory."

"Just be careful, is all I'm saying. Marching straight ahead holding your damn musket in front of you and the flag over your head may not get it anymore, Arden. You got to take the clue from your ancestors and start hiding behind rocks and planning your own little surprises for the damned enemy."

"I have heard you, wise one."

"Just eat your peas and let's get the hell on out of here."

"At least I know how to watch my language in public, while a guest of the South."

"What language?"

"You just said 'Christ,' 'hell,' and 'damn,'" she objects, laying her knife and fork across her plate. "We Southern ladies don't tolerate language like that." She rolls her eyes demurely in the direction of a placard over the cash register that reads, "I'm an organ donor. I gave my heart to Jesus."

Topaz chokes on iced tea, wipes his eyes. "Come on, you crazy thing, let's pick up some Tums and hit the road."

Arden raises an eyebrow to signal Glenda and says in a stage whisper that resounds throughout the cafe, "My brother is ready for the check now."

Oaxaca

SUZANNE PARKER

The Spanish laid out a new town around the old zocalo, clearly missing their hometown squares, their esplanades, their promenades. The zocalo is elegant in its dimensions. It takes a good amount of time, say half an hour with the crowded passageways, to navigate it. There is a comfort to be found in a square. After wandering the city's streets and alleys half lost and looking for a restaurant recommended for its cheap but good empanadas or after journeying on a crowded bus to the market town Ocotlán where no one speaks English and you speak no Spanish and the market is of a dusty, busy, hard-selling sort where people bring their bleating terrified goats and chickens hang by their bound feet beating the air with their wings, after walking out of town to find the artisan's shop and getting covered in mud from the cars splashing through the puddles and the looks of the people in the cars, staring, laughing, and the shop no longer exists or exists down an unmarked alley that is dark and full of mud and a smell of garbage leaks out from it, after all that and the bus ride back, breathing the fouled air and tired but jarred out of sleep at every rut in the road, after all that and then the trudge back through the heat and sun and now dried mud flaking from your ankles like a skin condition, and the beggars now beg in your own language and the children swarm you with arms full of trinkets, and the day has parched you and your feet are aching, and you are hungry, empty-handed, and no longer sure of the road you are on, after all that, to turn into the square, to look down the shaded walkway, the eyes lose their squint, shoulders release, you suddenly know where you are and where you'll be going and each corner leads to another corner and you cannot get lost and the toughest choice is which café but you know your favorite is La Primavera, just two turns to the right, the second table in the second row, the second seat from the left. You are in the square. There are four sides to a square and you will sit on one of them and drink a beer.

———

I was very sick by the time we arrived in Oaxaca. Not sick, as expected, from the water and resulting in a close acquaintance with a toilet but with a flu that steamrolled over and flattened me. By the time we arrived at our hotel, I was shaking and wanted nothing more than to sleep in a bed, any bed, no matter how flea-ridden or shared by a pack of street dogs. Luckily, the hotel was very nice—a gamble when booking from a website without pictures. The owner waited in the doorway for us, and we entered through a huge, wooden door as if a race of giants or giraffes lived behind. Maybe it was the fever or the frequency of churches we'd driven by with their steeples rising like conquerors above this three-story city, but as I passed beneath the door's arch I half expected St. Peter, with a smirk and his key swinging jauntily from his robe as he waited to pass on some bad news, but on the other side was only calm, cool, quiet, an inviting courtyard with a bubbling fountain in the middle and small boy tipping a jug of water into a pond that overflowed from its clam shell into a real goldfish pond below. This was the courtyard's focal point. The door to each room had a chair next to it so a person could sit and watch the fountain and the arrival and departures of the other guests. Finally, there were some stairs leading off the corners into dark turns and the second story. My girlfriend and I were staying on the first floor and could hear the boy's industrious pouring all through the night. The only thing to drown out the boy was my coughing, which I practiced frequently, hoping for just the right blast to clear out my lungs and be done with it all. In the morning, with me still coughing, we discovered that it was a lovely room—spacious, very white linens, Spartan walls but for a huge crucifix. The room also had a large shower with a skylight above it. The skylight opened on the roof, which was also the dining area so showering in the morning gave the questionable pleasure of knowing that anyone walking by with his coffee and plate of mango and sweet rolls could stop, look down, and, through a convex plate of mildly misty glass, watch as I dropped the soap, lathered up hair thick with dust and exhaust, stood still and let the water rinse me clean. My flu, if that's what it was, did not politely pack its bags and leave after a good hot shower but, like any unwanted houseguest, stayed far, far too long and made a huge mess and asked for butter when there was only margarine and then went on at length about how butter was the only true spread and was much better for your health and she could not, should not, would never substitute it when cooking her famous oatmeal cookies she was known for and all this passed on before breakfast had been cleared away. We suddenly had an unwanted traveling companion. At the Museo Rufino Tamayo, she announced art was boring. At lunch, she refused to eat the local cheese. In the sun, she swooned. In the cool corridors of the Mercado Juárez, she shivered, loudly. There was nothing to do but acquiesce, and so Lori went off to see the ruins of Monte Albán, an incredible Zapotec city, which I liked to think would have sacrificed my houseguest in an instant, something bloody and slow on an altar. I slept and sweated and listened to the maids. One had a very high voice, and since I couldn't understand their Spanish, they sounded like birds, a flock of birds, and I slept and dreamed of the Quetzalcóatl, the feathered serpent and Toltec symbol of life and fertility, and waited for Lori to return with fresh orange juice and tales of the dead.

———

There was some concern going to Oaxaca because I'd been there once before and there's always the threat of the return trip not living up to expectations, especially since I previously went with a lover who surprised me by professing devotion while sweating it out in the back seat of a cab. On this second trip, I was back with another lover, although we had long ago exchanged "I love you's"—so they were now somewhat commonplace, like a frequent rain in spring or an expected winter flurry. Useful, pleasant things but not a thrill, not a rush and like any rain or snow, if there's too much, it just becomes a bother although we weren't at the bother stage but certainly it wasn't a first time and so Oaxaca already represented something to me and didn't for her and the question was not what would she make of it but would I, could I allow it to be something new and something we shared and something that would obliterate the fond memories I already had of it for isn't that what happens? There's only so much storage space, and revisiting a place is like clearing out your wardrobe: fresher styles replace the old. Also, there's the threat of confusion—whom did I see Mitla with? Who was it who bought me the lemon ice? Who made love to me in a room with a wall of windows? I was in a constant state of translation, of revision. Who was it who lay down ten years earlier and who wakes up now to the sound of a different breathing?

———

The roof of the Hotel Azucenas was also its dining room. There was a little shaded area, a sort of cabana, built up there and then tables with umbrellas scattered about and a lot of pots with flowers and small trees. The breakfast would be the same each day: coffee and breads, some of the local Mexican rolls, which were white, soft, with a crusty sugary outside, or croissant, and fruit—papaya, mango, pineapple, melon. We would sit on the roof and drink and drink and drink coffee but one day, when I came up to the roof, Lori was sitting with two people. He was tall, red-headed, very thin, and very gangly in the way ropy, thin people are. She was the opposite. A decent height and rounded, not fat, but solid, full, curvy, her hips and rear circular, her upper arms like half moons. She was very attractive and I could see how at night after all the harsh edges his own body offered throughout the day she would be a pillow to him, all soft to sink into. Personality-wise, she was no pillow though. Both were professors, and she was talkative, opinionated, and sharp. He was quiet, slow to conversation, but smart as well. And he worked at the same school as Lori, in the physics department, which seemed right for him—all those angular proofs and theories, stripped down and tested. We had a meal together getting to know one another, and they became our traveling companions later in the week. They were good company, the kind of people who laugh at jokes and who can build on a good laugh to keep it going, so sometimes we'd start out chuckling about anteaters and end up hysterical two miles farther down the road over the desert landscape and the president's attempts at intelligence. It's important, or at least helpful, to travel with people who dislike the same politicians you do.

———

Then, there was the teacher's strike. They had arrived in town before us and set up camps around the zocalo. The center of the zocalo itself was walled off with boards to block the view. They had ripped out the beautiful old stone walkways and the central elevated bandstand. Everything was broken slabs and mounds of earth. The trees were the only things left standing, and they looked lonely and a little unsure of their future. On my first trip, I had strolled up and down the walks and spent whole evenings sitting on benches. We'd watched old women watching a young couple who were clearly in love, and we'd followed the strolling musicians, bought trinkets, and on one bench in the far corner dared each other to eat the local spiced grasshoppers dipped in a dusty red. The zocalo had been the city's heart, and now it was closed to its people, gutted, renovations planned, and the teachers were camping around it, spilling out and down the streets protesting their contracts and joined by others who had their own protests to make until each street leading from it was jammed with camps so when we walked down from our hotel we went through block after block after block weaving our way under tarps and around tents and sleeping bags and little rooms and villages made up for the different groups. We could not read the Spanish, but it all seemed very organized. There were posters and cardboard signs announcing each group's complaints and demands. There were meetings going on and what seemed to be lessons, which we imagined were on revolution but might just have been garbage removal. It was June, so very hot, and many of the protesters looked wilted and it was a maze winding our way through them to get to our coffee or, if it was afternoon, beers on the other side. Sometimes walking through at night, there would be singing and by a kerosene lamp someone would have a guitar and an audience that looked happy for the day's end and some entertainment. They were there all the time that we were and beyond, and we wondered if we should feel guilty or responsible. Somehow, they seemed like our responsibility, but it's tough not to feel that way about any place and its miseries when you're an American.

———

There were nuns in the street. A blocks-long parade of the faithful, banners waving, the Eucharist bouncing in its chariot, balanced on the shoulders of priests until the huge, stone, golden, still-warm-to-the-touch cathedral rose up, high above the town, and in front of this cathedral for all to see and hear—a mass. I couldn't imagine it, to stand there, feet hurting, maybe hungry, definitely cold, and stand, still, for a 10:30 p.m. mass. The fathers did not rush. The nuns did not sit. This was faith standing up, in Latin, under the black roof of the sky while the wind rolled down the mountain from where yet more directions for sacrifice had been found chipped into the stone. And beneath my feet, huge black elephant beetles covered the sidewalks, gutters, steps. They announced the rains and would, overnight, increase to thousands so their corpses needed to be swept away in great black drifts. All day, we had so carefully avoided them, selected a safe place to put each foot. I could not crush, crunch, flatten one with out wondering its name. But trapped by the candle-holding crowd, how could we jump off the wall we were sitting on? There was no way to see what was below or avoid what was passing by. We gave in. We sat with thighs touching, waiting, breathing in the heat of so many bodies, listening to their singing in a language I once heard and was taught a long time before.

As tourists, even tourists with good intentions to avoid the obvious places and buying the obvious things, we were still drawn to the artist's towns, for in Mexico there really are places that specialize in making one thing, and these places date back to pre-Hispanic culture and the artists still make the same objects their ancestors did, often using the same methods, and the work is beautiful. In San Bartolo Coyotepec, walls were filled with black pottery that was polished and thin and the light reflected off it so the dense coal black was still bright like an absence acutely felt. It was without color and the most colorful thing in the place. Floor to ceiling, there were plates, bowls, round vases like distracting moons, and everything smooth and cold to touch. In San Martín Tilcajete, painted lizards, butterflies, armadillos, anything that crawled or flew was carved in wood and colored bright green, purple, sky blue and then dotted with hundreds of white or colored points swirling or lining up like the henna-painted hands in Morocco or the tattoos on the faces of some African tribes. They were ornamental and extraordinarily pretty and happy in all the dust and brown distance and half-starved dogs and tattered chickens pecking around the courtyard we walked through to get to the shop, and the grandmother stopped her work in the kitchen and watched us, and the little girl rose off the stair she was sitting on and followed us, and the kittens sleeping on a bench even lifted their heads to stalk us. Everyone had awakened from a tired half-stupor and we were half-asleep ourselves from too much heat and walking and it was 2 p.m., and we should have been sleeping in the shade of a lovely tree or making love beneath the hanging Christ in our room, but, instead, we were out marching from shop to shop seeing the same painted animals but knowing someone had stooped over each one and applied a galaxy of color, and some were just rows of pigment slapped on for the tourists but some were artists and we saw the concentration and desire to provoke in how the swirl was sensual, lapping at the legs and curling under the chest like a receding tide and on the large lizard even the underside of the darting tongue was carefully telling its own story of being always hungry.

And we were artists as well and wanted to have a finished product so we bought three lizards and pictured them on our wall back home in the city and how they would be climbing up it, always returning to what they had known.

Not Viva in Las Vegas

KATE LYNN HIBBARD

*V*ulva in Las Vegas. Vulgar in Las Vegas. A place in the middle of the desert that uses too much water. Voluble Las Vegas. The loudest place I've ever been. The sounds of Las Vegas: bells bells bells bells bells, dinging machines, coins sliding into metal trays, ice clinking in glass or thudding dull against plastic, a thousand matches roaring up to light a thousand cigarettes. Music, horns blaring, showy show tunes, that lounge-lizard sound, jazz without soul, the faux butch ghost of Sammy Davis Jr., his flattop hair and cockeyed glass eye and a drink and a smoke in his hand. Cards being flipped onto felt tables, poker chips rattling, smokers coughing, a low constant hum, fake waterfalls, the gamblers' prayers, breath blown on dice. I walk through the casino to get to the elevator—there is no other way to get to the hotel room in Circus Circus—and I admire the brilliance of the man who named this place and I know that this is what hell must be like, trapped in a land of plastic where the sun won't go down. It's too easy to call it plastic. But it's easier than feeling. I can't feel what they're feeling. I can't feel what I'm feeling. I don't want to gamble, but I am so unhinged I eat constantly and buy makeup I will never wear again. All of my clothes are wrong.

I have no one to eat dinner with and order room service, watch the Oscars, and call my girlfriend who is always annoying on the phone. Tomorrow I'll go to the Baking Convention, the one that happens here every four years, and try to impress my boss with my dedication to wage slavery, my gratitude for this all-expenses-paid business trip to Las Vegas. Tomorrow I'll eat some honest bread and laugh at garish pastries. Las Vegas, the food capital of the west. Miles of banquet tables for people who don't care about what they eat. Married in Las Vegas. I can't get married here, or in most places, but if I could, would I go to the Drive-Thru Chapel of Love?

One of the first lesbian movies I ever saw was set in Las Vegas. *Desert Hearts*. I can't remember the names of the actresses, but I remember a couple of scenes. The dark-haired one flirting with the one who was still straight, driving her car in reverse at the same rate of speed the other one was going forward, which even at the time seemed highly unlikely to be possible. Like converting a straight woman to queerness, now that I think of it. The straight woman looking miserable, drenched in the rain, but I don't recall what she was miserable about, and what the hell, it never rains in Las Vegas. The hot hot scene of them fucking finally after all that emotional foreplay that women supposedly love. Her leaving on a train. A train. It must have been set in the '50s. She was wearing a nice gray suit. Maybe even gloves. *Leaving Las Vegas*. That insanely self-indulgent crap of a movie with Nicholas Cage, who drank himself to death because his wife left him. How original. Though the idea of purposely self-destructing as quickly and efficiently as possible does hold some appeal. A woman, of course, tried to save him. But he could not be saved. Dissolute in Las Vegas. Did Thelma and Louise drive through Las Vegas? Or was it a different Sarandon movie, one of that endless string of woman as irresponsible or bad mother, woman who won't grow up and be a proper mom and let her daughter become the sexually attractive one? Deluded in Las Vegas.

Las Vegas throbs shards of neon; it is a nuclear scab in the desert. The sun is too bright, and the earth is too flat. I never stop feeling like I'm on a movie set, like there are floorboards beneath the sidewalks, like all that dazzling could be turned off with a switch and a pneumatic sound like in all those movies set in football stadiums where the lights come on suddenly and the protagonist is blinded, silhouetted, and then the lights go down and there is nothing but the too-green grass gone black. There is no grass in Las Vegas. Being crass in Las Vegas is celebrated but doesn't seem like any kind of fun. There are white tigers and women in seven-foot-high ostrich-feather headpieces. There is no sense of irony in Las Vegas. Was it glamorous when it started? Why is it even there, in the middle of the desert? There is a university in Las Vegas, a good basketball team, churches and kindergartens too. There are actual people in Las Vegas.

The light in Las Vegas is wrong, the air flat and hot, and aside from the air conditioning there is very little difference between being inside a building and outside. There are no proper doors in Las Vegas. There are whores in Las Vegas, like there are everywhere else. There are sidewalks in Las Vegas, but they seem more like escalators. There are fake landscapes in Las Vegas, a pretend pirate ship and a pretend riverbank and a pretend palace for a pretend Caesar. The best Caesar salad I ever ate was in Las Vegas, when I finally had dinner with my boss and his wife. I let them order the wine. He ate osso buco, and I never had seen anyone eat that before. Strange in Las Vegas. He told me he wasn't sure I was really committed to my job and he was right and I didn't realize he saw me that clearly until that moment. He grew up working class in Pennsylvania and became someone else, someone who wore Italian suits and knew how to order wine. Someone with vision. Someone most people found impossible to work for. I liked him a lot because he was so ridiculous. I like ridiculous people, and I should have liked Las Vegas. I was too quiet for Las Vegas. I couldn't stop being myself, I couldn't stop thinking of myself as a self, I couldn't stop myself from thinking, long enough to be in Las Vegas.

What Happens after This Day

HANNAH TENNANT-MOORE

The last time I saw Ashley was the first cold Sunday of the year. I woke up at nine that morning, with red eyes and a throbbing head. Ashley's purple comforter was covered in sunlight. I got up to close the blinds, tripped over one of her shoes, and let myself collapse onto the floor. I sat below the window for what seemed like a long time. I crawled back into bed. At three, Ashley and I got out of bed and smoked pot out of her bong. By eight, we had finished a six-pack of Rolling Rock. We looked at the TV, not touching each other. At midnight, we each had a capful of liquid codeine and sprinkled Percocet on our bong hits. Ashley reached a tired hand over, touched me with one finger until the tremors came and went. We slept naked, tangled up in each other. I woke in the early morning and let myself lie still, look up at the ceiling for three minutes. I had another capful of codeine.

During the months I lived in a Buddhist monastery in Bodh Gaya, India, I became fascinated with the list of 227 disciplinary rules that govern the daily lives of Buddhist monks and nuns. Although certain rules have been modified over time (Western monks are not required, for instance, to squat while urinating, the traditional Indian way), most enrobed men and women still follow all 227. The English translation of the *Vinaya*—the book of monastic rules as explained by the Buddha and recorded by his disciples—is nearly two thousand pages long. A monk once told me the story of how a permanent schism leading to two distinct schools of Buddhism occurred over a disagreement about whether or not salt could be stored in an animal horn. (We were both cracking up when he got to the punch line.) The *Patimokkha*—rules governing daily life, including no eating after noon, no personal possessions besides a robe and a begging bowl, and no using perfumes or scented lotions—are recited twice a month to the entire community of monks and nuns. The word "Patimokkha" means disburdening, becoming free.

Being in love with Ashley was joints and cheap beer and Grey Goose vodka stolen from her mother and shrieking orgasms and drunken dancing and loud music in fast cars and milkshakes and french fries at all-night diners. She came into my life at a time when I spent most Saturday nights getting stoned by myself; I hadn't answered the phone for so long that it had stopped ringing altogether. I had no reasons for my misery and nothing interesting to say about it; it was just there, silently shaping all my days. Ashley had concrete problems, and she loved to talk about them until she gave them away to whomever was listening: she wished she was a boy and yet she bled every month, her breasts bobbed when she ran; her mom was nearly always drunk, her sister was angry and anorexic, and her father was perpetually, destructively cheerful.

I fell for Ashley so quickly partly because she had been my best friend in eighth grade and suddenly we were nineteen and gay and making out, and that always felt like one of the fun tricks life plays. We hadn't kept in touch throughout high school or college, until one Saturday night during my sophomore year when she called to tell me she happened to be at my school, and then there she was in my kitchen and we were hugging and laughing, exchanging phone numbers and free weekends. She asked me the second time we hung out, "Do you have a lot of commitments? Because I really can't stand that." I thought the answer was no; I didn't realize until they were all gone that my solitary activities—cooking elaborate dinners for myself, scribbling in notebooks at coffee shops, walking to the cemetery to watch the sunset—were all that was holding me together.

When I told Ashley I was planning to spend the following semester in India, studying and practicing Buddhism at a monastery in Bodh Gaya, the place where the Buddha attained enlightenment, her face went glum. "That sucks," she said. I was flattered in spite of myself.

Living at the monastery meant taking vows to follow the five precepts the Buddha taught as the path to a fulfilling, healthy life for laypeople. They forbid lying, killing (which extended to the hoards of mosquitoes that stuck their noses into our faces and shoulders as we sat in the meditation hall or tried to sleep), stealing, using intoxicants, and sexual misconduct (which meant abstinence while living at the monastery). A monk on pilgrimage to Bodh Gaya from Sri Lanka once told me, "There is no doubt: if you follow these five precepts, you will be happy. You will have a good life." Living at the monastery was the first time in my life that I slept easily and enjoyed waking up each day.

A few months after Ashley and I started dating, we were both home from college with no solid plans, sleeping together every night and driving around together every day. On her good days, Ashley was always laughing and pulling at my hand like a little kid: "Hannie, let's go swimming. Hannie, let's go out to breakfast." She used to fill in all the blank parts of my calendar, where I kept track of my babysitting jobs: "Babysit Ash." I was addicted to her need—how she would nearly crush me as she came, squeezing me against her, then burst into tears and lie under me silently sobbing for several minutes. I loved that she let me drink instead of cry, that she raided her mother's cabinet of prescription drugs, how much she hated her full breasts. The first time I saw her look at herself naked in the mirror and smile as she pushed her breasts apart, flattening them to her sides, I knew I would fall in love with her. I pretended I didn't have a choice.

My plane to India left at six in the morning on the last day of August. Ashley and I stayed up all that night in my bed. When my mom shouted from the kitchen, "Okay, Han, let's go," I felt all at once that leaving Ashley was more than I could bear. "I would give up the whole trip," I whispered, clinging to her worn cotton T-shirt, "if I could just stay in bed here with you for another hour like this." It was the kind of desperate-love thing she said all the time, to which I normally responded by smiling uncomfortably and asking if she was hungry or tired or ready to go. "Oh, Han," she practically gasped and pulled me closer, nuzzling her face into my neck.

Ashley stayed behind at my mom's house when we drove to the airport. After the car was packed, she stood on the porch in her oversized blue T-shirt and sweatpants and waved to us with one hand while she rubbed her drooping eyelids with the other. "She really is cute as a button," my mom said as we drove away. It was one of the only kind things she ever said about Ashley.

After days of traveling by plane, train, and bus, I arrived at the monastery in Bodh Gaya in a succession of jeeps carrying American students. It was dark when we drove in, and the only people out were a few old men sitting on upturned boxes, drinking chai on the side of the road. Panic set in at the thought that I would be living in this tiny town with one main dirt road, sleeping on a cot in one of these sweltering buildings. But then I got out of the jeep and was greeted by the monastery dog, her five puppies in tow, and the monks shouted *namastes* and welcomes as we unloaded our packs. I walked around the courtyard slowly, stopping at each peaceful, smiling Buddha statue. During our first dinner of rice, dal, and chappatis prepared by the local women who worked at the monastery, I remembered how it's possible to love something simple so much it makes your jaw ache.

One summer night, after we had spent every day together for months, I decided not to sleep at Ashley's; I would spend one night with myself. She called an hour later. Her mom was gone with the car, and there was an empty economy-sized jug of vodka lying on the living room floor. She picked me up and I hugged and kissed her and licked her wet eyes. We got high and drove around, listening to music so loud it busted the speakers on her car. She did not want to talk about her mom. Instead, she asked me to tell her all the reasons I loved her and then to think of more.

Her mom came home a few hours later, and then Ashley was all noise and sex and laughter again, and I had not slept in weeks. I used to stay up with her until four or five and then wake up at eight, either because I couldn't sleep or I had to babysit. Ashley slept all day. She had quit her job after a week because she couldn't stand being too tired to have sex with me after she got home from work. So the next night I told her that I needed to stay home. I needed to sleep. She called me at eleven: "I'm sorry, but I miss you. Can't I just come over and tuck you in?" I said yes because I missed her too; I could hardly stand to be alone and still, because it made me realize how long it had been since I had allowed myself to be those things.

A gong woke the monastery residents at five each morning. It began in the courtyard, then passed by each of our doors—slow footsteps interspersed with austere booms. I was always awake by the time the ringer got to my door, enjoying the coolest hour of the day, when I could stand to have a sheet on me as covering. I would look out the window next to my bed at the sky tinted yellow through the cocoon of my mosquito net, the call to prayer from the nearby mosque filling up the rice fields. Ten minutes before meditation started, I would get out of bed, dress into one of my three *salwar kameez,* and wait my turn at the sink to splash water on my sweaty cheeks.

Walking down to the Buddha hall, we passed the open-air kitchen where the nuns would be chopping vegetables and stirring lentils in huge copper pots. A dog or two would be curled up on the kitchen floor, waiting patiently for scraps. We sat down cross-legged on worn blue cushions and waited for our Burmese meditation teacher, Munindra-ji, to shuffle in with his swollen feet and white robes. He would take his seat before us and smile consistently for one hour, whether speaking or silent. Sometimes he would suddenly clap his hands together and shout, "Do not cling to the sound! Sound is gone! How can you cling to the sound?" He ended every morning meditation with the reminder, "You cannot jump from here to breakfast."

By the time we emerged from meditation, the little boys at the yellow house across the field would be playing cricket on the roof with sticks and rocks; the women would be hanging saris from second-floor windows to dry in the sun. We walked slowly to the dining room and took our time lining our sandals in a neat row at the door. We maintained silence throughout breakfast, a simple meal of fruit and sweetened rice gruel that lasted thirty minutes. I remember the sweetness of a single sugar granule melting on my tongue and the faint tearing sound when I pulled a slice of orange apart from the rest. For the first time in my life, I started offering silent thanks for my food before all my meals.

Our days were ordered by the deep resonance of the gongs, so that I never had to worry about how I spent my time, making it easier to locate myself inside the moments—the afternoons spent wringing dirty water out of my underpants and carrying buckets of shit-covered toilet paper to the trash heap to be burned, the mornings when it was my turn to sweep the Buddha hall before everyone else filed down for meditation at 5:30.

The hallways of the monastery were open air with no banisters, so we could sit on the edges, our feet dangling over the rice fields. I used to brush my teeth that way at night so I could watch my shadow multiplied ten times, my torso almost completely filling the field. I would listen for the sound of my spit splatting into the mud and then I would go up to the roof and lie flat like a starfish so I couldn't see anything but darkness and stars.

Ashley told me once during that first summer that she was falling for someone else. She made the announcement gravely as I sat at the kitchen table, making a list of things I still needed to get for India. I told her it was normal to have crushes, but she didn't have to tell me about all of them. She kept talking, explaining the details of her encounters with this girl—when she first realized she liked her as more than a friend, how honesty was important, how she would never act on her feelings but she thought I should know, how she thought about this girl all the time. I don't remember the point in her measured monologue when my hand flew out to her face, slapped it hard enough that her head shot back. I was horrified and curious by the print my hand left on her cheek. She seemed glad that I hit her. She had proof I had lost it over her; I cared that much.

I had been in India for two weeks before a craving for salty protein inspired me to brave alone the life-threatening obstacle course that was the walk to town. In the midst of dodging rickshaws, cow pies, and buses careening down the potholed streets, their passengers clinging atop them for dear life, I was accosted by barefoot children shouting, "Hello, friend!" and slipping their hands into mine, prepared to accompany me as far as I was going. The fabric store owners shouted to me, "Look at the beautiful Indian girl!" since I was wearing the sari I'd bought from them the day before. They beckoned me into their store, offered me chai, and told me how "luck" I was to be in the holy town of Bodh Gaya.

When I finally arrived at the food store, I bowed to the owner and wiped the dirt and sweat from my face with the edge of my sari. "*Apka pas peanuts hai?*" I asked him hopefully. He smiled at me for about a minute, bobbing his head lightly in the Indian manner, before announcing, "No peanuts, no problem." He shrugged and offered me instead a chocolate bar filled with paraffin wax to keep it from melting. I bought the waxy chocolate and headed home.

I was chuckling to myself on the walk back, thinking how I would tell this story to the other Americans at the monastery, how "No peanuts, no problem" would become a familiar refrain, since, without intoxicants, laughter was the lubricant that brought us together. Suddenly the rickshaw driver who was normally stationed outside the monastery stopped beside me. For once he didn't ring his bell in my ear over and over, saying, "Burmese vihar, good price." This time he said, "You—so smile, so happy," and then biked away, leaving me to navigate the cows and their shit on my own.

I got ready for my trip to India by smoking pot in Ashley's sports car—a brand-new black Acura her dad leased for her—and driving around till one of us stumbled on an errand we had to do. One Saturday we found ourselves parked in front of the post office, where I was supposed to get passport photos taken. But I didn't feel like talking to strangers or smiling for the camera, so Ash suggested we drive to Rockport instead. We had one mix CD and a day-old bottle of water with us. After we merged on the highway, Ashley slipped one hand down the front of my shirt, veering slightly toward the median as she squeezed my breast. "I just like knowing I can do that," she said as she returned both hands to the wheel. I smiled at my reflection in the rearview mirror.

In Rockport, we ate fudge and taffy and picked snails off rocks. We made out in a public restroom and laughed at the nasty looks we got from the older woman waiting in line when we emerged holding hands. We smoked more pot and ate more fudge and taffy. On the drive home, Ash was sullen and wouldn't talk. "Nothing, nothing," she kept muttering when I asked what was wrong. I knew she wanted me to push her to talk about it or at least put my hand on her thigh as she drove, but I also knew she was sad for no reason or for the same old reasons, just like me, and I was bored of our stoned sadness. I lit another bowl and turned up the music. When I started belting out, "Driving so fast I felt like I was drunk," Ash let her foot fall heavy on the gas pedal, pushing the speedometer past ninety. That was when I put my hand on her thigh.

The day monsoon season started, I was squatting in a monk's tin roof hut, drinking warm, flat Coke out of a bottle. Joti, a monk about my age, was explaining to my friend and me how he fell in love with meditation during a ten-day retreat. "I could really feel my whole self for the first time," he was saying as the sky that had been a hazy gray every day since we'd arrived in India suddenly opened up. The three of us sat in silence for a while, watching the water drench the parched earth and listening to heavy raindrops on the roof, so loud it was like being trapped in a snare drum. When it became clear the rain would not let up anytime soon, Joti insisted we take his umbrella. We bowed to each other and headed out.

About a half hour's walk from town, Joti's temple was the only structure in the middle of a giant grazing pasture for cows. Within minutes, our *salwar kameez* were soaked through to our skin. The flimsy umbrella was completely helpless against those torrents, but we took turns with it anyway to express our gratitude to Joti, who was watching us from his doorway. Knee deep in mud, we had to run back every few steps and wrestle with the thick goo for our shoes. Being drenched in cool water felt so good after months of suffocating heat that even when the lightning started we kept holding that umbrella up toward the sky, laughing so hard we couldn't catch our breath as manure oozed between our toes and the sky's electricity contemplated using our heads as conductors.

After the rains started, there were evenings of fog so thick you couldn't see six inches past your nose. I would go into town anyway, to hear the Thai nuns chant at the main temple, the Mahabodhi, and walk home in air so condensed it felt like swimming. Even in the pitch darkness, I knew the restaurants were being converted to families' bedrooms, the mangy dogs were prowling for scraps, and the store owners were sitting around in the dark, drinking chai. High-pitched Hindu folksongs were broadcast almost constantly on speakers throughout town, and confused roosters crooned all night long. I was never afraid in Bodh Gaya. The constant sober chaos made being alone feel so safe.

Ashley and I used to drive to Concord to go swimming at Walden Pond after I finished babysitting. Dropping our towels on the sand, we would run and dive, swim ferociously until we got to the very center of the pond. We would reach for each other underwater, my hand slipping under her navy trunks and her fingers pulling aside the crotch of my black one-piece. We swallowed pond water as we kissed; we stayed under for as long as we could. I liked when it rained. All the families and couples and fishermen cleared out, and we were alone with the water. We would chase each other in the shallows and spread our arms out wide, twirl until we collapsed, laughing. We opened our mouths to drink raindrops. When the lightning started, we dove deeper.

In the beginning, letters from Ashley were like drugs: an irresistible promise of temporary escape that always made me feel worse after I was done with them. Seeing the envelope with my name scrawled in her mousy handwriting, I would feel a surge of gladness at the reminder that I had someone saving space for me in my "real life." But after reading her words—pages about how much she loved and missed me and how my absence had convinced her we were meant to be together forever and school was boring and she had to go now, some girl was bringing her to a party—I felt so distant from the life I had waiting at home that I forced myself to remember things I should miss. I would will myself back to the lazy Ashley afternoons, lying in each other's arms with nothing but pot and bed and sad songs by narcissistic women, the way Ashley's faith in love—violent and hedonistic as ours was—gave me permission to let myself go, do nothing with my life but fall into the situations she offered me.

I always felt a sense of relief when I could conjure up longing to attach to those memories, because the deeper I fell in love with Bodh Gaya, the more terrified I became of going home. So I reveled in the fact of her letters, piled up on my desk like down payments, even as I began to respond less and less frequently, knowing it would require something I could only access with great effort.

And then one night a monk came to the restaurant where I was eating vegetable curry for dinner to tell me I had a phone call. "Aslay, I think," he said. We walk-ran back to the monastery and he pointed to the office, where a giant antique phone was sitting off the hook. "Ash!" I exclaimed. "I can't believe you called!" After a pause, her voice came back to me casual, subdued.

"Hey, happy belated birthday. Did you have a good day?" she asked.

"It was the best birthday of my life," I gushed, and told her about how it was on the last day of our forty-eight-hour silent meditation retreat, and baby goats were born during our final walking meditation, and how to break the silence, one boy began singing "Happy Birthday" and everyone else joined in, belting out the words with voices that hadn't been used in two days.

She said she was glad I was so happy. But that wasn't really why she was calling. She had to ask me a serious question, and she couldn't talk for long, it was so expensive. "See, there's this girl I'm becoming really good friends with," she began. I leaned my weight against the office desk as she continued, hearing the words almost before she spoke them—how they'd had sex the night before and then Ash felt so guilty that she just had to call, but this girl was so cool, and it was just friends with benefits. "That's okay, right? You'll still be my girlfriend when you get home, right?" I looked at the floor at the orange robes swooshing in and out of the office as she spoke. A couple of American students walked by the open door, laughing. I remembered my vegetable curry. I told her I would write her a letter. "I love you," she said. "I love you so much."

The next afternoon I went up to the roof of the monastery and stared down at the rice fields. I was gripping the smooth ceramic railing with both hands and rocking back and forth on my heels over and over, when I heard footsteps behind me. Leah, an American girl I'd never really talked to, came up beside me and asked if I was okay.

"I'm breaking up with my girlfriend," I blurted out, and was instantly irritated by the words' mundanity compared to my inner panic.

"Oh, shit" was all she said in response, so austere that I knew I was telling the truth. I remember that moment with crystalline clarity—the hot sun on our backs, the absurdity of the two of us strangers gripping this railing, looking down into rice fields where an old woman was squatting in the mud and threatening her grazing buffalo with a stick. I remember thinking, "This is pain's arrival," and there was something in that acknowledgment that made the period to follow less excruciating, as if I were watching the drama of letting go wash over me from afar, with something close to curiosity.

I cried silently for two weeks during meditations after that, lifting my hands slowly from my knees to wipe my face with the corner of my *dupatta*. I cried loudly for those two weeks on the roof at night. I would go up there after I had brushed my teeth and beaten the insects out of my bed, and lie there under the stars, inhaling Bodh Gaya's constant burning smell and listening to the crickets singing from the rice fields. Once the tears started, I would sit up and rock myself in a ball. I remember looking up on one of those nights, seeing the nearly full moon rising from behind the Mahabodhi temple and thinking, "There is nowhere else I would rather be," even as I rocked and sobbed like a catatonic psych-ward patient, imagining Ashley in someone else's arms and silently singing those lines from the Sarah McLachlan song she used to blast every time she felt namelessly bad, which was often: "You hurt me more than I ever would have imagined. You made my world stand still." It was that kind of soppy, narcissistic broken heart.

And then it lifted. I began to hear those lines play over in my head less and less frequently; the images of Ashley in bed with someone else began to die out almost as soon as they entered my mind. Meditating for two hours a day in the same room, with the same people, on the same blue cushion, I got to witness my inner world shifting before my eyes. Soon all that mattered as I sat watching my breath was the trickle of sweat dripping off my nose into my lap, the erratic whir of the ceiling fan, the puppies yelping outside.

I used to go to the roof of the monastery to dance alone after evening meditation. I could see the Mahabodhi to the west, commemorating the place of the Buddha's enlightenment. To the south was the long bridge that leads to the place where the peasant Sujata offered the Buddha rice milk, breaking his fast and waking him up to the Middle Path—not too much leniency, not too much austerity. I would raise my arms up to the sky and leap and twirl and skip to Tom Petty and

Belle and Sebastian songs playing in my head. The glass bangles on my wrists—twelve on each arm—would cling together like wind chimes. I became so embarrassed by myself that I couldn't stop laughing. I covered my arms in kisses. I stayed up there until the sun had completely disappeared behind the yellow house at the edge of the rice fields.

Once, seeing a plane pass overheard, I was immediately assailed by the wistful ache planes have awakened in me since I was a little girl and first understood those lights in the sky meant travel, being far away. But in India, the vague longing that arrested my dancing for a moment was not to be inside the plane. For once, I was sad for the time when a plane would carry me away from the exact spot I was in.

The day I left Bodh Gaya, I sat alone on the roof until the final gong was called. I did three slow prostrations to the Buddha statue in the meditation hall, and then I got on the bus to the train station. I tried to stay awake to look out the window, but soon I no longer recognized the barefoot boys running and waving, or the women carrying naked babies or baskets of dried cow pies, so I closed my eyes. Getting on the plane to Boston was a sudden divorce from joy. I called Ashley an hour after I got home. I watched myself smoke a bowl and lean in to kiss her in the car. I heard myself tell her it was alright now; things were going to be okay with us again. When she dropped me off at home that night, I sat outside in the snow for a long time. I told myself I was just confused and jetlagged, that mistakes like that don't matter, that they only last the one night.

I tried to continue meditating at home, fifteen minutes in the morning and evening. But at night I was usually too drunk or stoned, and in the morning I was too cloudy. And I felt weird sitting on a pillow, cross-legged and straight-backed, with Ashley nearby, waiting for me to finish so we could go to bed or go get breakfast. Each time I let myself give in to those hollow moments of lying with Ashley instead of meditating, I would remember Munindra-ji telling us, "When your mind is clear, you have easy solutions." But if I had to be a real person, trudging through schoolwork and depressing news stories and sharp, cold faces, I didn't think I could bear to have a clear mind. It seemed so much easier to be cloudy, and, in a way it was: it made the moments pass so easily it was like they were nothing at all.

The summer after I got home from India, Ashley's grandmother had to move full-time into a hospital, and Ashley got the keys to her apartment. We would go there late at night or during the day, between my babysitting jobs. We took shots of the rum we kept in the freezer, next to the Tyson chicken dinners. We never found any glasses among the cans and cans of Campbell's soups, so we drank it out of the bottle. Then we would get naked in her grandmother's bed, which we liked because neither of our beds at home had a head-board. We would tie each other to the metal flowers and fuck so hard the bed came away from the wall. After I came, I would hold her lips tightly together with my other hand over her eyes, then lay very still until the last peace-seconds drained away. Afterward, we would crawl under the bed to retrieve bras and socks from amongst the rows of yellowed shoes and slippers.

The first night we slept over there, I lay awake in that sheetless bed and listened to the sound of the air conditioner. As the first light came through the blinds, I shook Ashley gently and said her name. She looked at my wet cheeks and turned her back. I hit her with a pillow until she sat up. We had sex until early afternoon.

One night as I was stumbling around in the bathroom of Ashley's grandmother's apartment, my last glass bangle from India broke off my wrist. Tiny pieces of blue glass scattered all over the pink granny tiles woke me up enough that I stopped and looked in the mirror for a long minute and wondered if that had really been me dancing on that roof in Bodh Gaya. But I was so drunk and the image was so coated in sober longing that I bent down, picked up the pieces as quickly as I could, and threw them in the trash. Then I walked straight into the bedroom, where Ashley was waiting for me.

We kept fighting all that summer, and drinking and smoking pot and staying out till dawn. One Thursday night we collapsed. We were dancing at a bar, so high on beer and pot and so full of our own emptiness that we could no longer hide the damage we were doing to ourselves through each other. So when Ashley spent one song too many dancing with another girl, I got so angry that I would not let her touch me. She started grabbing at my arms and I swatted her away. We were screaming in the middle of grinding couples. The big man grabbed us and led us to the door. And then we were in the nighttime city lights and I was running and she was chasing me, grabbing at my wrists as my arms flailed and punched wherever they landed, until Ashley was up against a brick wall and a police officer was saying, "Did I tell you you could move?" and I was trying to make myself sound sane for the officer—"No, this is not a domestic dispute, sir. We just met. It's fine now"—and then we were shaking hands, being ushered into a cab. We had no money for the kind Pakistani driver because Ashley's house was locked and neither of us had keys. I got his address to send the money, but I lost it and he never got his thirty dollars. He told us to go to sleep as he pulled away, that sometimes it is better in the morning.

The next night, I walked in my sleep. My mom found me standing in front of the window, shrieking. I tried to end it after that. But Ashley begged me not to go, and I remembered how I could laugh and go to parties and wake up in the morning with someone to talk to when she was there.

The real ending happened very quickly and oddly a few months after that, when we were both back at school and visiting each other on the weekends. The only way to explain what happened is that Ashley just left. She had spent almost two years telling me that I never gave her enough, that all she needed was to be with me always and then she would be perfectly happy and I wouldn't give this to her, why wouldn't I give this to her, and then suddenly she was gone: refusing to kiss me as I touched her, coming with her arms limp at her sides, bringing me to her parties only to leave me in the corner to drink alone while she flirted and laughed and made her jokes with everyone else. So I ended it, and this time she did not stop me.

My meditation teacher in Bodh Gaya used to tell us that we die in each moment, only to be reborn in the next. Reminding myself of that sometimes helped a little in those weeks after Ashley's need passed from me to something else, and so I had to be alone with the mistakes I had made. But of course I could not forget that it *was* me who had done those things, who had slept and woken in that closet of pain and done nothing to get out of it. I had known the joy of living by rules that make sense, and I so easily traded it away for something I knew I did not want.

But then a few more weeks passed, and I let myself remember the first full day we spent together—how it was warm enough for skirts and T-shirts and driving around with the windows open while Ashley played song after song that I loved; how she was the only person I'd ever met who listened to music as loudly as I did and wasn't bothered by spitting windblown hair out of her mouth as she shouted over it; how she lay her hand over mine as I drove, moving with me as I shifted gears; how I learned what it felt like to share the feeling of not caring what happens after this day, and how it felt so much better than not caring alone. We drove through Connecticut and Massachusetts, stopping at coffee shops along the way, never once mentioning that it was finals week at school, that I had a ten-page paper due in the morning. We laughed so hard that twice Ashley spit coffee all over my new white skirt—once hot, once iced—and I told her with complete honesty that I didn't mind at all. When I let myself remember that, I can understand how I was able to convince myself that I never made a choice at all, that this was just there, and it came with hitting and yelling and drugs and lots and lots of crying.

I once asked my TA in Bodh Gaya, who'd spent most of her twenties traveling back and forth between India and the States, "Is it very hard to go home?" I was hoping her answer would surprise me, that she'd sound like my mom trying to get me to start writing a paper for school: "Dreading it is always worse than doing it." But instead she smiled in that removed way she had of leaving us to face the problem of the moment head on. "Going home is the hardest part of the whole trip," she said.

Four years later, I still think of those words every time I remember the novel joy of that first trip to India, the safety of drifting off to sleep cocooned in my mosquito net as familiar voices whispered over cups of tea, roosters crooned in the courtyard, and Bollywood music absurdly blasted from town. So I see how I felt at the time that it would be impossible to be happy anywhere else, and I may as well let myself fall back inside nothing Ashley days. I will probably always ache for "my India," as I used to call it to myself, walking around Bodh Gaya with my bangles jangling on my wrists, stopping to chat with monks I knew or hold friends' naked babies. My panic to leave Bodh Gaya may have derived from an intuitive understanding of the truth: that those really would be the happiest days of my life.

But I don't wonder about that anymore—an unanswerable question that is irrelevant to my current life—just as I almost never think of that first day with Ashley, the coffee and laughter. What matters now are the months after we broke up—the endless hunger from lack of appetite and insomniac exhaustion and crying so frequently I hardly noticed when the tears started or stopped—and how all that was such a small price to pay for reclaiming my days, ones where I say my silent version of grace before every meal, remember to eat slowly and taste sugar melting on my tongue; sit quietly for a few moments each day and watch the constant arising and passing away of breath, sensations, moments; lie flat under the stars to feel how tiny I am and yet part of it all, to remind myself that no matter how cramped the quarters seem at times, there is always some plane overhead, flying through infinite space.

Shopping

LAUREN SANDERS

$\mathcal{V}$eronica, descended from the shopping gods, was a sprightly figure who donned trendy clothes as comfortably as most people wore pajamas. She loved trying things on with the dressing room curtain half open, and had a talent for plucking the sexiest items from the rack. Shopping was for her an act of rebellion against years of Catholic school uniforms and religious convocation. Her mother thought she was in Rome to study with the nuns.

We met in that ancient city, at a tiny boutique with rows of fake snakeskin pants and sweaters that looked like trench coats. She stepped out of the dressing room in a tight denim skirt and baby T with sparkles and crescents between her breasts, and I imagined tracing the waves with my pinkie. The thin, angular salesgirl yanked down the skirt so it hung low on her hips. Veronica eyed herself in the mirror, palming the vulcanized fabric as if it were a sheath. As if she were on a photo shoot. I wondered what the denim felt, sandwiched like that between her hand and thigh.

She pivoted to look at herself from behind. I was mesmerized.

I like that word.

Franz Mesmer was an Austrian physician who believed all ailments stemmed from a misalignment of internal magnetic energy. Patients seeking realignment attached magnets to their limbs and drank iron or held ropes tied to a magnetized tree. Mesmer would swing his hands close to their bodies in a series of furious passes, conductor of his own symphony. In his care, people were said to faint, convulse, speak in tongues. He called this animal magnetism.

Veronica, head twisted over her shoulder, caught sight of me in the mirror. She turned around, and in an American accent, as if we'd known each other for years, asked me if the skirt was too revealing. I felt a rumbling in my chest, was afraid my face might betray the heat beneath my skin. A vestige of pediatric trauma. As a child, I was constantly pink-skinned and sweaty-palmed. Boiling from the inside out. It grew worse whenever anyone looked at me.

Veronica's stare was magnetic, mnemonic. I found it soothing. Like a nursery rhyme. My words came involuntarily. I'd been hypnotized . . . *mesmerized.*

I said: "You should buy that outfit and never take it off."

My father is a shopper. He can spend hours sifting through aisles of suits, coats, ties, and slacks. He loves the feel of virgin tweed between his fingers. The starchy smell of fresh cotton shirts. He also likes to watch people shop.

When I was thirteen he bought me a red dress. It was short-sleeved, silky, and to the knee. A sash of white satin belted above my pubescent hips. They were round and embarrassing, normally buried beneath layers of corduroy and flannel, but in that red dress there was no hiding the peaks and curves. Trying it on, I saw myself in the mirror: cold and goose-fleshed. My face was no longer pink. Three years earlier, I'd had an operation that left my skin as transparent as cigarette paper. But my forearms and shins bore the purplish scars of one who'd started shaving too young. I was on the swim team. They said without hair you swam faster. The other girls in my dormitory at boarding school shaved too. For boys.

My father watched me throw back my shoulders and suck in my stomach as if seeing me for the first time. My body was a surprise to him. It was surprising for me to surprise him. An uncomfortable tingling crept into my neck and cheeks. I wanted to cry: I'm turning pink again. But I'd barely cried. Not from the burning of my soggy, red face, nor the wet palm prints I left on the surface of everything I touched. Of the estimated five million sweat glands in the human body, two-thirds are located in the hands. As a child, I couldn't understand what made my millions of glands different from everyone else's. I was afraid to touch anything that didn't belong to me. Afraid to write on the chalkboard or return a rubber ball that had been kicked out of bounds. I thought I would never hold another person's hand.

Doctor after doctor said the condition was benign. My father—himself a doctor—didn't give up. He carted me to specialists throughout the world, daring anyone to fix my skin. At ten years old, I had experimental endoscopic surgery in Germany.

My mother returned to the States a week after they'd sliced into my back and severed the sympathetic chain; my father stayed the whole four weeks. Afterwards, we visited Berlin. Before the wall came down. My father explained about borders that pitted brother against brother. He cursed the war that had taken his father. He promised he would never let anything like that happen to me.

Remembering his words, I relaxed into the red dress and saw in my father's eyes my transformation from tomboy to young woman. At that moment I knew what I'd felt for a while. Something other than a child, I was ripe. Blistering in hormones and curves. My father told me this without words. He knelt down next to me and lifted the hem above my knees. His thumbs grazed my skin. He smelled like a Christmas tree; I was his ornament. He smiled up at the woman who owned the store. A short hem is the style these days, they agreed. How he knew so much about style my mother and I never asked. He spent most of his time in surgical scrubs.

That day, both of us staring at my lustrous red reflection, my father told me red was the color of revolutionaries and romantics. The two together made love, he said. To wear red was valiant, risky, and seductive.

My father knew about these things. He worked in trauma.

I had only the vaguest ideas about life then. Could barely make sense of my father's words. His gray-green eyes sparkling at the sight of me all dressed up and no place yet to go. The red dress. I knew only that when I peered into the mirror at the dress shop I saw someone different from the girl who slouched across the hills of the academy in old corduroys and bit her fingernails until they bled.

Down the street, we bought a pair of white patent-leather pumps that matched the belt and stitching. The heels were too high. Back at school, I practiced walking in my dorm room. Thirteen is not a good age for anything. My roommate told the other girls I was training to become a prostitute.

Every day, I practiced my walk and talked to phantom dates in the mirror. They wore tuxedo jackets with jeans and smelled like my father. I quit the swim team to devote myself to them, ripped the pages from my text books and replaced them with lyrics from gloomy love songs. At the end of the year, I was shipped home after a phone call proclaiming I was not to return unless I attended summer school, and even then I would probably have to repeat the seventh grade.

I wore the red dress and white shoes on the bus ride home. My father met me at the train station. He said I looked smashing and took me home. Told me to splash some water on my face but keep on the dress. My mother was away on business and we were going out to dinner. I was elated. I loved being with my father.

At one of the fancier restaurants in town, my father ordered expensive meats, shrimp cocktail, sparkling water with slices of lime. He let me sip from his wine glass. He was handsome in his trimmed beard and tan. I'd brushed my lashes with mascara and dabbed my cheeks with the rosy blush my mother had given me the first time I wore the dress, to a family wedding.

All the men in the restaurant gawked; the women looked askance. Were they staring because my dress was wrinkled from sitting two hours on the bus and there were sweat stains under my armpits, or was it something different?

I didn't finish my steak. My father helped me after he'd eaten his venison. Between bites he told me I wouldn't be going to summer school. The academy could kiss his public-school behind. He said he would explain everything to my mother who'd had the idea to send me away, though she could be quite single-minded when she had an idea. Shopping with her was like an archeological dig—hours spent sifting through racks at discount department stores searching for the one item she had to have. My mother was brilliant and tenacious. She always found what she needed. Sometimes without even trying it on.

What if communal dressing rooms were more like bathhouses? With jasmine incense burning and smoky lighting, shadows that would make anyone desirable. Walking in, a clerk takes the items you've selected and gives you a steaming cloth for your hands as flight attendants do after a long journey. The clerk hangs your clothes next to the mirror. Your fingers bathe in the warmth of the towel. A deep breath and the sweet spices flow down your spine. In the mirror you see you are beautiful. So is everyone around you. You are not afraid of watching them. Of being watched. Everyone is steeped in the erotic ritual.

Several years ago, I found myself alone one night on a dark industrial street by the river. I'd just ended a brief affair with a boy who was barely legal, almost a decade younger than me, and had gone out looking for excitement. I went to a women's bar. Everyone there spoke of a back room. I made my way inside. A few women stood fully clothed against the walls, others breezed back and forth, haute urbane, and I remembered I'd once fallen in love at first sight. Many years before. With an older woman who fed me equal doses of madness and literature. She took me shopping for second-hand cardigans and made me memorize "The Love Song of J. Alfred Prufrock":

> In the room the women come and go
> Talking of Michelangelo.

I imagined spray-painting the words on the walls of the club.

Finally, a minor celebrity decided she'd had enough talking. She peeled off her dress and lay down on the floor. Another woman removed her clothes and slid on top of her. They kissed. A third woman joined in, a hand on one's breast as her mouth found the neck of the other. Three became six, then seven, then eight . . .

I lost count as their bodies slithered into a sac of limbs and liquid, one living, breathing organism. A few of us stood off to the side, watching. I held an internal debate. Nobody knew me. Nobody would know I'd done it. But I couldn't bring myself to remove my clothes. Nearby, a voice led the chorus of hollers and moans, this heaving, pulsating thing so close I felt it on my skin. I could have stepped down and grabbed it, but my feet were bolted to the floor. The air was heavy, like summer in the South. I couldn't breathe, caught in the middle of a steam room in my street clothes. Beneath the outer layers, my body began to evaporate. I lost my neck, my arms, my stomach, my thighs.

The cuffs pulled at my heavy wool pants. It was all I wore then, when I'd shaved my head and was experimenting with androgyny. Never in my life had I been so consistently approached by both men and women. The streets and stores and bars and buses had become a back room on the go. Looking down, I saw a hand wrapped around my ankle. My pulse quickened. I felt another hand between my thighs and with the grip tightening around my leg rocked into a deafening orgasm.

I bolted from the source.

In the room the women come and go . . .

At the bar, I caught my breath and ordered a club soda. It was dark enough to hide my dilated pupils and rubbery knees, cool enough to nurse the hole in my heart. I wanted to be back in my apartment, where isolation wasn't so conspicuous. I am not a good candidate for anonymous sex. When I come I fall in love.

Before I left, I looked for the hand. Through one of the holes someone had drilled in the wall. Attrition had befallen the organism. But it was no less dogged in its pursuit of pleasure. Its noises were more dire, the keening of banshees. .

Another group of women—the deconstructionists—had gathered to observe through the holes.

"This isn't erotic," one said. "Do you think this is erotic?"

"No," said another.

Then another: "Not at all."

All night they kept their eyes plastered to the holes talking about how un-erotic it was.

We set out for Milan in a car Veronica borrowed from her Italian cousins, stopping one night in Florence to buy leather gloves for her mother. Veronica loved to imitate her mother—she was a caricature or cliché. The Italian American with her scoured face and fingers scrunched together, her thick accent and unbalanced stride. All she'd wanted from Italy was a pair of gloves and a rosary blessed by the Pope. She wore the same housedress every day. It drove Veronica mad.

Florence was congested. Veronica had difficulty navigating the pools of summer tourists. We parked the car and stepped from its air-conditioned cocoon into the smothering maw of the season. I needed water; Veronica wanted a gelato. We walked a few blocks to a café and eyed the fantastically colored ice cream behind the glass, convinced only the Italians could make a museum-worthy exhibit out of milk and sugar. Outside a young man in a tank top rubbed soapy water against the window, sweat dripping from his temples. Even in the heat, life went on. I ordered a large bottle of water and a yellow pineapple cone. Veronica was already licking the deepest brown chocolate I'd ever seen. We sat down next to the window, the two of us tonguing our cones as the young man made rainbows out of soap and water on the windowpane.

The seventeenth-century scientist Isaac Newton studied rainbows in soap bubbles to prove his theory of white light. Before him every scientist believed white light simply was what it looked like: white light. But by passing a beam of sunlight through a glass prism, Newton discovered a spectrum of colors. He concluded white light concealed a rainbow of refracted streams, each comprised of tiny corpuscles. Like blood.

We spent the night in a cramped room with white stucco walls and two double beds. Veronica opened her suitcase and removed a silky red nightgown. She undressed in the bathroom. I stripped down to my underwear and put on a T-shirt. It was hot in the room. I opened a window, which made it even more stifling. Veronica snored all night. Her nose in the moonlight looked almost phallic. I studied her face, wondering what sort of streams and corpuscles lurked beneath her skin.

The next morning, we woke with the sun and hit the market before the heat set in. Veronica honed in on a pair of mauve gloves, while I modeled cashmere sweaters over my clothes. After making her purchase, she found me perspiring in a snug V-neck sweater with three-quarter-inch sleeves. "You look lovely," she said, and somehow I stayed calm, pretending I knew it too. She grabbed me by the elbow to look at my figure in the dingy mirror. The sweater over my long tubular skirt reminded me of a mermaid. I was blushing. She thought I was lovely.

I bought the sweater, and we set off to see David. By the time we arrived at the museum, the line was already massive. Veronica said we should wait, but I was afraid I might pass out from the heat. She wanted me to see David's hands; the biggest, sweetest hands she'd ever seen. I said of course he had big hands, he's fourteen feet tall, but I felt dizzy. Veronica said his nose was also big, and my heart jumped. Had I spoken aloud about *her* nose the night before? She said David looked Jewish or Italian. I said he was Jewish, in the hands of an Italian, and like that we left Florence, two American women talking of Michelangelo.

There is an intimacy to car travel. For me, it is the perfect merging of public and private space, at once enclosed and exposed. A veteran of marketing and sales, I have spent much of my time alone on the road. I often pick up hitchhikers—women only—and am amazed what people reveal once the rhythm of wind and wheels takes hold.

We told each other things in Veronica's car. We talked about how we'd been hurt. Exchanged stories. There was an immediacy to our conversation, as if in a few hours of driving we could condense the decades. We arrived exhausted in Milan and checked into an elegant hotel with air-conditioning. Again, the bellhop led us to a room with two double beds. Again, Veronica changed in the bathroom.

I remember that bathroom as much as anything else in the city. So clean and bright, with a bidet and no standing shower, it seemed like the city itself, an icon of modernization and tradition.

I remember the beds with their ornate coverings and rubbery foam pillows. The construction men in bright orange hard hats working outside our window. Veronica insisted we keep the curtains open. They couldn't see us through the fog, she said.

I remember the stores we strolled in and out of. Along the avenues, hidden in cul-de-sacs, Veronica found them all. She'd been living in Italy more than two years, but it was her first time in Milan. She hated shopping alone.

We went one afternoon to a little shop with tinseled windows. Inside were short, short dresses, iridescent halter tops, shiny synthetic jackets, and rows of black trousers that caught Veronica's eye. The first pair flared above her ankles like a couple of clarinets in repose. They were all the rage that season. The shop was packed with prowling young women modeling clingy garments for each other, their hair and skin and clothes multiplying in the mirrors like a Cubist painting. A city of women.

Veronica and I took turns using one of the two dressing rooms. Once, we met in the stall. She giggled, and turned her back to me before wriggling out of a shirt. I watched her shoulder blades spread, mesmerized. They formed wings beneath the tattoo on the back of her neck. The Hebrew word *Shalom.* Peace.

I asked what I'd been wondering since we met. "Why the Hebrew?"

She laughed, and told me Hebrew was the language of the Bible. Even Jesus spoke Hebrew. By the way, did I know she was named after the saint Veronica? The woman who met Jesus on his way to the crucifixion and handed him her veil. When he returned it, his face was etched on the cloth. Veronica had seen the cloth at St.

Peter's, she said, slithering into a hot-pink halter top with strings that crisscrossed down her back. She asked me to tie the ends. I stepped closer, heart pounding, a feeling less instilled by her bare back than by her reconfiguring five thousand years of history to suit her own purposes. This was very sexy. I wiped my sweaty fingertips on my pants and took up the strings.

As I tied, Veronica told me the holy cloth was also called a Veronica, a name biblical scholars said was derived from both Latin and Greek. *Vera* meaning true, and *ekon* or icon, as we know it, being an image. True image.

I looped the strings beneath her ribs, giving the bow a final tug. She turned around, raised an eyebrow, and pulled back the dressing room curtain. Once again, I stood captivated by her figure in the mirror. This woman, this image. *Vera Icon.*

She moved her hips from side to side, pivoting to check out her back as was her habit. She knew I was watching.

"So?" she said, and I knew what was coming next. "Is it—"

"Too revealing? Never."

"But do I—"

"Look fat? Absolutely."

Ignoring me, which she could do because she knew she wasn't fat, knew she had the kind of body designers envisioned when their ideas were nothing more than charcoal sketches and swatches of material draped over a mannequin, Veronica slipped her hands beneath her breasts. A slight pout to her lips, she wondered whether a push-up bra might help.

I shook my head no. The color was all wrong.

She smiled, and asked me to untie her.

To this day I crave the rush of shoplifting. Those last strung-out seconds before the door when nothing registers but the stereophonic thump of your pulse. Then, a couple of small steps, and you're lost in the weekend crowd, sprinting through the streets with your best friend as if you'd just crossed the border during wartime—any war, any time. Sammie and I knew nothing of politics; our parents had money. We were mercenaries.

Afterward, we bought onion rings and chocolate milkshakes and finished them on the walk to the bus stop. On the ride home, as dusk cradled up against the frosted windows, we giggled uncontrollably and copped furtive drags from a cigarette, our bodies tingling with life.

We stole everything: gold-filled bracelets, plastic rings, thick lip glosses, toe socks, sunglasses, halter tops, hats, gloves, paperback novels, cassette tapes, candy bars, and whatever else we could fit into the pockets of our oversized coats or slip beneath our baggy pants. Soon our heads grew larger than our clothes. We thought ourselves invincible. We left the house in old sneakers and came home with new ones. Walked out of stores in jackets with the price tags clipped. Our parents hardly noticed. We told them we traded clothes since we didn't have sisters; they told us how lucky we were to be teenagers in America.

The year we were thieves summer came too quickly. Early in the season we went shopping for bathing suits and found the store so crowded the saleslady let us share a dressing room. We jammed inside the white cubicle with its silly shutters. Down the row, we could see the heads and feet of other women, most of them my mother's age, one to a dressing room like something out of another era, backstage in a dance hall or at summer camp in the 1950s, without boys— the kind of places I'd only seen in black and white on television or in my mother's photo albums. Adulthood had always seemed monochromatic to me.

In the room the women come and go . . .

They peeked at us over the tops of their stalls. We were too loud for the dressing room. How dare we disturb the lackluster chore of trying on clothes?

We were fourteen and finishing each other's sentences. We sang dirty words in limericks and rhymes, words we'd looked up in the dictionary. We shoved each other back and forth like boys on the football team, as we surveyed the rainbow of suits—one-pieces with flowers, tropical fruits, and zebra stripes; bikinis crafted in macramé or clipped from sheets of psychedelic nylon. Even the boring Speedos in our hands radiated with possibility.

Our clothes dropped like petals from a dying flower, our bare elbows and shins bumping against each other as we tested one suit after the next, determining how many we might be able to fit beneath our clothes. Some we knew wouldn't fit. Others we held up for each other's inspection. We were determined. Methodical. If my mother had taught me systematic shopping, then this was systematic shoplifting, the layering of bikinis under one-pieces under our clothes. Only the black suit with the big hole in the center presented difficulty. It was one of a kind, unclassifiable, and we both loved it. Sammie said we should shoot for it. Odds or evens.

I picked odds. I won. But the suit made my stomach look like a swollen dart board. Sammie said it wasn't my look. A million times she'd said I would know my look by the feel of it. I knew it was more complicated. A look was who you were *and* who you might want to be. A look was about possibility.

Sammie tried on the black suit, and if the sweat between my legs had seeped from my underwear into the crotch she didn't say anything. I watched her step into the leg holes and squeeze the clingy fabric over her thighs and chest and shoulders. It fit her snugly, and seemed to have been designed for her flat stomach and conical breasts. Her look.

But, for the first time, I saw something else. Something knowing. Something I wanted to know. In those few seconds it took her to try on the suit and confirm its perfection in the mirror, she had transitioned into the black-and-white world of adulthood. A world she would enter on her own.

When I think of Sammie, I forget she's married with three kids and remember that day in the dressing room. The day she wore the bathing suit that framed her belly button and made her look like a pinup girl. A suit so great we couldn't risk stealing it. I put it on my father's credit card as a decoy.

She wiggled out of the nylon tube and stood in front of me, naked except for a pair of white cotton panties with little pink hearts that said LOVE. Like Valentine's candies. She was so close I could see the tiny pores in her nose, smell the sweet scent of bubble gum on her lips, and I knew then—although I had no words for it—that I loved her completely and unconditionally. A love that hijacked every muscle in my body. A love like shoplifting.

It was Sammie, as much as my father, who fused love and shopping for me. That day in the dressing room when she pinched my thigh and told me I would outgrow my baby fat. At her touch, I felt myself drowning in colors. Like a canvas with Sammie squirting paint at me.

I lost my balance and prayed for gravity.

Einstein spoke back to me: Gravitation cannot be held responsible for people falling in love.

Our friendship shifted that day. The day she wore the bathing suit that changed the way we looked at each other. We'd sipped from the forbidden goblet and were finally caught, not for any of the bathing suits beneath our clothes—they were never even discovered—but for a gold bracelet Sammie had slipped into her bag at the cash register, breaking the cardinal rule of shoplifting in department stores: never lift anything once you've left the fitting room. There were too many guards and cameras and mirrors. Someone had seen her. They shoved us into the back office and emptied our bags. There was the bracelet with the price tag intact.

She did it on purpose. I knew; she knew I knew; but we never spoke about it. We drifted apart without ceremony. Without resolution. Most of my lovers have gone that way.

Sammie left me with the intimacy of dressing rooms. How two girls together can get away with certain things. Why Veronica and I shopped in three different cities before I found the courage to kiss her in the room with the two double beds. We'd been shopping for days by then. I knew the Italian words for hips, stomach, and thighs. Knew how to say, "How much?" I could have made love to her in Italian. But she wanted it in English. American English. "Fuck me," she whispered. "Fuck me like you've been dying to."

After that dinner with my father, I wore the red dress only one more time. The summer after I'd been kicked out of school, before I started shoplifting. It was my father's birthday and we were having dinner with a few of my parents' friends. This memory, of course, is black and white except for my crimson dress and wine the color of juice from steak. They let me have my own glass, agreeing it was very European.

The friends said I looked older, was going to be trouble once the braces came off my teeth. My father nodded. He told them that the last time we'd gone out together everyone thought I was his lover. Coming from his lips, the word evoked mystery and romance. It also felt sordid. My cheeks flushed redder than the dress.

They all laughed. My mother was last and loudest before she settled into a long sip of wine. I wanted to hurl the bottle at her, at all of them with their teeth and gums stained ghoulish purple, their faces red with celebration.

When we blush, our capillaries dilate, trapping blood beneath the skin. Whether from arousal, exercise, too much wine, cold weather, or embarrassment the skin responds unwittingly. It gets hot and, depending upon your natural hue, changes color. On me the blood brushes bright pink.

The British naturalist Charles Darwin was the first scientist to connect blushing to our emotions. Blushing, he noted, was the most peculiar of human expressions because it was involuntary and ungovernable. Our nerves could not assess the stimuli and decide whether the context was appropriate. Only the heart stored that information.

I did not want to think about being my father's lover. Or anybody's lover. The word sounded too intimate. *Too revealing.* I started going out with older boys. Boys who carted kegs of beer for a living and drove souped-up automobiles. Boys who wore thermal shirts and would never be caught shopping for them. Boys who liked me in tight jeans and wouldn't know what to do with a red dress beyond getting their callused fingers underneath the hem. I never liked any of them.

What if I lined up my old lovers like shoes in a closet? Would they say anything about my style in love? Perhaps we shop for lovers as we shop for clothes. Sometimes determined, knowing exactly what we're looking for; other times wandering into stores half-oblivious and gravitating toward whatever we find attractive—impulse buying.

My mother, as I've mentioned, does nothing on impulse. She has had one lover her entire life and never shops with friends. She doesn't have to. She married a man who likes shopping more than she does. But she's good with makeup. She was the one who'd started me on mascara and a little concealer at thirteen, when I was skittish about rubbing anything on my skin that didn't sound clinical, terrified the wrong chemical might rouse the disease the Germans had excised with a thoracic sympathectomy. *Sympathectomy.* The word is not as congenial as it sounds. There is nothing congenial about having a metal tube shoved only inches from your heart.

Sounds as absurd as clipping magnets to your skin or holding ropes attached to an electrified tree. Being *Mesmerized.* But the surgery fixed my face, and I am now as normal as the next light-skinned mammal. Except when I fall in love. Then the worst sensations of my youthful condition return—the hot, pink skin and sweaty temples—refracting my body through a prism. Even with makeup, I cannot not shrink from my desire. It is written all over my face.

That was how I met Veronica, my face wide-eyed and flushed as she stood in front of that very first mirror modeling the shirt with the price tag hanging from her armpit. She cost fifty thousand lira.

> And would it have been worth it, after all,
> After the cups, the marmalade, the tea . . .

I would have paid fifty billion lira just to sit across from her in the café with the colorful gelato, even knowing what I know now. That the cloth at St. Peter's—the *Vera Icon*—is probably a fake, although it still seems miraculous behind its Plexiglas screen, hermetically sealed like a love affair in Italy. That loneliness comes from opening up and not shutting down, and there is no easy way to squeeze the sweet revelations, once divulged, back inside. Instead, they lie in front of you, little mausoleums of who you were *and* who you might want to be. Love is about possibility.

I also know that the word "lover" is more sad than sordid, for no matter the circumstances most lovers end where they began: alone. And missing a lover is the meanest kind of longing. It's ungovernable and involuntary. Worse than blushing. You become a shadow figure, an etching on a cloth.

This, contrary to popular belief, is the worst time to go shopping.

You Can Take Me to the Shrine, but You Can't Make Me Pray

LOUISE A. BLUM

I wake to find myself in the middle of a quest that I did not realize I'd undertaken. I am standing on a hilltop outside Mexico City, before the shrine of Guadalupe, the wind whipping through my hair, overlooking a great, vast city with which I am unfamiliar. Gold-leaf turrets shimmer in the sun. One cross after another pierces the sky. Rooftops empty into rooftops as if to form a set of stairs. Below me, in the courtyard, tiny, wrinkled women work their way across the cut stone on their knees. I can imagine the blood, stinging their skin, even though I cannot see it.

People are everywhere around me; we are shoulder to shoulder along the wall overlooking a city of twenty million people. There is no place here for solitude. We are all drawn by a similar need. Languages float around me on the air, a medley whose individual tones I cannot discern. A hush beats against us, in the form of a great wing that shields us from the city, the smog, the dead dog covered with lye that rots in the corner of the courtyard below. It shields us from the honking of horns, the screech of tires, the muffled swear of a cab driver, the symphony that is Mexico. Here on this hilltop, we are all the same. We are all on a quest. We are all immersed in our lives, our individual preoccupations. We are knitted together by the thread of our solitary wanderings into one great quilt of desire. Our heartbeats meld. I want to hold the hand of the woman next to me. Her head-scarf caresses her brow. She is unconscious of me, as if she were here alone, yet I can hear her breathing. My heart throbs in my chest, an open wound. What was a vacation has become a sacred offering. All that I have buried has been unearthed. The dirt sticks to my tongue.

This is the last place I ever thought I would find myself. I never intended to come here. In fact, when my lover, Connie, and I discovered that the tour we'd signed onto for the pyramids stopped first at the Shrine of Guadalupe, we decided to talk our fellow travelers out of it. We tended to approach every situation with the assurance that we could control it. It's almost as if we thought we could hijack the tour bus, subject everybody in it to our own agenda. "You don't really want to go there!" we'd tell them. "Just follow us." And they would, of course, comply. Given our individual compulsions to control our lives and the lives of those around us, it was no wonder that we'd spent as much of the last year and a half we'd been together fighting as we had making love.

We'd met in March, become lovers in December, and moved in together the following October. By traditional lesbian standards, I guess we moved pretty slowly. I had, however, spent the previous four years steadfastly avoiding any commitments. Now I felt as if I'd leapt onto a speeding bullet train, James Bond–style, and was currently clinging to the roof for dear life.

We failed to take Mexican men into account in our hijacking plans. Seasoned despots though we were, we were no match for these men who had been the bane of our existence since we arrived in this country. From the sultry young men who lounged around the Zona Rosa calling, "Hey, señorita!" in suggestive tones to the disapproving tour guide who had already asked us just why it was we *didn't* speak Spanish, we were continually on the defensive. The tour went to Guadalupe on schedule. I crossed my arms and sulked. Fine, I thought. You could take me to the shrine, but you couldn't make me pray.

This was our first vacation together. It was May, and Connie and I had come to Mexico for a month. We'd never traveled together, we didn't speak Spanish, and neither of us had ever been here before, but we didn't let that stop us. Blums are born to travel, my grandmother had reportedly said, a prediction that saw one of my older brothers to the jungles of Vietnam and the other to the frozen tundra of the Northwest Territories in 1968. Maybe Connie had never been out of the country, never even been further west than Michigan, but surely I had enough traveling experience under my belt for both of us. At twenty I had taken my bike to Europe, secured a job as a mother's helper in southern Germany, and spent five months speaking Schwäbisch. I took my notebook and wrote on the steps of cathedrals, the windowsill of an ancient monastery, cafés in Munich and Salzburg. I fell in love with a world that appeared to view time differently, as something to be treasured, not counted down as if to a shuttle launch.

I'd driven from San Francisco to Boston and back, awakened with the bells of a monastery on a mountaintop outside Taos, watched bats pollinate the saguaro in the Sonoran Desert. I'd slept in my truck, hiked Red Rock canyons in Utah, and driven through Kansas on roads that had no names to find Lorraine, the town where my father was born. There was a diner and a post office. Both were closed. There was no one there to speak to me; it was as if the town had frozen when my father left it, the inhabitants lifted out, the houses left intact, still filled with the dust of the Great Depression. I returned home empty-handed.

I suppose every trip I've ever taken has become a pilgrimage, somewhere along the line. But I still wasn't prepared for the journey that was Mexico.

Connie and I hit foreign soil in the midst of an argument, and if we thought a new locale would bolster our flailing relationship, we were wrong. All it did was provide a more exotic backdrop for our arguments. We fought in front of all the best-known tourist attractions, and then some. We fought in our rooms, we fought on the streets, we fought when we were hungry, we fought when we were tired. We fought when we were drinking, and the more we fought, the more we drank. The constant attempts to communicate wore us down. The night before the Guadalupe tour, we went out to dinner in the Zona Rosa, the wealthiest and most touristed area. When my dinner came, it was swimming with pork. I was sure, in my frantic perusal of our Spanish-English phrase book, that that wasn't what I'd ordered. My stomach turned. I signaled the waiter. He ignored me. I took a sip of wine, put my glass down. I could feel a tightening in my head. I signaled the waiter again. This time he came. I tried to send the food back. He shrugged his shoulders and began to turn away. "Do you speak any English?" I asked. I felt desperate.

"No," he said, and then, in Spanish, "This is Mexico."

I looked at him. Our eyes locked. I felt like a bull, pawing my foot on the grass. "Louise," Connie murmured. I seized his arm, went through my phrase book until I had something resembling the right wording. "This is not what I ordered," I said, enunciating carefully. "I want to send this back." I'd gotten close enough.

"No!" he said, again. He shook off my hand, turned and marched away.

I was shaking. "Don't make a scene," Connie whispered. I stared at her. I could feel an irrational anger rising in me. I pushed the food away. "Don't be angry," Connie begged.

How could I not be angry? "Let's go," I said. Inside, my anger raged, impotently, like a caged panther, seeking one loose bar to make an exit through. It occurred to me that Connie had been telling me not to be angry the whole time we'd been together.

Only recently out of the closet in our country, we were at a loss to reconfigure our relationship on turf so foreign to us it might as well have been Mars. A man trailed us as we left the restaurant. "Hey, señoritas," he called. "How was your dinner?" Men had been propositioning us since the moment we set foot in the country. This was one time too many. I turned around and gave him the finger. "Señorita," he cautioned, "I do not like that!" I shot back: "That's the fucking point!" Connie seized my arm to silence me and I shook it off angrily. I'd had it with pretending I suffered some low-level hearing loss, and diplomacy had never been my strong point.

The more frustrated we became with our surroundings, the more heated grew our arguments. "Fine," I'd say. "Let's just break up."

"You always want to break up!" Connie protested. "You're always ready to give up."

And she was right. I suspected deep down that I was not cut out for this kind of partnership. I had only to look at my parents to know that the talent it took to maintain a healthy and loving relationship did not necessarily run in our family. I longed for my solitary days, conveniently forgetting those many lonely nights. I yearned for my old autonomy, but at best it was half-hearted. Having come this far, I had the nagging sense that I could never go back. I had tasted what it was to be a couple. All the gritty ash of it. The more time I spent with Connie, the less I truly wanted to be alone. The train was moving too fast for me to jump. This relationship had become a part of me, and me a part of it. I could no sooner give it up than I could cure myself of cancer. For better or worse, we were in this together.

Perhaps if we had chosen another part of Mexico, a more touristy part, like Cancun or Cozumel, things might have ended differently. As it was, however, we chose the arid alien north of Mexico. Instead of beaches, we chose smog. We might have been drinking margaritas. Instead, we found ourselves sharing buses with chickens. And we couldn't just go for a week; it had to be a month. It was more like boot camp than a vacation.

I had thought I was a seasoned traveler, but Mexico is a language I do not speak. Everywhere I turn in San Miguel de Allende there is a cross, a testament to a faith I do not have. Cobblestone alleys plunge down hills I never even knew were there. We turn a corner, and the road drops away beneath our feet. Our lungs fight for the thin air that is afforded us. Arid hillsides open their thighs to the sun, eschewing rain. A niche cut into the stone of a street corner confronts us abruptly. Jesus stands poised on the globe that is our earth, one hand half raised, as if he had been interrupted, mid-thought. There was something he had to say—did anyone catch it? Frescos peel from grey stone ceilings; the bones of a saint peek out of windowed boxes carved of cedar. One man, all in black, gazes at me from a picture frame, surrounded by naked cherubim, penises discreetly garbed, who unfurl a banner that is always wordless. The bougainvillea chokes the pathways, pervades me with its scent. A push through a dark alley, and we are in the midst of a parade. Flags stream across the streets; the people are cloaked in the colors of flow-ers. Huge papier mâché puppets lead us dancing down the street; a mariachi band brings up the rear. At any moment, of any day or night, there can be a mariachi band. We are immersed in a swell of people who could be celebrating anything—a revolution, an insur-rection, a saint. Two sticks meet to form a cross above my head.

An American woman mourning her son's death greets us in a cantina buried deep in a side street. She has been here twenty years. It's a self-imposed exile. She is one of the expatriates, those who have come here and cannot find their way back. She loves the woman she lives with, who does not love her. Her son's needled veins wrap around her heart so that her lungs are trapped. The skin around her eyes is weathered with pain. She continues to call us long after we have stopped picking up the phone, stopped drinking in cantinas and begun instead to find quiet rooftops where we can sit and watch the stars. The woman's pain is too much to embrace. Connie and I have spoken often of having children, broaching the topic even before we brought up living together. We bring it up, then back off again and again, wary as wolves circling the tainted bait of a hidden trap. This relationship was hard enough, but to throw a child into the mix was unsettling enough to make me nauseous. I had trouble keeping friendships going through the years. What could be more long-lasting than parenthood? I thought of the woman whose com-pany we were avoiding. Her grief was so raw I could smell it on her. The depths of such a commitment are unfathomable. People cause each other pain, even on the best of days. What would be our future? What would be our legacy?

Three burros stand, unblinkingly, beneath our windows for just under an hour. Desert green is everywhere—in the scrub pines that dot the hillside; the cactus that yawn from the dirt, arms outstretched and reaching for the sky; the palm trees that cool the air. Jacaranda and eucalyptus scents eddy on the breeze. So much growth in a place of little water.

In Guanajato we see the mummified bodies of the poor, dug up to make room for those who could pay for graves. Once destined to be burned, they are now on display. An accident of climate has preserved them for inquiring eyes. I see a woman's labia through a sheet of glass before I turn away. In Antotonilco, we see a parade of mourners flagellate themselves, swinging their ropes across their own backs, again and again. A wood cross wavers before them, hesitating, as if God had doubted, mistrusted His creation, this line of ardent followers who crowd the doors of His church, hungering for the flesh of saints.

So many crucifixes; they crowd me, invoking all my latent claustrophobia. I sneak a glance here and there into the face of Jesus. His patiently suffering countenance does nothing for me. The thorns that twist about his head and pierce his brow appear contrived, as does the bloodless gash in his side. Why is he not howling in pain, writhing in unspeakable agony? I know that pain is neither stately nor elegant, yet his appears to be exquisite. Of course, he had an assurance that we do not—that his suffering had a purpose. We have only our lives, and no guarantee that we'll ever be called to anything greater than our ordinary fears and joys.

In Mexico City, the zocalo calls, in a voice as lilting as a distant flute. Mayan men populate the Diego Rivera murals that surround us on the walls of the Museum of Popular Cultures, foreheads sloping beneath their golden headbands. Outside on the plaza, drummers are warming up. The dancers' ankles are sheathed in weathered hooves. A hand pushes my camera from my face. There are things we are not meant to take away. A dancer's eyes are closed; her tongue lightly touches her teeth. Her face is poised mid-breath. The song ends before I am aware it has begun.

Stones litter a killing field that predates our own bloodshed. One head at a time is entered into sport. Giant warriors chiseled out of stone surround us at Tula. Their silences clamor with conflicting legends. The ball court stands cloaked in an ominous silence. Stone steps close us in. A hollowing in the stone above two skulls—How many have lain here, before us? Did they give of themselves willingly, or were there screams? The stones do not tell us; they hold the terror of a final witness; they will not give it up. The silence alone is testament. Every new generation comes up with its own manner of torture and enslavement, its own means of eliminating those it deems extraneous. The eternal one-upmanship.

Ten million Arawak Indians when Columbus landed in Haiti— twenty thousand left enslaved in a matter of years. Six million Jews obliterated by the Nazis. Seventy thousand Japanese civilians killed instantaneously when we dropped the bomb on Hiroshima. Countless dead in Iraq. Smart bombs. Daisy cutters. Depleted uranium. We get better and better at this. Besides—those old gods had nothing on ours. Our God's blood sacrifice called for no stranger, no enemy. His demanded nothing less than His own son. For the life of me, I cannot grasp the meaning of this.

I stand on a continuum of atrocities. Everywhere I look, I see more opportunities for horror. This is the world I want to bring a child into?

A wide-eyed feathered serpent snakes around three sides of the pyramid in Tenayuca, evoking the Toltec rulers some nine centuries before. Quetzalcoatl is everywhere here—a holy man who became a god, who put an end to human sacrifice, whose teachings transformed Toltec warriors into peaceful farmers, who upset the old guard and led them to drive him out into the wilderness, where he lived for twenty years before sailing away, promising to return. Everywhere we go, we hear about him, read about him. I look around me uneasily at my fellow tourists. Am I the only one to suspect that he *has* in fact come back, maybe more than once? It's enough to make me reexamine those crosses all around me. Maybe Jesus is only part of the progression. Maybe salvation is possible, but only with our own evolution, only by our own hand.

Tequila burns my lips as I climb steps never meant for feet the size of mine. The alcohol stuns my lungs, tricks my muscles into complying. The pyramid of the sun permits my ascent. I close my eyes, the throbbing of my temples the beat of drums. The sunlight burns me. No one climbs the pyramid of the moon, the monument to fertility. The Avenue of Death precedes it, fittingly. Its stones radiate a certain darkness. I hesitate for a long time before launching my assault. When I lift my foot to the first step, I have the sense of no return. The pull of the moon is all around me; it pulses in the air, bathes my skin, relentless, careless with its strength.

When we reach the Basilica of Our Lady of Guadalupe, it has rained in the night. The streets are washed clean; the sun is shining brightly. Connie and I have been up all night, fighting, exhausted. As we approach, the tour guide tells us what we already know from our tour books: the appearance of the Virgin to a newly converted peasant, the cloak of roses, the request that they build her a church.

I look at my watch, pointedly.

But when he keeps talking, I learn what the tour books have left out. The Virgin appeared eight years after the Spanish destroyed the ancient Aztec temple to the goddess Tonantzin on the very same site. "People come from all over the world to worship here," the tour guide tells us. "They ask the Virgin for something, and if their request is honored, they repay Her, often by promising to return the following year." I am intrigued, if not convinced. I shut the door on religion long ago, back in college. There have been times, however, I have to admit, that a slight draft has let me know the door had not been sealed.

Connie and I climb the hill together. We pass people of all ethnicities, coming back down. Some hold hands, some are smiling. The air is clear, free for a moment, it seems, of the smog that clings to the streets of the city. As we climb, I can feel something stirring within me, a creaking of old hinges, Lazarus fumbling for the crack in the tomb. The air whips around me. Mary stands with her arms outstretched, palms open. I study her face. It occurs to me what her draw is—that she survived. She had to keep on going, after inconceivable loss. She had to age, her skin becoming wrinkled, ravaged by the desert sun. Neither jubilant, palm-waving crowds nor murderous, whip-wielding officials ever awaited her. Her lot was to persevere. No wonder she graces so many alcoves. No wonder her face has always seemed familiar. She is us, doomed to keep on living, with every year of life bringing us more to lose. I think of the woman we left behind in San Miguel, her mourning so old it has become ritual. I wonder what could comfort her, if not another mother's similar loss.

Connie and I separate without even speaking, she to the old church, and me to the stone wall that overlooks the city. I always found my God outside, back when I was looking. Even as a child, taken to church every Sunday, I took to the woods alone for real worship as soon as we got home. I find a spot at the wall and fold my hands. The wind seems to tear at my heart. It has been a long, long time since I have prayed. It used to come to me effortlessly, the way that language did, when I was a child. I used to plug right into God, the minute I lay down to sleep at night. Now my brain sputters like a wet match, refusing to light. I unfold my hands, then fold them again. My palms are damp. My heart is beating rapidly. I used to memorize psalms; now I can find nothing to say. What do I want? The wind ripples my hair. My eyes are wet.

What is it that I want so badly that I will cross that pavement on my knees, allow these stones to lacerate my flesh? Mary holds my life in her outstretched palms, and I never even realized it. If she is looking down, I must look up; otherwise, how would I see her face? A falcon cuts into a dive before my eyes. Just as swiftly, I am made aware. My bandages unwinding, I come into the light. If I open my mouth, I will taste it on my tongue.

Lover, relationship, child—the rosary of my desiring. No sooner do my lips form the words than my heart holds the answer. The past opens itself to me, and I see its progression like waves of the same ocean, each dying out upon the same sand. Those who are making their trek across the stones already have what they want. They prayed for it last year. This year they pray to thank Her. That torn flesh is not from sacrifice, but from thanksgiving.

She is a woman. She doesn't ask for blood. She has shed enough of that herself. She asks for nothing, except that we return. Like any mother. I open my eyes. The rail is warm beneath my open hands. Connie comes up beside me and takes my hand. We walk together toward the stone steps that will lead us off the hill. I know what I want, and it is what I have. It has been there all along. The calmness in my heart is like the fall of rain. I have only to come back, to this place where I do not belong, to Mexico, this country in which I have no roots. No language. These traditions are not mine, and yet they take me in with open hands. Anyone can walk here, drink of the blood, the air that is ripe with a singular grace. *You have only to say the word.* It is mine to claim. My lips part, mouth open. The pearl of my desire appears upon my tongue. I will be healed. I walk, and the stone awaits my step. I add my body's weight to those that have graced this path before me.

$\mathcal{L}$ooking for the $\mathcal{U}$

SANDRA GAIL LAMBERT

Withlacochee River—North Florida
Full Moon Weekend
Water Levels: 54.94, 54.39

"*T*hey're having a fight," Alice whispers into the dark car where Jackie and I are sitting. It's six in the morning. "Should I offer to separate them?"

I'm not sure. Who wants to start a camping trip riding with the pissed-off half of a couple? But Jackie leans across me, pats Alice's hand, and tilts her head. Alice nods. Their fifteen years together has just allowed them an entire conversation.

Alice walks back to the other kayak-topped car with an offer to switch places with Beckie or Madeline. Alice can attest to the value of this technique and not just because she's a psychologist. On our last camping trip as a group, it was Madeline who reported that Jackie and Alice were yelling at each other in their kitchen. They chose to separate themselves for the two-hour drive, that one to the St. Mary's River, and by the time we finished loading the gear into the boats (a task that can be delicate for an off-kilter couple) all was well.

This time Alice returns alone and wedges into the pile of dry-bags, coolers, and life vests in the backseat.

"They said that they're fine."

"Oh yeah, fine, right." Jackie and I mutter the words in unison.

"Do you think I should go ask again?"

"No, no." Jackie lowers her voice and adds, "We could give them the name of a good therapist and leave them." We laugh the guilty laugh of friends of quarreling couples everywhere. "But really, can we go now?"

Here is the part of the trip where Jackie gets impatient. She doesn't want anyone to take that last bathroom trip, chat too much, or look for sunglasses. This morning none of that happens, and within a quarter of an hour we've left Gainesville and are headed north on I-75. I adjust the passenger seat, put my feet on the dashboard, and think how being a single person has many pleasing moments. I have a code for them in my head: "Happy, happy," I think to myself.

Before we reach our exit, they already have to stop for gas. After corralling everyone into cars, it is never a good idea to let them out, and, sure enough, everyone scatters. Except me, since my manual wheelchair is buried in the trunk under the rest of the gear—I don't want to do anything to slow us down even more, and I don't have to pee anyway. Madeline taps a Candy Red nail-polished finger on my window and waves as she goes by. I tap my Baby Peach polished one back. Our home spa date was weeks ago, and they're a bit chipped. I see Beckie on the far side of the cars. She's using her height to reset the kayak ropes.

Eventually, everyone is back in their places. Alice and Jackie say they didn't dally, but there must have been some wandering down the aisles, since they report to me on a variety of Florida souvenirs, including the horrifying dried-alligator-foot backscratchers. They have also bought more coffee, which I know will only lead to more bathroom stops. This is the part of the trip where I get irritated. I practice breathing deeply until we're going a satisfying sixty miles an hour.

In our car the *Big Chill* soundtrack is playing, and we're dancing in our seats to '50s tunes. During the slow songs, we discuss the perennial camping questions: if we can hardly find room in the car for all this gear, how are we going to fit it in our boats? Where is the cooler, and can we start eating now? And does that left rope look loose to you? We decide it doesn't, and I relax into our consistent forward momentum.

Reading from my slip of directions, I get us off the freeway and over to the 150 bridge where we slow to see the river for the first time. I lean out the window and look into patterns of reflected light and shadow. It smells green and wet, and my heart invents its own skipping pattern the same way it does when a handsome woman leans in close. It's hard to leave the river, but a mile later we arrive at the meeting place for the shuttle service.

Jim the Outfitter is waiting for us and has a million river details to share. Everyone else leaves the cars to find a bathroom while Jim leans on the car door beside me and keeps talking. I'm surly because I'm still stuck in the car, but I remember my responsibilities as trip planner and begin to listen. It's obvious that he loves this river. I find my map, and he shows me where things are.

"Go to the right at this shoal, to the extreme left on that one. Here's where the power lines cross seven miles down. Three more curves in the river, and you'll see a good camping area on the east side."

I make marks on the map.

"I could put you in a little north of here—it's closer but steep. Maybe we should go to this other one, or there's this real easy one, but it's a few miles away."

I'm thinking: shut up, take me to the closest place, and throw me in. "Well, Jim, that first one sounds just fine."

My weak-bladdered friends herd themselves into cars, and we follow Jim down a sandy trail on the northwest side of the bridge. It's not long until Jim pulls over and stops. I look out the car window at a fifty-foot drop. The river's edge is thick with cypress knees and brush. Jim is standing beside my window again.

"Now, there's this other place we could go look at and then come back here if we want to."

"No! I mean, I'm sure this is good."

Jackie has clambered partway down the hill.

"No problem, Sandra. We can get you down fine." She's a mid-wife and thinks anything is possible. Neither of us cares if she's lying.

Everyone starts throwing things out of back seats and trunks. My wheelchair reappears, and I'm finally free of the car. I turn my chair so I'm backed up to the drop. I lean forward over my knees, brace my arms against the sides, and wrap my fingers around the footrest tubing. I am locked in. It's understood that Beckie will back me down the hill. She's the athlete and always knows exactly where her body is in space. And I've known her for twenty years. Jackie moves behind to help, and we start down the hill.

Midway, my right wheel runs high onto roots, and I'm dangling sideways, strands of my hair sweeping along the ground. I mention, maybe in a loud voice, that if they can't hold on to let me know. I want to have some control about how I fall before the chair goes over. Beckie assures me, maybe also in a loud voice, that they've got me, and the wheels bump off the roots and the chair levels again. I think I hear "drama queen" muttered. When we reach a small flat area a few feet above the water, I let myself fall onto the soft sand.

The wheelchair is whisked up the hill and folded into a car. Alice and Madeline are going to follow Jim to the takeout ramp, which he assures us is paved, and drop off the cars. Everyone helps bring the kayaks down, and I get my first good look at Beckie and Madeline together. Their faces are tired and post-crying, but they are being sweet to each other. Nevertheless, as the cars leave, I'm glad that all couples will be separated for the kayak-loading phase of the trip.

Jackie comes down the hill with life vests in each hand and paddles sprouting at all angles from under her arms. Beckie follows with drybags perched on each shoulder. They surround me with piles of stuff and are laughing as they tromp up the hill, arm in arm, for more loads. I start strapping, snapping latches, and hooking on the bowline, seat, and paddle leash. I listen to the two of them go on about their girlfriends.

"Look, she's packed this plastic in plastic."

"Oh, that's nothing. Here's an umbrella—no, I'm wrong, two umbrellas. We already have three ponchos. What is she thinking?"

"Five gallons of water!"

"We have a rule about this—if you don't use it on a trip, you can't bring it on the next one. I'll never have to see these umbrellas again."

"Did we each bring a full set of cookware?"

"Where am I going to stuff this pillow of hers? Really, a pillow. On a camping trip."

I tighten the strap over my big drybag with the two pillows in it and think, "Happy, happy." Scooting to the water's edge, I calculate which cypress knees I can squeeze between.

"Can one of you push my boat down to me?"

Beckie steps close and squats to control the slide of the boat into the water. I lean one hand on a cypress knee, pivot off the bank, and land in the center of the kayak seat. After arranging the binoculars around my neck, I tighten the paddle leash and squirm to get the seat just right. Then I put the paddle in the water for the first time. I'm floating. My shoulders fall away from my ears. All worries about water levels, weather, and camping sites dissolve into the current. I look at the bank where my friends are bent over their boats. I love them; I love everyone. Gently back-paddling, I hold still in the stream flow. I don't know what's past that first curve, but I reassure myself that I've done every bit of planning and research that is possible. Now, there is only the river.

I spin the boat and paddle upstream while I wait on everyone else. I stop at the bottom side of a set of shoals. They look manageable, but I've never been in any rough water before, since it's not something we have much of in Florida. I've read books and know you're supposed to look for the V, the "vee"—whatever that means. Jim the Outfitter said this stretch of the river has a set of Class I shoals each mile.

I hear a car engine downstream and paddle back to the launch site. Alice and Madeline are waving goodbyes to Jim. I watch them slide and skip down the hill where they immediately reorganize how their respective girlfriends have loaded the boats. I stay out of hearing range, but the tones of voice sound fine. Soon boats are going in the water, and I let the current take me. Jackie and Alice are next. Beckie and Madeline stay behind, kayaks close, talking.

Since the drought, our Gulf rivers have been low and slow, but not here. It's been a long time since I've had the luxury of a strong current. The banks are high, wooded, and empty of people. The sun is perfectly hot. We're passing a patchwork of state forest and privately owned land. The private lands are obvious because of the cows that stand huge in the water as we float past, their eroded paths to the river scarring the bluffs behind them.

One by one we hear it. Jackie cocks her head, and Alice shrugs her shoulders at me. I think it's a road, but I can't find one on the map I have strapped onto the bow. It gets louder, and I'm thinking planes or tractors when the water begins to ripple. It's the shoals. Alice goes first while Jackie and I hold our kayaks in place and watch. She bumps up and down, lurches once to the side, and she's through. I square my shoulders, paddle hard, and look for the V. For ten seconds I'm surrounded by rocks and swirling cowlicks of water. I never see a V, but I make it anyway, and at the end I raise my hands and take a bow, accepting the accolades from my friends.

While we wait to make sure Beckie and Madeline are successful, Alice decides it's snack time. First snack and first lunch are my responsibility. I always bring boiled eggs. They aren't fancy, but they're a perfect protein boost, and I present them with flair by peeling each one and passing it over with a portion of salt mixed with hand ground pepper. As much as it gives me pleasure to serve women in this way, I have another motive. I think traceless camping means traceless, and annoying bits of egg shell can tempt even the most conscientious camper to toss them overboard—despite the foreknowledge of my judgmental stare.

After eggs, we are a lively group of paddlers. Madeline and Jackie are laughing together. Beckie compliments Alice on her shoal navigating and then brings her boat alongside me. We try to remember where this river comes from—somewhere in Georgia, Tifton maybe? Alice speeds ahead to look for the next shoal. Beckie follows. Jackie drops behind to take photos of the walls of exposed limestone, and Madeline and I paddle beside each other, comfortably silent.

We continue to see no one. I look over, and Madeline is naked and in the water. She's like one of those two-year-olds who, every time you turn your head, strip down and leave a trail of discarded clothing. Soon I'm surrounded by bare-skinned, cavorting women. I have on pants, a long-sleeved shirt, a sports bra, and a wide-brimmed hat. I am not modest, but I burn easily. I decide to get wild. I remove my shirt and slide into the river mostly clothed and still fully hatted. After finding a submerged rock, I sit on it chest-high in the water. Madeline floats by with only her toes, breasts, and face visible. Jackie is swimming across the river, showing white buttocks and an occasional kicking heel. Alice wanders the shore in her sandals, bending over to look at butterflies on blooms. And Beckie still isn't all the way in the water. She's beached her boat and has ventured in only calf-high. As usual, she is immersing herself at an excruciating pace, holding her arms stiff and straight with fists clenched, grimacing and then squealing as the water level reaches each tender part—or as she calls them, her "important stuff."

Jackie returns, and group consensus thinks it's time for lunch. I've brought homemade pimento cheese and fresh-baked onion bread along with celery and carrot sticks, apples and a Scharffen Berger bittersweet chocolate bar. Everyone says it's my best pimento cheese ever, but they always say that.

I tuck away our remains, and each woman wanders over to her kayak and pushes off. We're quiet as we paddle intermittently and take the kayaking equivalent of a nap. It's difficult to tell mileage because of the current and no roads or bridges to serve as markers, but it's a twelve-mile trip, and we're supposed to find a good camping spot at eight miles. When we pass a sandbar, segments of the group think that this is the place. I'm tired as well, but I know we haven't gone far enough and override them by continuing downstream. They have to follow. So much for consensus.

When we hear the loudest roaring so far, we all hesitate until our boats come up even to each other, as if we were at a starting line. We sit straighter, tie down water bottles, and grip our paddles. Alice sprints ahead, pulls over, and slides out of her boat to walk past the shoal. She's scouting. She returns to her boat and paddles to the extreme left. She makes it. Jackie's next, and she hits something hard and jerks sideways, almost overturning the kayak.

Then I go, avoiding Jackie's route. Water is flipping over itself in all possible directions, and everywhere I look there are flat, angled patches. Are they the famous V shapes or the tops of rocks? It doesn't matter since the boat is being pulled, pushed, and twisted, and paddling is a joke. At the end, I am shoved sideways into a calm spot. I take my bow.

It's late afternoon when we go under the power lines. The river curves three times, and on the east bank is a sweet sandbar. We start to unpack, and my life goal has become to get the air mattress inflated, take off my wet clothes, and lie down on my two pillows. Alice helps me, and soon I am resting and listening to everyone else assemble all their comforts.

Alice and Jackie have a tent smaller than mine, and Beckie and Madeline have what we call "the little Hilton." Their double air mattress fits inside it, with plenty of extra room. Madeline passes by my tent door from time to time. She is stripped again and intersperses her chores with jumps in the water. By this time, it is clear that Beckie is ailing with a sore throat. She wanders slowly, picking things up and then putting them down in other places. When her tent is ready, she announces that she's going to steal Madeline's pillow and rest awhile. Alice is exploring the woods behind the sandbar, but Jackie calls to her, and they cavort in the water, kissing and laughing. They swim to the far bank and climb the bluff, and I watch their bare forty-seven- and fifty-four-year-old backsides bend to climb the narrow path. I think of wood nymphs, Imogen Cunningham photos, and the places in the world where women taking off their clothes can stop a war—their naked bodies the ultimate authority. Madeline alternates between playing in the river and checking on Beckie.

I'm rested enough to be hungry when Jackie and Alice swim back. Jackie starts fussing with her pots and coolers, and I move out of the tent to watch her. Dinner is her responsibility, actually her and Alice's, but Alice does the cleanup. The meal starts with an appetizer of cream cheese, cocktail sauce, and crabmeat on crackers. Everyone except Beckie gathers around, but a plate is prepared and placed by her sick bed. We are munching, heads bent over the plate, hands reaching for more crackers, when we feel a cool wind.

A dark cloud comes fast over the trees and blocks the sun, the wind is harder and cooler, and a few fat drops of rain land around us. Jackie starts to cover food, I zip my tent, Madeline gathers her scattered clothes, and Alice gets a gleam in her eye. She rushes to her kayak and returns with the two umbrellas, handing them to me and Jackie with a flourish. We huddle under them expectantly, but the rain slides by the side of us, and the sun shines again. Alice insists that it still counts as using the umbrellas.

Jackie finishes unpacking her special camping cookware and utensils. She's especially fond of her collapsible spatula. I've had so much good food from these pots that I get hungry when I see them. Beckie crawls out of her tent just as the asparagus finishes steaming. She's feeling better. The tang of bay and onion hits the back of all our throats, we smell rice, and soon I'm leaning against my kayak and eating shrimp jambalaya out of a plate propped on my belly. I pause intermittently to moan words of appreciation. Jackie is perched behind her stove, Alice is handing around food, and Beckie and Madeline are seated on their life vests. By the end of the meal I'm listing sideways, and they are lying down, life vests now serving as pillows. We don't sit up again until Jackie heats the lemon sauce to go over the gingerbread she has, like a magician, revealed from the bottom of a cooler.

After dinner we talk about how good the meal was, Beckie feeling better, moonrise, and what to do with food scraps and grease. Alice says bury them; I say pack them out. Beckie also says to bury, but above the high-water mark. Madeline says isn't that the moon between those trees, and why does it look bigger sometimes? Jackie thinks it's because the moon is closer to the earth. I say it's only an optical illusion caused by seeing it low in the sky with trees and houses in front of it. Someone says it's because really the world is flat. Alice experiments, holding her thumb in front of the moon and squinting. She says when it's higher in the sky she'll see if it's still thumb-sized. We start measuring things with our thumb. It seems that with this system Madeline's tush, the saucepan, my tent, and the moon are all the same size. Alice points out satellites and planes and names planets.

When the moon shines on our tents, we go to bed, proud that we've stayed awake until past eight. I hear extended goodnight kisses from Madeline and Beckie's direction, and farther down the sandbar Jackie whispers, "No flashlight? We have all this crap but no flashlight?"

During the night, I hear a large splash in the river. When I open the tent to look, the river is calm, but the color-leached brightness along the far bank throws strange shadows.

The next morning I'm awake, completely repacked, and loaded before the first coffee addict crawls out of her tent. Jackie gets the water boiling, and soon the sound of zipper comes from the other tent. After caffeine fortification, Beckie and Madeline start breakfast by laying out soy milk cartons in a variety of flavors, since we all, except for Jackie, have entered the hot-flash era. We're in various levels of undress, eating oatmeal, when we hear trucks across the river. Doors slam, voices carry over the water, and there he is waving—Jim the Outfitter. He calls to us over the water. He tells us that this bluff is a popular weekend launch site.

It's odd to remember that there are other people. After two loads of canoes put in and are carried off by the current, we forget again. Jackie wants a picture of the campsite. She gets naked, puts her camera in a drybag, holds the bag in her teeth, and swims across the river. She's standing on the far bluff when a fishing boat rounds the bend. Those little electric motors are quiet. When I look from the guy-filled boat to the far shore, there's nothing left but a camera on a tree stump and Jackie's head bobbing in the river. The guys are polite. They pretend they haven't seen and keep their heads turned our way and chat about the weather as they pass by.

After breakfast we play. Alice sits on a bent tree trunk in the shade and watercolors, Beckie and Madeline are romping like otters, with much splashing and laughing, and Jackie is inspecting the bottom of her kayak for gouges from the day before. "How thick is this plastic?" she calls out.

Intermittently, tents are collapsed and packed. Some of us brush our teeth, some of us don't. I decide I don't have to conserve strength because I'm packed, only have to paddle four miles downstream, and don't have to drive. So I practice getting in my kayak from deep water using only my paddle float until I'm able to throw myself into the boat with not much thought required. I'm satisfied and exhausted and wondering how big the bruises along my arms are going to be when I remember the leftover gingerbread.

All I say out loud is, "Gingerbread," and Alice lays down her paintbrush to scrounge in the cooler. We gather around the pan. Alice shows her painting, and Beckie reads us a bit of Buddhist philosophy, and then, ironically, for me the feeling of endless time ends, and I want to go. I say pointedly that it's already 1 p.m. I say we don't really know what lies ahead. I say we might have to drive home in the dark. I say to myself how obnoxious I'm being and that there's no reason I can't go ahead on my own.

I float downstream, alone, calmer. Houses are visible from time to time, along with more trash and signs of campfires. Before I get to State Road 6, everyone else has caught up. The final miles flow through high, fern-laden banks seeped with water that forms miniature spring-fed grottos. We develop the skill of listening for the music of water bubbling into rocks. If fairies exist, this is where they live. We pass rust-red rocks carved, inexplicably to us, into massive shapes. This restarts the discussion of how I need to help out and get a geologist for my next girlfriend. (Sometimes a herpetologist is suggested.) We pass a section where choking swaths of an invasive climbing fern line bank after bank. We pass two more spring heads, stopping at each for Madeline to take a naked dip. After a final boat-twirling set of shoals, we arrive at the concrete ramp. Gear is tossed into cars, kayaks are strapped in place, and we are on the freeway.

It's dark when they drop me at my house, and I am out-of-my-mind tired. I put on Aretha Franklin and wander from room to room. I wipe down the binoculars, wash water bottles, and empty the cooler. I open mail, listen to messages, and make a trip to the hamper each time I find another piece of dirty clothing. On the porch, I un-stuff the wet tent and drape it over the railing, releasing a shower of sand. Exhaustion makes me feel drugged and feverish.

During my bath the hot water stings my arms—my moments of partially undressed abandon have led to a sunburn. As I brush my hair, I look around and realize that everything is either put away or ready to be washed tomorrow. I go out into the night and the still-full moon. I slap the tent and listen to the next layer of sand fall onto the wood deck.

Happy, happy.

The Gift Shop Is Never "Fermé"

JANE CHURCHON

I dozed most of the way to Chartres, waking up every now and then to a few fat, white cows. I would stare at the stone houses, mortared with history. More than a few sported small satellite dishes on roofs, like crowns on royalty. I would sleep for a few more minutes, then wake to small fields of withering grapevines or to bursts of white sheep on rolling, storybook hills.

My partner, MK, and I were on day eight of nine in Paris, our first trip to Europe. We were tired: In those eight November days, we'd squeezed in the Louvre, the Orsay, the Picasso museum, the Pompidou, Versailles, and enough walking to slim an elephant to gazelle proportions. Our American, middle-aged bodies, used to cars and convenience, ached night and morning; only the beauty of the city lured us from our warm bed each day. Though we would miss Notre Dame, this train ride came as a welcome respite. We had only to sit and take in the countryside as we ventured to the cathedral at Chartres, its legendary stained-glass windows and its labyrinth — the labyrinth I'd waited seven years to see.

When I first saw a labyrinth, I had just left my husband, a man with an overwhelming Judaic spirituality that eclipsed my own, less-acknowledged Jewish heritage. A friend drove me to San Francisco and the labyrinth at Grace Cathedral Church. The choice seemed odd: Why bring a semi-Jew to walk a crooked Christian mile?

"You have to do this," he told me as we entered the sanctuary. Before us stood a large stone basin of holy water, and beyond that stretched a small sea of maroon shag, embedded with what looked like dark brown crop circles or a medical text's drawing of fallopian tubes. I wondered how I could "do" a piece of art. Without a word, my friend took off his shoes and began to walk the path.

Grace Cathedral's labyrinth curves like a country lane, neither maze nor puzzle, with no secret passageways or tricks. One need only put one foot down in front of the other and follow the path. A spiritual journey, the labyrinth moves the walker through straightaways and curves into the rosette-shaped center, a symbol for Mary, "the rose of creation." Here, the walker might meditate before retracing the same course, ending where she began. I took the walk on that day in 1997, and I emerged with an overwhelming sense of peace. I was hooked.

My own life had gone through some surprising twists since that first go-round in Grace Cathedral. I surprised myself by dating women. In 2003 I married MK, short for Mary Katherine, in Canada. Two years after that, I lost 150 pounds through weight loss surgery. Around these milestones, my path wound through more usual curves and straightaways: our daughter's teenage crises, my mother's death, our son's new love for reading, one cat's death and the arrival of two more, the pounds of fruit from our tomato plants, a new house.

Through it all, about twice a year, I'd go to San Francisco and walk the labyrinth at Grace Cathedral. By the end of those walks, after the curves and the straight path through the center, after brushing against people on the way, standing to the side to let others pass, looking at the cracks in the walk, and hearing the sounds of the city, I'd find a tranquility that normally eludes me. Each brush against my sleeve reminded me of the daily touch of others; each pause and hurried step reminded me of the staccato and vibrato of my life. Walking the labyrinth was like standing at the ocean, sparkling and vast, on a sunny morning. The enormity and the insignificance of who I was in this world became clear. I was a miracle. I was ordinary.

Labyrinths have their roots in antiquity. Only happenstance, not design, preserved the labyrinth at Chartres, constructed around 1200. Most labyrinths from that era or before have been torn out in deference to changing decorative styles. Medieval pilgrims walked or even crawled the length of a labyrinth—about 850 feet in Chartres—as penance. The Chartres Cathedral nave boasts eleven layers of back-and-forth quarter-circle paths, eleven layers of fallopian tubes leading to the uterine rosette. The world's more modern labyrinths, including Grace Cathedral's, are reproductions of it.

For seven years, I'd looked forward to walking the labyrinth at Chartres, the mother of all modern labyrinths. I imagined that as my feet trod the fallopian path, I would invoke those pilgrims from centuries ago. My ancestors, Jews, did not seek spiritual redemption, did not crawl on hands and knees over granite to find the center of the labyrinth, or their metaphorical centers. Jews bow and sway in prayerful meditation, but do not make sacrifices of themselves to follow their God's example. Yet I longed to feel those ancient French stones underfoot, to rub against the ash, dust, earth, and skin still clinging to the rock from 1,200 years of pilgrims' soles. I wanted their devotion and faith, if only on my toes.

The trip that day in France started oddly, with the woman at the train ticket counter telling us that MK's debit card would not work. We shrugged and paid with cash. But once on the train, alarm grew; I would doze, wake, and need to say, "I'm letting that whole debit card thing go." The labyrinth would clear my mind of the ordinary, and what could be more ordinary than money?

Later that evening, we would find out about what I feared that day on the train. Our U.S. bank had mistakenly rejected a large deposit; we couldn't pay our hotel bill. We would argue with the American bank from our hotel room, after enduring repeated, nasally recorded French warnings that we were dialing incorrectly. Eventually, we would surrender, scrounge our remaining Euros to pay for dinner and breakfast, and charge our hotel bill to a card that could barely support the freight. But that would come later. On the train under a blue sky, we tried not to worry. The labyrinth and its still center waited.

As the train pulled into Chartres, we saw the cathedral on a slight hill a few blocks from the station. Its two towers—built three hundred years apart, one Gothic, one Romanesque—blithely claimed the town's sky, mindless of their asymmetry. It was a brisk day, and my enthusiasm hurried our walk through the town square—picturesque, I noticed faintly.

We entered the dark cavern of the sanctuary. As my eyes adjusted, I walked forward, looking for a clearing large enough for the labyrinth. Tourists clicked their awed cameras at the front of the sanctuary, at the stained glass. I didn't have eyes for stained glass. I was there for the labyrinth.

"You're going to be really upset," MK said. "Look down."

The pavers on which I'd been walking, their unevenness rolling my feet forward, *were* the labyrinth. Wooden chairs, bolted together into pews, covered all but the rosette. I stood on my spot and looked at the chairs. It was impossible to walk the labyrinth.

MK went to the information desk. No one spoke English. "*Je suis un pilgrim,*" I heard her say, and then she made the Yellow Pages sign of walking fingers. "Walk le labyrinth?" she asked.

"*Le labyrinth est fermé,*" the woman said. We'd learned that word. The Turkish Baths at the Louvre were *fermé*. The Matisse exhibit at the Pompidou was *fermé*. We had traveled five thousand miles, but the French close holy things without much warning. Sometimes it seemed as if all of France was *fermé*.

I started to cry. "At least take pictures," I told MK, and so she did, blurry photos of me standing in the rosette, smiling inexplicably as if my dream had not just evaporated. "Take a picture of my feet." And now we have a photo of my two shod feet, standing in the glow of those multifarious stained-glass windows, an artful, triumphant sham of a photo.

We went to the bookstore, in the way that Americans will go to the gift store after any experience. The gift store is never *fermé*. We found a glass labyrinth and some key chains with a labyrinth design. Our debit cards were rejected again; something had gone terribly wrong with our account. We paid with ragged bills and walked back to the station. Above our heads, the ancient cathedral towers loomed, their intricate stonework angrily unmatched, both beautiful and terrifying in their homage to God and Church. We boarded the train. My spiritual pilgrimage was *fermé*. On the hills, no fat, white cows.

And life continues. Since we returned from France, I've lost another fifteen pounds, and our daughter turned eighteen. The house needs a new roof. I received a promotion. We attended two weddings and a funeral.

The other day, MK bought a rug. I came home from work feeling cross and full of the workday, vaguely registering the new rug in our entryway. Its blue and cream design clashed with the room's orange-sicle tiles. MK asked, "Do you like the rug?" and I said, too politely, "It's OK."

But a few minutes later, almost tripping on the rug's upturned edges, I suddenly recognized the pattern: a miniature Chartres labyrinth, too small to walk, but a perfect representation. It was MK's attempt to make up for what I lost that day in Chartres.

I cannot walk the small path in our entryway anymore than I could negotiate the chairs bolted together across the labyrinth in France. The rug reminds me that not all paths are walkable, not all ways lead to our center. Sometimes the road is *fermé*. Yet, there is always some path. I may not know where it leads, and I may not know I'm on it, but all I can do is keep walking and find out. So I share the rug with MK, and when I look at our own miniature labyrinth, it reminds me that she loved me enough to want to give me something I thought I lost that day in France. It reminds me to look out the window and be grateful for the cows.

Playing with Fire

PATTY SMITH

In Senegal, in October, the mango trees turn yellow. Heat, like a veil, hangs between you and the air. Between you and the unpaved roads. Between you and the Senegalese themselves, gorgeously black-skinned in vibrant colors of waxed cloth made by the Dutch and sold in yards in Lebanese shops in Dakar and in market stalls here in Ziguinchor, the capital of the Casamance region of Senegal.

Ziguinchor. Where it is *hot*. Where, in October, there is no hint of fall, the air thick and gauzy. It is the kind of heat that flattens, gives headaches, rots the mangoes as soon as they fall to the ground—a searing, blinding heat that makes you think the end of the world will definitely come with fire.

I'm new to Ziguinchor, to Senegal, to all this. I'm twenty-seven, a French teacher in a Massachusetts private school. I have come to Senegal for one academic year on a Fulbright Teacher Exchange with Jim, a Midwesterner who at forty-one is fourteen years my senior and has been a French teacher for longer than that. For now, in Ziguinchor, while the house that will be mine sits full of water—built over a rice field, it floods every rainy season—Jim and I are thrown together in a government-owned apartment in the building Étage Ibra Seck across the street from the village artisanal and just down the paved road from the lycée where we will both teach English.

Jim had confessed on the plane ride over that he almost refused the Fulbright. He questioned how being in Senegal would improve his French.

I told him, truthfully, that I had been excited, that I had just that year completed projects with my seventh graders focusing on French-speaking Africa, about which I knew little. The students cooked food, learned about the governments, prepared presentations in French about geography and weather. They wrote to embassies and travel agencies, scoured the libraries in their hometowns and in our school. Still, it seemed resources were few. In spite of all their good efforts, my students wrote reports that said *we all danced to the beat of the drums.* I knew there had to be more. I knew that if I wanted to teach about French West Africa, I needed to gather resources. I could hardly believe it when the call came from USIA in Washington, D.C., with an offer to go to Senegal, to West Africa, to the very part of the world I was trying to discover with my students.

"We're starting a new program there," the official said. "So you'd be the first teachers to go, pioneers."

I spent the months from April, when I was officially notified about the Fulbright, until September, when I left, getting all the necessary shots—yellow fever, cholera, gamma globulin for hepatitis—and reading whatever information I could find: David Lamb's *The Africans,* David Else's *Backpacker's Africa,* Kim Naylor's *Guide to West Africa; The Niger and Gambia River Route.* I met with friends of friends, former Peace Corps volunteers who taught me to eat with the right hand only, to greet everyone whenever I entered a room, to remain at a host's house until the third glass of tea was served in the after-meal ritual of Senegalese tea-drinking. I convinced my family and friends, many of whom saw my going to Senegal as a crazy move, that this was a once-in-a-lifetime, not-to-be-passed-up opportunity. Convinced myself, too, not because I was nervous to go so far, which I wasn't, but because I was still reeling from the breakup of my first long-term relationship. My friends knew this. They knew that I might see the Fulbright as nothing more than a chance to bolt.

After four years together, my girlfriend, Bianca, had left me the previous February, and in those months before I heard that I'd been granted the Fulbright, I lived shell-shocked in Boston, in the little basement apartment Bianca and I had rented together, while she moved across the street and in with another woman. At twenty-seven, I was young enough to feel that my life was over; I couldn't imagine a future now that Bianca had erased the life I had imagined with her. So my friends were right. I was thrilled to be given this opportunity to go halfway around the world, to see what it might be like to start over, to begin again, to get the chance for rebirth.

The apartment is big enough for the two of us, and so far, Jim and I get along. Although we've known each other for less than one month, we don't mind living together. Jim doesn't ever say it out loud, but I'm certain that he is as happy to have me by his side as I am to have him when we try to get the electricity for the apartment turned on and cannot, or when we venture into the market to look for mosquito netting, cooking pots, a spoon.

Both Jim and I had applied for teaching Fulbrights to take us to France. We imagined Paris or Provence or coastal towns in Brittany. We fantasized about weekends in Amsterdam and vacations in Spain, afternoons at the d'Orsay, and red wine in cafés. Art museums; *boeuf bourgignon;* good, hot coffee; purple Bics. Both French teachers, we have separate ongoing love affairs with France and each have spent several years traveling and living there. I've lived in Belgium, too—four months of teaching for an American program at the International School of Brussels. We are travelers, Jim and I, and yet we have not in our wildest dreams imagined any of this.

How could we?

Reading about Africa gives a conflicted view of what to expect. Ethnic warfare and sophisticated cities. Villages with no running water; gold jewelry. Government bribes and American music. The tourist books tell of pristine Senegalese beaches and describe the maze of mangroves in the Casamance and the gnarly roots of the sacred and mighty banyan tree. You see pictures of the fiery red flamboyants and the blazing pink bougainvillea. The books tell of how friendly the Senegalese people are and of the strong Muslim influence in the north, but nothing in the books prepares you for the actual landing—the actual moment when you take your first steps into the blinding glare and chaos that is an African city. And nothing you read can help with the reorientation that is necessary when all your usual ways of figuring out your life don't seem to work anymore, when the usual rules as you have always understood them do not seem to apply.

There aren't Yellow Pages. No telephones. No street addresses, and in 1988, when we arrive, no Internet.

Most of the time, Jim and I feel helpless.

Luckily, upstairs from us, there is Royo. When we mention casually where we are living, the Senegalese smile and nod. *Oh, Royo,* they say. *You live with Royo. He will be a big help.* Everyone mentions him—the teachers at the lycée, the *proviseur* and *censeur* of the school, even the Peace Corps volunteers we meet early on. They mention Royo in that Senegalese way of using only last names, a habit I will have a difficult time getting used to—as if the country were one entire football team.

Royo turns out to be Michel Royo, a French physics teacher who has been living in Ziguinchor for four years now but is currently nowhere to be found—away, apparently, on vacation, and when he returns will be anybody's guess. *Soon,* the Senegalese tell us. *He will be here,* they say in that calm, unnerving way they have of speaking, vague and Zen-like. No one seems worried that classes begin in mere days and Royo is not around. *He will be here,* they say. *Royo.*

When we are not dragging ourselves to Senelec with the dim hope of getting electricity, Jim and I spend our time in these early weeks wandering the hot, dusty streets, buying Cokes or Orange Fanta at the boutique next door, owned and run, as are most of the boutiques in Ziguinchor, by a Mauritanian. At these convenience stores—wooden shacks with one long counter and flimsy shelves lining the rear wall—Mauritanians, or *Nars* as the Senegalese call them, sell anything from a single Marlboro cigarette to warm Orange Fanta. Condensed milk, eggs, long and crusty baguettes, kola nuts, single cubes of sugar, vats of palm oil. Light-skinned, the Mauritanians look Tunisian or Moroccan. They wear long, white robes that flutter behind like sails when they walk, their feet covered by pointy, elfin-like shoes. It's a daily diversion for me, this dip into the boutique, and I'm developing a craving for the warm, sugary fuzz of Orange Fanta, a drink I had never tasted before arriving in Senegal.

Inside our cool, dark apartment sans electricity, Jim and I read or talk about lesson plans. I have none—at least nothing specific, but Jim has plenty. He has brought several cassette tapes to use in class and magazine articles he thinks the students will enjoy. I am at a loss. I'm not sure, really, how to teach English as a foreign language, not to classes of sixty-plus students. There'll be some group response and *repeat after me,* vocabulary games and verb conjugations. It will be similar to the way I teach French, but *how* exactly, I don't know. I'm hoping—Jim and I are both hoping—that the school will give us some sense of direction.

Early in October, we report to school for the official opening—a mandatory faculty meeting for which only two-thirds of the faculty show up. We are supposed to hear a speech from the minister of education, too, but he never shows up and we're told to go home.

We have heard word of a possible student strike in support of Abdoulaye Wade, the presidential candidate from the opposition party, at the very lycée where we are scheduled to teach, where the previous year has already been declared *une année blanche,* literally a "white" or "blank" year. Out on strike, the students didn't attend enough classes for the year to count. So it seems that detailed lesson plans might be a bit premature. It's hard to gear up when we just don't know *if* school will start, let alone *when.*

At least this is what I tell myself.

At least this is what I say when I leave the apartment for another aimless stroll on the hot, dusty streets or head to the Hôtel Nema Kadior for a swim in the outdoor pool, the cost of a swim the equivalent to one dollar. I can't get in a rhythm. I can't yet believe that I'm actually in Africa, actually here, no longer in Massachusetts reading about this place I could not picture in my head. That school won't start is Jim's greatest fear and perhaps mine also, because what will we do with ourselves if we don't teach? Out loud I say that we have so much to discover, it won't matter whether or not school ever starts, but secretly, I'm nervous too—nervous that without the routine and anchor of school, we, too, will have a blank year. We won't ever know what to do with ourselves here, who to *be*.

We are relieved, finally, when one evening, after we have returned from our nightly excursion to the Oasis restaurant for steak *frites*— still without electricity, we cannot cook in the dark—from upstairs, we hear music, salsa or soukous, and we realize that our mystery neighbor, Royo, has returned.

Eager to meet him, both of us feeling that at last, our difficulties navigating this place are over now that Royo is here as promised, Jim and I climb the stairs to introduce ourselves. When he opens the door, it becomes clear that Royo has already heard about us.

"Ah, *les américains*," Royo says, smiling. I had pictured him a much older man. Instead, a skinny French surfer boy with a blond shag and brightly colored pants waves us in and shows us to his roof deck, a *paillote* surrounded by tall, green lemongrass plants. As if he has been expecting us all along, Royo hands us each a glass of rum. "Welcome," he says in English and clinks our glasses in a toast.

It's dark on the rooftop in Ziguinchor. Still, I can discern the outline of things below: the ditch that runs alongside the road, a gutter for when the rains come; the fence that surrounds the village artisanal across the street; the tiny wooden restaurant on the corner, *cheb u jen*, fish and rice, their specialty; the Mauritanian boutique next door. At this hour the boutique is closed, but still, people mill about on the street, the sounds of their voices muffled and dim. Up here, it's the men's voices you hear, the French words distinguishable from all the rest—Wolof, Diola, Mandinque, Pulaar. Up here, you hear the scruff scruff of shuffling feet, flip-flops dragging against pavement and packed dirt.

The Senegalese live outside. They sit in plastic chairs in the spaces outside their houses—square, earthen buildings with corrugated tin roofs. Or they crouch in doorways, making tea over coal on small hibachis. In this heat, people will drag their mattresses outside to sleep. Jim and I might consider it if it weren't for the mosquitoes. As it is, without any mosquito netting, we burn coils on the floors of our bedrooms next to our mattresses, trying to keep bites to a minimum.

Here, on the rooftop, the lemongrass seems to keep mosquitoes away.

Jim wants to know about the strike.

"*C'est l'Afrique,*" Royo shrugs. Royo turns then and introduces us to Baccary and Lamine, two men, friends of his, hidden there in the shadows of the *paillote,* one a drummer and the other a dancer, all white teeth and blue-black skin, their voices so low I can barely distinguish their words. They're folded into the chairs they're sitting in and lift themselves up, extend their hands first to Jim, then to me.

"*Bonsoir,*" we greet them. Baccary is the shorter one, his face round and grinning, mischievous. Lamine stands tall, serious. I'm struck by the hardness of Lamine's skin, his fingers so long and slender circling the glass of rum. He mumbles some kind of greeting to me in French. *Happy to meet you. Enchanted to know you.* I can't make it out. He is long and lean, dressed in crisp, ironed pants and a white T-shirt, not the waxed African cloth that Royo wears.

Baccary's head is covered in dreadlocks, each capped with a bead, and Lamine's hair, stiff curls cut close to his head, is nearly covered by a white cloth hat like the one worn by Gilligan on *Gilligan's Island.* The hat slips over his eyes when he sits back down, and now and again, he pushes it up, when he says something else I can't make out or laughs at something Baccary or Royo says. I sip the rum and try to follow the conversation, wipe the sweat that keeps beading on my forehead and drenching the hair at the nape of my neck.

Lamine teaches African dance, Royo says.

"Really?" I pipe up. "I'm very interested." I wipe again at the sweat.

Lamine pushes his hat up then and looks right at me, the black center of his eyes fixed on mine, looking, he will tell me later, all the way into my soul. He doesn't say what he saw that night, but I wonder if he discovered then the tender spot I knew was there but was trying to ignore—me, untethered except for the convenient friendship I had with Jim, far, far away from anything familiar.

Days go by in that African way that feels like months. Heat and slowness and dark quiet nights, though after all our weeks in Ziguinchor, after so many varied efforts at asking politely, Jim and I finally have electricity. One afternoon, when I return to the apartment from a long, meandering walk, Jim looks up from his plan book where he has already outlined weeks of lessons and hands me a rolled-up paper bag, heavy with fat, juicy limes, and says, "Oh, this is for you." He wags the bag. "An African," he says. "I don't know who it was. He said these were for you."

"A man?"

"He said, '*Donne ça à mademoiselle.*'" Jim shrugs.

"But that could be anybody—"

"He said 'Pa-tee.' '*Donne ça à Pa-tee.*' He knew your name." Jim turns back to his plan book. Jim's fan is blowing, but it feels hot and stuffy in our dark brown apartment. "I don't know who it was," Jim says. "An African." He takes a sip of water. "I didn't recognize him."

In the slow days that follow, students filter back to Ziguinchor from their villages. The strike is delayed at least for now, and school opens. I hear word of dance class starting at the African Cultural Center, and I show up, excited to add a new activity to my days.

We are a dozen white women, two of us American, but mostly French teachers at the lycée or wives of French expatriates. Through the hanging slats of the broken French shutters, warm night air filters in with the chattering of birds and the movement of people heading home for dinner, their voices rising above muffled sounds of feet shuffling on pavement. Already it is getting dark. The market will be closing. Soon, the streets will be empty. We push the rickety table to one side in the small room of the Cultural Center.

Baccary hits the skin of the drum, beats out a simple rhythm to get us warmed up. I'm surprised by the sounds—deep, resonant, sharp. *On commence.*

Lamine's long, taut body moves easily, without effort, hands loose and expressive. As Baccary drums, sending an explosion of beats into the floor, the air, our feet, Lamine responds. I watch his hands. I watch those fingers and remember the feel of rough skin. Watch his arms, slender and black, his body limber, supple.

We dance barefoot on the dusty wooden floor. Lamine dances

shirtless. His muscled back curves down, arches upward. Blue-black skin curving and arching, those legs in navy-blue stretch pants. I feel shy, have to look away. We women are in lines behind Lamine, imitating his moves. Some of the others are already good at this. They leap and stretch and reach with grace. But me, I sweat within minutes. I drink half my water before the warm-ups are over.

Le Kotéba, Lamine announces. A Mandinka wedding dance. He demonstrates by bending and scooping air with his hands then pushing the air up and away from his head. He lifts his right foot in time with the drum.

We try. Laugh. Try again.

Lamine urges us to bend. "*Il faut baisser,*" he says over and over, crouching low. But only his body can move like that, elastic, fluid. The rest of us stand too tall. Stiff. "*Écoute le tam-tam,*" Lamine says.

We bend, scoop, stretch, push. All in the rhythm to the drum. But I am too big. I don't feel graceful at all. I feel lumpish, American.

Baccary smiles, hits the drum with frenetic energy. His headful of dreadlocks flop and twist, the leather amulets on his arm pulse with the flex of each muscle. I am drenched. Thirsty. Tired.

"*C'est bien, Pa-tee.*" Lamine appears beside me, bending, pushing.

In the dim light of the room, I watch him. His skin glistens and I stomp alongside, awkward and pale. I try to imagine myself beautiful. I try to imagine that I am wrapped in a batik *pagne* in the midst of the village women, the drum calling only to me. I try to imagine that I am able to do more than keep the beat—that I can dance, that I am fluid, that I have grace.

"*Et les citrons verts?*" Lamine looks at me, hands on his hips.

"*You* gave me the limes?" I ask. I stop dancing, bend over to catch my breath, wipe my forehead. I watch Lamine glide his way up to the front of the room, his whole body an expression of Baccary's drumming.

One night, after I've been going to dance class for a couple of weeks, Lamine takes me to his troupe's performance at the Hôtel Nema Kadior. I watch him before the show, behind the hotel, as he bends over the drums, warming them up in front of the fire. No lights—just the bright moon and fire glow. The *djembés* lean in toward the flame, the drum skins tightening.

Lamine and I don't speak. I watch him and feel a tug deep in my belly, a longing to reach over and touch Lamine, crouched there in front of me, turning each drum to warm the skin. I want to run my hands along Lamine's sides, feel his back, each muscle. I want his hands to touch me again, want to feel the hardness of his fingertips.

It has been so long—months—since I've felt any desire. But this man before me now, I want to touch. I want him to touch me. I picture us making love. It isn't the first time I've been attracted to a man, but the feeling still surprises me so much that I don't admit to it right away. And then I tell myself it's because I'm not in my real life that I'm thinking like this.

"Come," Lamine says getting up from the drums and offering his hand. I love this walking hand in hand in the dark. I feel chosen, singled out, beautiful. Lamine introduces me around to the other dancers—men practicing footwork in the shadows, tall, feathered hats like drum-major helmets on their heads, and women lounging in their costumes of black bras and short skirts. The women mumble hello. They barely acknowledge my presence, and I sense their disapproval, feel their hostile stares after we walk away, my white hand in Lamine's.

When the time comes for the show, I sit alone at a table where I can see both the performance and the audience—French tourists with fruity drinks and video cameras. You can see it on their faces, what they can't wait to tell friends back home. They are planning the party, waiting for the moment when Lamine eats fire, his body sleek and lithe. *There,* they'll say, *see? Look at him.* I wonder if I'll be in the background, if the tourists can tell what I'm thinking, the white girl off to the side, if they can see how much I want to blend in with this scene, to feel as if I belong here with Lamine. I wonder if they can see the desire that is clearly there, even before I admit it myself.

By November, I am at last moved into my own house, in Santhiaba, a neighborhood not far from the market, in a house owned by a general in the Senegalese army. A supporter of Abdoulaye Wade, the general is in jail, and his house is used for official guests—Peace Corps volunteers and visiting Fulbright teachers. I am settled, too, as much as I can be in the routine of my life here in Ziguinchor—teaching, dance classes, trips to the market, an occasional movie, dinner with friends, camping trips to the coast at Cap Skirring, visits to villages.

My house, like Jim's, is an *étage,* the French word for "floor" or "level." This house is split into two residences—divided in the front by a metal fence and burning pink bougainvillea. My life, too, feels split into *étages*—there is the life I see myself leading at home—Patty, the feminist, the activist, the lesbian—and the life I lead here— Pa-tee, a dancer, a drummer, a conjurer of fiery ancestral spirits.

In her memoir *French Lessons,* Alice Kaplan says that people want to adopt other cultures because there's something in their own that doesn't *name* them. In French, I can see myself with a man. In Senegalese French, there is no other possibility. But in English, I am someone else entirely. Someone I felt sure of before I left the States. Someone I can't begin to explain to this man I am slowly drawing close to.

The first time he stops by my house in Santhiaba, Lamine says he wants to show me dance steps, which I think is odd, since I'm not the best dancer in the class or even the third or fourth best, and when we're saying goodbye and Lamine holds me and whispers that he doesn't want to go home, I'm caught off-guard. It has been weeks since his dance troupe performance, but the feeling from that night returns. I imagine us together in bed and I hear myself telling Lamine he can stay. I know right then that I will sleep with him, and I do.

I'm nervous that first time, not confident about being sexual with a man. I'm embarrassed by my inexperience, but Lamine doesn't seem to notice or mind. I'm self-conscious when I take off my clothes. I feel too fat. But Lamine tells me my body is strong. I discover that in general, Senegalese men prefer their women bigger than American men do. Wide hips and strong thighs are sensual here. I discover that this is a place where I can feel beautiful.

Afterwards, when we're talking in bed, Lamine asks me how long it has been since I've slept with a man.

"A pretty long time," I say. I don't tell him that he's the second man I've been with ever. He tells me that it has been a while for him, too. He tells me he was married once and that his wife left him a few years ago to move to Dakar. He tells me he has a son and daughter.

"Where are they?"

"In the village. With my uncle." He says this matter-of-factly, without sounding sad or regretful. "Some day," he says, "I will take you there."

The following day at lunch, Lamine says, "I love you." We're at his place. In his one room on folding wooden chairs, we eat *cheb u jen* with our hands, scooping from a large metal bowl in the middle of the floor. A thin foam mattress takes up most of the dark room. Across from me, taped to the wall, are magazine pictures of Nelson Mandela, Michael Jackson, and James Brown.

"You hardly know me," I remind Lamine. To myself I say, *Do I even know what love is?* Bianca and I often said *I love you* to each other. First loves, we said. We'll always love each other, we said.

"I know who you are. I know you are an artist. From my heart, I tell you, I love you."

This is crazy. Love. "Is that why you gave me the limes?"

"Pa-tee," Lamine says with a fondness in his voice that makes me blush. I look away.

"At home, you know, my lover is a woman." I am trying to lessen the tension, to cut down the seriousness of I-love-you. I don't know why I keep the present tense. I don't know what I'm waiting for or if I still expect anything from Bianca. I know that I miss her—more here than after our breakup in those long months leading up to my departure.

Lamine frowns but looks at me steadily. He cups his right hand, keeps the rice from dropping on the floor. "*Une fois,*" he says after a long moment. He shakes his head. "Once," he repeats. "I think I have heard of a woman like that." *A woman like that.* I must look startled. "In the Gambia," he adds. He licks the oil from the outside of his hand.

I don't know what to say. It's clear that lesbians are not in Lamine's worldview, and he seems unimpressed that I have been one of these women. Lamine says, "Does she still love you, this woman? Do you love her?"

"Not any more," I tell him. I don't tell him what a lifesaver this Fulbright has been. Or how fresh and deep the wounds still are, how I boarded the Air Afrique flight in New York still feeling ragged, drawn out and empty. I don't say what I'm thinking—that I'm playing with fire here, getting involved with a man.

We make love again that night on my bamboo bed, under the canopy of mosquito netting. I run my fingers along Lamine's arms, down his sides, smooth and hairless, and against his spine. Lamine smells of sweat and the sweetness of herbs inside the *gris-gris* he wears on a string around his waist. I picture him when he dances and the muscles in his back as he warms the tam-tams by the fire before a performance. I think of how he brought to me a bag of limes when he knew little more than my name. From the mattress, I lift one of Lamine's hands and hold it in mine. The tips of his fingers are tough, like the summer feet of my childhood.

"*Le feu,*" he says and smiles. His hands are hardened from handling fire. He has burned off his body hair, too.

Afterward, I can't sleep. I lie on my side in the crook of Lamine's arm and listen to the drone of mosquitoes hovering beyond the screened-in window. I think of the relentless, hot sun that will rise exactly at seven, the shrill call to prayer two hours before that. I think of Jim—whom I've hardly seen these past weeks—and his plan book, the tapes and the magazine articles he meticulously photocopied before leaving the States, my empty notebook, general lack of plans. I wonder about the women I have been with before and this fire-eater with me now.

The first time he saw me in a bathing suit, Lamine told me he loved seeing the form of my body. This is a first. I have never felt beautiful before in my life, and here with this man—this dancer, this fire-eater—I do. I feel beautiful in a way that is completely new, in a way that has never before felt possible, in a way that makes me feel like I am somebody else, a newer, better version of me.

It's all new—the heat, my being with a man, this way I feel, my life.

Five Days in Palm Springs

REBECCA CHEKOURAS

Day One

This morning I rise with the burning sun at the Bubble Up Hideaway Motel in beautiful Palm Springs, California, where, as the old song goes, the skies are not cloudy all day—resulting in temperatures of about 120 F by noon. The F in this instance means Fahrenheit; as opposed to any other F you might associate with temperatures in the 120s by noon. I look out over the pool and wash down some beta-blockers with Diet Coke. I am visiting my friend of more than half my life, Gypsy Bailey, who recently purchased this small motel on an all-or-nothing gamble. We met at university in the heady seventies, marching, chanting, calling for the takeover of key departments and offices, and producing the campus lesbian newspaper. After graduation we were pulled in different directions, and eventually there came a long stretch of years when our friendship was little more than my peripheral awareness of her life in Memphis and her loose tracking of my life in Chicago. As the wildly unpredictable result of taking one day at a time, Gypsy became a shop owner and I became an advertising executive. One day I woke up wanting to dodge middle age and escape the vortex of karma that was running me into wall after wall. I moved to California, where people go to reinvent themselves as their id. Almost a decade later, Gypsy arrived in the Golden State to pursue her own dream of running a little resort that paid for itself as she rented out the rooms and presided over a glittering salon of artists and intellectuals in the evenings—a grown-up version of the tea parties she gave as a little girl. The Bubble Up, so adorable behind its For Sale sign, is not, as it turns out, the little moneymaker Gypsy thought she was getting. Every day some new thing goes wrong, gives up, breaks down, or blows a gasket. But it is sweet in its own disheveled way.

It feels right to find each other again in the desert. Meeting Gypsy all those years ago, now that I look back on it, launched the slow deterioration of my tolerance for the prevailing cultural and societal norms and for the office in particular. I have definitely reached the end. I have tagged along as far as I can—three decades of deadening corporate life. Now, a twenty-first-century Whitman, I loaf and invite my soul by wandering in the desert.

We are both adjusting to life in the Mojave and to Gypsy's new M.O. as motelier. A wicked wind keeps the fierce heat pressed up against my skin as if it were trying to get inside me. We have had to put Marlon on ice. Marlon Brando is Gypsy's nineteen-year-old Chihuahua; fat as a football with legs so rickety he resembles nothing more than a rotting burrito on wobbly toothpicks near the end of the party. When we go out (and Marlon goes everywhere with Gypsy), we load Brando into his special monogrammed canvas carryall, where he sits on a brick of blue ice wrapped in a towel, another towel thrown over his head to discourage him from calling attention to himself. The tremendous heat causes steam to vaporize from Marlon's iced bag so it appears he is smoldering in there. We rotate the blue ice packs in the freezer, so Marlon is always good to go.

We're on our way to the AIDS consignment-resale store on Palm Canyon. Gypsy is fascinated by the store's extravagant castoffs and goes every day to see what's new. On a deeper level, retail is still more familiar to her than the hospitality industry, and she feels at home in the store. Vintage retail is big in Palm Springs, and you never know when an amazing find will present itself to the savvy. The employees reinforce this feeling of imminent bargaindom by wincing when I ask about something.

"Do you have any Tupperware carriers for deviled eggs?" I ask, innocently hopeful. We have an invitation to a weekend BBQ at a storied home that has been on many magazine covers. A friend of Gypsy's owns it—one of the A-list fags this town is full of and Gypsy's first friend in this vast colony of transients. The party house sits high in the hills overlooking the 111, near Bob Hope's old place. We need to bring something to the soirée. Gypsy would never show up anywhere empty-handed. It's just is not who she is.

The floor clerk shoots me a big wince as if he'd just seen a seven-car pile up on the 10 at speeds of over 90 mph; he has to turn his head away. "We just got one in this morning, but it was snapped up immediately," he says from some emotionally disturbed place. All snapped up, none for you—the sorrow of the late shopper.

So I wander off to look for Gypsy and her smoking dog. As I spy her across the floor, I receive sudden and alarming proof that I have become the kind of woman children point at. This one just reaches for a handful of her mother's shorts. It makes me wonder if everyone can see how badly I've failed at the simplest thing that everyone else can do. From the outside it doesn't seem that bad: a tall, thin, middle-aged woman with short blonde hair and blue eyes, tan from recent afternoons on the golf course, slumped shoulders from a decade at university followed by a life that evaporated behind a desk while thinking up marketing campaigns for products no one really needs. Maybe I'm okay. Children don't yet have the blinders adults use to breeze through public places filled with hollowed-out souls.

Distraught with a vague but persistent spiritual malaise I cannot identify, I sometimes wonder if this is how homelessness starts. A-okay one day, then sliding down the razor's edge the next, the reasons in there somewhere just out of reach. I sigh and inspect Gypsy's shopping basket: a pair of socks that has "Shut Up Bitch" knit into the cuff, a beautiful pair of tan suede slides, and an elegant silver cream-and-sugar set. How does she find treasure when all I see is crap at every turn? I persevere and find two pairs of shorts in mint condition for $5 and $3 respectively. I "snap them up" as is the practice here. The eighty-something queen who volunteers at the counter looks at my price tags and says, "Three plus five, that's eight."

"Yup," I reassure him.

"You come back now," he chirps as we are leaving.

While I'm pocketing my change, a young man with dozens of squares of aluminum foil in his wet hair comes racing up to us, his cape of bright yellow sunflowers on a sky blue background luffing in his breezy wake. "Oh! Hi! I saw your dog from across the street. I'm getting my hair done for the party this weekend. But your dog! I know this dog's soul mate, and she is in trouble. You have to rescue her!"

Leaving the store, I smile and wave to the little knot of concern at the counter. The plate-glass window reflects a steady stream of Mercedes and BMWs arriving to drop off the discards of wealthy gay men who own vacation homes here. Later, when it is dark, this same stream of cars will troll for different treasure using Red Bull and Viagra as bait.

Deciding to check out the Tin Man's story, we steer over to Pretty Pet on Tahquitz Canyon where a longhaired Chihuahua puppy brought in for grooming has been marooned. Her owner, one of the hundreds of octogenarians dying off to make room for the sex-o-gregarious party boys replacing them, met her maker as the pup was going through the wash. Adored by the staff, the six-pound nugget of hyper-personality cannot stay in the shop forever. As I'm thinking "cute pup," Gypsy and Marlon are hearing wedding bells. Thirty minutes later, we are heading home with Brigitte Bardot.

Day Two

Another day rolls over the hills toward us. There are no guests at the motel. It is the depth of the low season, and Gypsy still has not got the gestalt of the business down after six months of holding on to this tiger's tail of surprise, remorse, and extensive repairs that started out as the simple purchase of a small motel. She was a major collector of Americana in Memphis, where she had a store and became something of a cult hero due to her quirky sense of merchandising. She had an unfailing eye for what would appreciate quickly, that and a flat out, go-for-broke lust for life. Her spirit is bigger than her five-foot-seven frame; more importantly, she has always refused to compromise her vision of what she wants from life. And in that sense she became mythic. Gypsy lunges at life, cannonballing into the pool, falling in and out of love with dozens of women, heart a million miles out in front but tied to her sleeve by a gossamer thread as strong as kryptonite. I wish I could be as brave.

A woman I'm dating, Ginny, will be arriving late tomorrow tonight. But today is occupied with a quick trip to town to pick up paint supplies, following the game plan we'd laid down last night, while drinking and smoking pot, to release the id from the savage tyranny of the superego. That's when Gypsy decided to redecorate.

The old motel was built in the early 1950s, like much of the Las Palmas area, and is painted a soulless white, a fact that disturbs Gypsy far more than the complete lack of paying customers in the high heat of the desert off-season. We've loaded ourselves, Marlon, and Brigitte into Gypsy's ancient Buick Roadmaster to make a run to the hardware store.

Palm Canyon appears through the windshield as an endless succession of hotels, apparel shops, restaurants, and midcentury modern resale stores along a broad avenue lined with palm trees reaching up through sidewalks adorned with names of Hollywood legends framed in stars. While Brigitte and Marlon hump enthusiastically in the back seat, Gypsy gives me a quick run down on the Palm Springs mise-en-scène: old people loopy on too many contraindicated prescription drugs; middle-aged people on maintenance medications or an Rx to ease the pain of recent cosmetic surgery—one of the town's main industries—and young gay men on ecstasy and cocktails. Apparently, the secret password of the town is "portal." Everyone seems to be looking for the door to some new state of being.

"Well, it's a fag resort tucked inside a retirement village," Gypsy offers, as if that adequately explains Palm Springs. "Everybody's on vacation and Viagra, or life support and Lipitor."

"Hey! Swing into Starbucks," I cry, sighting the familiar logo. "I need coffee." As we wait for sugar and caffeine, I try not to stare at the two men in front of us. Both are short, maybe five foot five with muscular torsos propped above rear ends that are not the usual male square, but rounder. And it is hard to find a square jaw line on either of them. The unwanted intimacy of standing in line erodes my determination to stay out of their business.

"I thought I'd have more arm and leg hair," says one.

"Yeah," says the other, "and somehow I believed I'd grow taller even though my surgeon told me that wouldn't happen. You just believe what you want to believe, regardless of anything anybody else says, you know?"

As the men laugh, I keep as much polite distance as I can, but Gypsy, suddenly aware of the conversation, steps right in.

"Hey, hi, I'm Gypsy Bailey and I just bought the Bubble Up Hideaway over on Tamer Lane. And this corporate stick-up-the-butt is my assistant." I roll my eyes but Gypsy continues undistracted. "You know, I'm curious about this whole FTM thing."

"We are the answer men," they reply genially, looking more feminine behind their sweet smiles. "Whaddaya want to know?"

"Well, okay."

I brace myself, remembering how Gypsy can attack a conversation like a kamikaze diving right to the most vulnerable point. "Where does the dick come from?"

Aicheewahwah! I cringe. Isn't that what the Internet is for? Jesus!

"It's made of a roll of skin and tissue drawn from the stomach area," they reply, talking effortlessly about their metamorphosis. Gypsy, unaware of any protocol surrounding the phenomenon, has grabbed a sizeable roll of her own midriff. Looking at them both, she asks, dryly, "You mean I could be a penis donor?"

Back on track, tooling through town where misters deplete the aquifer to cool empty patios, Gypsy cranks the wheel on the Roadmaster and turns into the hardware store's parking lot. It is filled with rainbow windsocks and patio furniture browsed by women holding hands and men eyeing each other up and down. Breezing past the popcorn machine, the rainbow flags and key rings, rainbow baseball caps and T-shirts, cock rings and silicon vibrators that can be cleaned in the dishwasher, we stand before endless racks of paint chips and get to the work of transforming the motel into something more in line with Gypsy's worldview. Gypsy is making a stack of chips in colors I can't believe are even produced, let alone seriously considered for purchase.

"Don't let the exteriors fool you," Gypsy confides. "The interiors here really pour on the color."

We arrive back at the Hideaway loaded with cans of paint in shades that have never been mixed before and, I feel reasonably certain, will never be mixed again. After lunch, Gypsy is determined to bake a cake. Nothing signals home like baking a cake, and, she reasons, it would be better to heat up the kitchen now instead of this evening, when we will sit at the green Formica table there pondering our future. Once the pale discs of batter are in the 350-degree oven, we head outside into the triple-digit afternoon and begin painting the one-story, six-room motel a screaming pink.

We are comfortable, working quietly side by side, despite our many differences. I haven't seen Gypsy since last winter, when she tripped over the cribbage board and opened her forehead on the edge of the baby grand during a cocktail hour that lasted from 5 p.m. to about 2 a.m. It took seven butterfly Band-Aids to close the wound, but it has healed nicely, leaving only a thin white vertical grimace above her left eye. I also talked to her the day her car was stolen but found abandoned only a few blocks away, a child at the Bubble Up suffered a burst appendix, and her handyman needed emergency-room care for an ingrown hair on his ass. It was apparently quite severe, as a week later he was still wearing a maxi pad to catch the draining fluid. I am discovering it takes a determined sangfroid to keep the faith at the Bubble Up Hideaway. Gypsy is a believer. I used to be. C'est la vie, it is cocktail hour, and we must do what we must do. Can we really have gone through all the olives so soon?

Evening, Day Two

We have reached some point of no return as evidenced by the disco music we have loaded into the boom box in the kitchen and the bong passing between us. With Sylvester's "You Make Me Feel Mighty Real," the gay national anthem, rattling the dishes in the cupboard, we enthrall ourselves with a push-puppet dance contest. I find it is an almost Arthurian test of dexterity, while Gypsy skillfully makes an elephant with a serpentine trunk shake his puppet bootie to the disco beat. Concentration makes her eyes bulge, and sweat forms on her upper lip, but the behemoth seems alive in her hands snaking his trunk up and down while moving his Leviathan rump back and forth in perfect rhythm, responding to the slightest movement of her fingers on the disk that relaxes the elastic string holding the puppet together. We are screaming with laughter. She switches to Felix the Wonderful Cat, the star of her collection. Standing upright and being the most anthropomorphic of the puppets, Felix provides endless entertainment as he snaps his fingers, rotates his hips, and lays down the funk and jive like the hepcat he is. He is groovin'. He is mighty. He is bitchin'. We are wrecked. Just when I think this Faust of funk can't get any more entertaining, Gypsy rotates his head so that it is on backwards and his tail becomes an ersatz penis swinging and circling with the driving beat. Now we are on our feet, snappin', bumpin', feeling the music in us and dancing in the midnight kitchen.

Just at this moment, Gypsy takes a super-sized hit from the pipe and I remember that I changed the screen without telling her. Changing the screen without telling anyone is like sneaking fresh tennis balls into Wimbledon and not holding them up at the start of play—bad things can happen and those who are on the receiving end can seriously misjudge a critical calculation such as speed (in the case of tennis) or smoke flow (more relevant to the pot pipe). Gypsy's head instantly expands to Tweety Bird dimensions as sideways atom bombs smoke out of her ears. Her eyes, bulging out of their sockets on bungee cords, fly across the kitchen, slam into the opposite wall with a wet slap, come springing back home to the vacant holes of her skull, and her eyelids roll up like a cheap shade flapping when the spring breaks. Now we struggle with the simplest things like checking e-mail or mixing a cocktail. We've developed a curious inability to use aluminum foil. We eat the layer cake by the handful.

Day Three

Life is exquisitely slow at the Bubble Up Hideaway, one of the pleasures of being without deadlines but also due in no small part to our persistent stupor. Due to the ancient mercies of the San Gorgonio mountains, sunset happens at about 6 p.m., when that yellow coin slides behind the tallest peak, signaling the arrival of our happiest moment: cocktail hour. We begin with wine and beer poolside and inch our way across twenty yards of cement, flagstone, the faux leopard wall-to-wall carpeting we just installed, and linoleum, upgrading with every change in flooring to stronger mood enhancers until we find ourselves seated at the green Formica dinette in the kitchen, holding martinis while rummaging for the bong.

While the kitchen at the Bubble Up may be only twelve feet by twelve feet, it is an improbable cosmos of infinitely extendible dimensions, every nook and cranny packed with the memorabilia of a 1950s middle-class childhood. Long a nationally recognized collector, Gypsy has many of her hundreds of vintage lunch boxes and thousands of juice glasses lining the tangerine shelves of her kitchen cabinets. It can take me away in a moment to a place buried deep in my heart, a memory that crystallizes some understanding of the archetypal stuff from which my life has been constructed. I find myself wondering what, exactly, a broken heart is and where salvation comes from.

Stoned and drifting, I come to realize the Bubble Up is a wormhole to a lost innocence, where one may idly open a cupboard only to have a universe fall out, its arrival heralded by a perfectly preserved ceramic Tinkerbelle, wand poised to grant your every wish, a smile of genuine goodness on her virginal lips. In goes my hand to the farthest kitchen drawer and out comes whatever I can find . . . a cigarette lighter shaped like a woman's torso—when you flick it, the nipples and crotch light up in red bulbs like miniature Rudolph noses. And that is the essence of Palm Springs: the inseparability of good from evil, the senses from the spirit, the place where hope and doom meet in a longing for redemption through ordinary things.

We are completely alone and naked by the pool, where the thermometer has cooled down to 95 degrees. Brown as a caramel, still gorgeous at fifty-five, with no tan lines, long, silver hair, and eyes the green of chameleons, Gypsy illuminates the five-foot tall, plastic soft-serve ice-cream cone she rescued from a fast food demolition site. A mountain of faux vanilla softly blunts the evening shadows. Birds sing themselves to sleep in the palms, and the sky grows purple then gray then deep midnight blue and the stars shine down on us as we sing songs we loved as children. The question of collecting moonbeams in a jar is discussed to an absurd length. Shrouded as I am in a life that started in a state of grace and then crashed due to forces as mysterious to me as Area 51, I decide yes. Yes, I would chase after those beams.

Third Night

The big party is tonight, and I am open to whatever comes my way. We don't know any locals and I am curious about who lives here as opposed to who comes to vacation here. We cross the valley floor and snake up the face of the mountain, winding around to a trim gate featuring a for-sale sign. Everything is for sale in Palm Springs. It is on permanent flip.

Behind the gate, a lushly watered lawn of closely clipped grass spreads evenly across a smooth, flawless yard. The home presents blindly to the street. On either side of a massive doorway a window-less wall stretches away, framing the towering cathedral entrance of metal. From what I can see, the glass panes above the doorway are the only source of natural light in front. We can't see in. These midcentury modern homes give Palm Springs its distinctive look. Most of the other $1.4 million houses on the street are similar: bland or architectonic fronts, lawns like fairways, dramatic entrances, and private. Palm Springs was made to keep secrets.

Inside, wealthy gay men from LA and their hairdresser or interior designer boyfriends are eating caviar on endive standing around a sunken bar in the middle of an eleven-hundred-square-foot living room. A glass wall looks out over the Coachella Valley. Just beyond, a pool with sight lines to infinity shimmers with underwater lighting. The stars are white in an indigo sky. It seems I could reach out and touch them.

But things often are not what they seem in Palm Springs: women are men in drag, lush green golf courses lie on top of desert rock and sand, huge homes in walled compounds sit empty for months, tended by servants and lawn crews. There's a lot of surface in Palm Springs. The city was originally built for trysts and hiding away; it's a Kasbah in the middle of nowhere between LA and Las Vegas. Yes, there are hardware stores, podiatrists, supermarkets, and kids playing league baseball. Under this civic veneer, the city can hide people when those people don't want to be seen doing what they are doing. This is especially true for public people who wrestle with private demons. Drying out, rehabbing, getting facelifts—these are all better done in seclusion, and, like the ancient *abbas* of the early Christian church, seekers of redemption still enter the desert asking to be saved. After rigorous trials, they emerge new and transformed.

Day Four

A hatchet of sunlight is splitting the drapes in my room, creasing the skin between my eyes at 7 a.m. Head-splitting, apparently, is a signature amenity of the Bubble Up. Beside me, Ginny, the woman I've been dating, is still snoring, her faucal breathing the sound of a carpet being torn from nails. Using deductive logic, I can conclude she arrived last night sometime between the last martini and lights out. I met Ginny through one of those mail-order bride services for lesbians, an online dating site. It is impossible to take those things seriously, and so we don't, instead rolling along in the moment.

Ginny is having her fifty-first birthday, and she has caravanned down with Lili, to observe the turn. Lili is a vagabond who lives with me the four or five months out of the year when she can sit still. She is one of those complete surprises the universe will sometimes throw my way: in her early thirties, straight, glamorous, nerves of steel, intrepid globetrotter. We met reaching for the last box of chocolate-covered orange slices on the shelf at Trader Joe's. We avoided a fight by instantly becoming friends. She moved in about a year later when Simon, the love of her life up to that point, dropped a surprise breakup on her in Kuala Lumpur, leaving her stranded and bewildered. Now we are an odd entourage of older lesbians and their Kato Kaelin on vacation in Gomorrah.

Life has been easy for me in many ways—breezing through university at the head of my class, scholarships, fellowships, you-name-it, nailing the perfect job just before graduating, switching from painting to big business with the greatest of ease, multiple feats of derring-do—no hands, no safety net. Just don't ask me to maintain a family. That mystery is beyond what my decade at university taught me. I can't keep failing at this and still believe in myself. At fifty-two, I am running out of time.

Day Five

Because of our efforts with a can of paint and a brush, the Bubble Up Hideaway has developed a decidedly red interior; a red as vivid as anything imagination will allow; think shiny new bike mixed with a semigloss candy-apple red. It is an industrial color, not meant for the home but for NASCAR hotrods or detailing on the Space Shuttle. Against the deep milk-chocolate ceiling, it evokes memories of the candied cherries that made my childhood Christmases so meaningful. The leopard carpet now covering the living room in the owner's unit was salvaged from a supper club we discovered just before the wrecking ball did. Gypsy clearly has a direction in mind here, someplace she wants to take us visually and experientially. If I had to say what Gypsy does for a living, I would say she creates free space—places that are the outward manifestation of her capacity for enchantment and whimsy, her delight in life and the people who dare to really live out their visions of themselves without apology or regret. No one is judged here. Her home and store in Tennessee and now the Bubble Up are testimony to this woman's desire to appreciate everything she encounters. She has never, to my knowledge, been afraid, and I am drawn to almost any expression of fearlessness, whether it is throwing everything on red seven or a color choice that would drive most people from the room.

The pervasive red theme even bleeds into Ginny's birthday cake, a three-layered pink whore whose blotchy rose frosting, though excessive, can no longer hide her spreading fault lines. It is concocted of strawberry Jell-O powder mixed into sugar complemented by more strawberries steeped in more sugar and mortared by butter. Gypsy's recipe is out of her mother's cookbook—a woman who won the Pillsbury Bake-Off more than once in the Kansas regionals. She taught her daughter everything she knows about baking. The cake is sensational, and, after the singing and candle blowing, premenstrual Lili furtively eats half of it to satisfy her biological craving for sweets.

Evening, Day Five

I cannot even begin to describe how magical it is to be stoned and floating in a pool of 90-degree water when the ambient night air is still close to a hundred. I lie on a foam float staring up at the desert sky filled with stars and swirling planets, holding onto Ginny's foot as she swims gracefully around the painter's palette pool, and young, mischievous Lili, who cannot swim, sits poolside chucking red devilducks at my head. I can hear but not understand the pleasant patter of her conversation with Gypsy while devoting the better part of my attention to the underwater lighting of the turquoise pool. It is sublime and I am idly content watching my pink toenails trail after me in the slow circling of Ginny's swimming. It's working, right? We're okay?

Each evening at the Bubble Up is rooted in its own soundtrack unconsciously chosen through the popular vote of "share of play time" on the motel's sound system. Previous nights have seen this prestigious spot held by Big Momma Thornton, Shelby Lynne (who fended off a strong challenge from Sheryl Crow), Susan Tedeschi, and, in a precipitous decline from which Gypsy had to be saved, Leonard Cohen. But tonight, having gone completely native, the overwhelming choice is the late Israel Kamakawiwo'ole, the Hawaiian mezzo-soprano whose shimmering rendition of "Somewhere Over the Rainbow" accompanied by ukulele is breaking my heart. He has a woman's voice combined with the earnest purity of a child. We play him incessantly, singing along into spoons and fists, attempting our own comebacks on the wings of his music. What is salvation, who can bestow it, when does it take root, what makes it grow?

Veteran of parallel worlds that I am, I drift, enchanted, across the universe, borne along on restless winds of memory and desire. Israel's plaintive voice echoes down the halls of everything I have ever wanted.

And I know what I want; I want to tell someone about everything.

A Friend in America

GILLIAN KENDALL

───

I held the secret letter deep in my raincoat pocket as I approached the hostel warden. "Excuse me," I said, obviously American but at least polite. "Are you busy?"

He gave an impression of youthful surliness: intimidating glasses covering small eyes, bangs falling across his face. "Not terribly, at the moment."

"I was wondering if you could help me find someplace—a village called 'Shanaheever,' or something like that." Aware that I was scrambling the pronunciation, I produced a note—not the letter—from my other pocket and pointed to the name of the village. The note was an e-mail, pulled from my printer just as I'd left for my flight to Dublin. It read:

> You follow the Skye (sp?) Road up from town, from a pub, I
> think it's called the King's Arms or something, and go about
> two miles until you're in the village of Shanaheever. There
> are no shops or anything to indicate a village—you have to
> ask. You'll see the castle gates on the left. Sort of opposite
> them is the lane to the Sayers' house. If you go too far you'll
> see a big white house. In other words, turn before the castle
> and you'll see his cottage. Of course, all this is from 20 years
> ago, so it may have changed. Oh, Jill, I hope you find him!

My friend Adrienne—a nurse in Little Rock with twin toddlers and a handsome, delinquent teenager—was the author of the note and the secret letter. In her hurry, she had neglected to mention from *which* town you took the Skye (Sky?) Road. I had come to Clifden, a coastal town in County Galway, because I remembered hearing the name in conversations with her. I supposed that Shanaheever—unmarked on any map and probably hugely unknown—lay outside another, smaller town to the north. Or possibly the south, there being no land west of Clifden.

The warden peered at my e-mail. "Shanaheever," he said in a way that sounded correct. "No, never heard of it."

"Oh, dear," I said. I had picked up the expression in England; it was useful for conveying all sorts of emotions, from sympathy to outrage to self-pity. "I really need to find it."

The warden tried to hand me back my paper. To hold his interest, I blurted, "I have to tell a man there about his nineteen-year-old son in America."

"Have you, now?" The warden glanced down again at the note. "God, it wouldn't be John Sayers, would it?" Behind the glasses, his eyes rounded in sly delight. "I know John. He's a bit of a flirt."

"Oh, shit," I said, accidentally reverting to American. "Sorry. I just—I wasn't supposed to tell anyone. Please forget what I said. How do you know him?"

"He lives just up the road. Here, the Skye Road—that's just up that hill on the left. It is John, is it? This is fantastic." In Ireland, *fantastic* can mean "incredible" or "unbelievable" rather than "great."

"Please, please, don't tell anyone," I said. "I thought the village was miles away from here. I have a big mouth."

"Every time I see John, he's talking to at least two American ladies," the warden mused. He sounded envious. "Not one, two. Sometimes more. He likes the tourists."

"He sure liked my friend." I was bursting to tell the story of how, twenty years ago, Adrienne, my older sister's most glamorous friend, had met John in the Dublin pub where she was barmaiding the summer before her senior year in college. How he had been charmed by her thigh-length red hair and Southern accent, and she by his pirate's beard and complete collection of Van Morrison, which they spun on a little hi-fi in the whitewashed cottage where John lived with his father. (I think mainly Adrienne fell in love with "Moondance" and rural Ireland. And Bushmills whiskey helped.) In the six months before her tourist—"employment prohibited"—visa ran out, she moved into the cottage loft, got a job in another pub, and got pregnant, although she didn't find out about the last until she was back in Arkansas, a college dropout carrying a large Gaelic fetus.

She named the child—who had his father's deep, powerful eyes—Seamus, but at thirteen he rebelled and demanded to be called Steve.

"If you want to meet John," the warden said, "just take another American girl down to the pub with you tonight and sit at the bar looking like tourists. I guarantee—"

"Which pub?"

"Ah, that's a point." The closed look on the warden's face was gone, replaced by interest. "I often see him at King's, and Mannion's. I have seen him at Humpty's, but not often. Then there's the hotel, where they do poetry on Wednesday nights; he always reads there."

It was Tuesday. "But I need to find him tonight; I have to leave tomorrow."

"Ah, well, then you won't hear the poetry. Pity, that. He's not bad. But as to tonight, there's no telling. He'll probably be at Mannion's."

"Where's that?"

"Just up the road. It's not difficult. Listen, I'm free about nine-ish. If you like, I'll take you round the pubs and we'll find John. That suit you?"

It was well into the evening, but the sun slanted in the pub windows as bright as afternoon, reminding me how far north I was. We sat on low stools at Mannion's, waving away the smoke. A white-haired fiddler, an even older man on spoons, and a woman singer in print dress performed ballads and unhappy love songs. I bought the warden a Guinness with a smile drawn on its thick, white head. "Thanks again," I said. "I would've had no idea which man was John. All Adrienne said was that he was tall, good-looking, and had brown eyes and brown hair."

"I don't know about the good-looking part," the warden said, "but the rest describes half the men in here."

"Right. Oh, and supposedly he has nice hands." Also, Adrienne had guessed that, in the maddening way of men, John would have aged well. She hadn't allowed me to bring a picture of her—forty, short-haired, and solid. I picked up my half-pint of Carlsberg and clinked it against the warden's glass. "To John, wherever he is."

"John Sayers, indeed," he said. "But that's a very touristy drink you've got there. Lager and lime, is it?"

I nodded. "I don't like the taste of Guinness. Dark beer—"

"Don't call it beer!" he said. "That would be sacrilege."

The oak door swung open and four men crowded in. All were tall, had dark hair, and could have been dapper two decades ago. I glanced at the warden, who shook his head.

He continued to shake his head about all the tall, dark, and handsome locals who entered Mannion's. Then it was on to the King's Arms, were the warden peered into every smoky corner of the cloistered, cluttered little rooms, but to no avail. He asked the barmaid if she'd seen John. "Not tonight," she said.

As we crossed the street to the hotel, the sky was still yellow-blue and bright, though it was nearly 11 p.m., closing time. The hotel lounge contained only a pack of Italian tourists listening to a dreary country-western cover band.

Finally, we tried a pint in Humpty's, a rock pub full of teenagers, but when the last call came we still hadn't found John. Taking his leave, the warden thanked me for the drinks and wished me luck. "I'd go with you back to King's," he said, "but I've got a busload of school kids from Limerick coming in late tonight."

My escort gone, I sauntered back to King's, feeling the lager's effects, and planning how to explain my indiscretion and failure to Adrienne. In the small front room of the pub, I spotted two Australian women from my hostel leaning chummily against the bar on either side of a stunning, six-foot-plus man. He wore long sable curls, a beard no less lustrous, and a black leather coat (though the pub was plenty warm). One of the women recognized me and waved drunkenly. "Hullo! Come and meet John—Jesus to his friends."

"Jesus to everyone," the man said. He gazed at me with a combination of lust and Guinness, his eyes as compelling as Steve's. I remembered Adrienne saying, "If you've seen Steve's eyes, you've seen John's." She also claimed that they laughed alike, but I had never heard Steve laugh. Mostly he was a shadow going in and out of his mother's house by the back door.

"John Sayers?" I said.

"Och, no, not Sayers. Owens, I am. That'd be my cousin, now."

"Sorry." Of course. This character with the Celtic cross around his neck and a scar on his nose was the age John had been when Adrienne had met him. The man I wanted would be graying, balding, or at least slightly stooped.

Forgetting the two women he'd been chatting up, Jesus focused blearily on me. "How do you know Johnny? Is he about tonight?"

"I don't think so; I've looked in every pub within walking distance. I have a letter for him, from a friend in America."

"You could give it to me." He tried to make his wizard eyes sincere. "I live near John. I'd see that he got it."

Adrienne had said her relationship with John had provided great gossip in the village for years. Having already revealed John's secret once, I didn't want to risk doing so again. Besides, Jesus seemed a little creepy. "I was told to give it to him directly," I said, apologetically. "Could you tell me where his house is, exactly?"

"Of course I could," Jesus said, "seeing as you don't trust me. It's up the Skye Road, a couple of miles. You'll pass a great stone barn near the road, with pony carts in it, and then look up the hill."

"Is there a number?"

"Och, no. No numbers on the Skye Road. But if you're afraid of not finding it and you don't trust me, why don't you just slip it in the post? You could just put 'John Sayers, Poet, Skye Road,' and he'd get it."

But every letter Adrienne had sent in twenty years had gone unanswered; she wanted to know that he received this one. Besides, this quest was too romantic to end at the post office. I had to at least try to find the cottage.

"So, is John married?" I asked. Adrienne was hoping that John had paired up with a local girl, Mary O'Something, and that they'd bred a dozen children.

"No, not John. He's a writer. And a wee bit of a farmer." Jesus said this as if writers and farmers never married. "And his friend in America?" he said, leering now. "Is she married?"

"Yes," I snapped. "Happily. With children." I wanted him to know this was not about an unrequited love.

"Ah, that's grand." Jesus turned to one of the Australian women. "Would you marry me tonight?" She giggled, and he leaned toward me and said, "I think she likes me."

Realizing how tired I was, and how early I'd have to get up, I said goodnight and thanked him for his help.

"And thank you," Jesus said, raising the dregs of his pint in my direction, "for not trusting me."

In the morning, the Skye Road lifted me with every step. I was alone on the narrow lane except for dozens of indifferent sheep roaming about the heathery enclosures. The arms of oaks and beeches bent overhead, making a green tunnel for me to pass through. Around the bend in the hill, the trees thinned, revealing brown cliffs, down which rocks and clumps of grass tumbled into the sea. Daisies grew in the cracks of a stone wall, and wild fuchsia bushes, as big as houses, dangled fine pink flowers.

A few hundred feet above sea level and rising, I began to pant. Adrienne must have walked this road every day, going down to Clifden for bread and milk, climbing back up in time to make tea and bring the dog in from the rain. No car, no TV, no central heat, no worries—except staying warm and dry.

When Adrienne had returned to the States, my sister had brought her home to stay with us. The first night, seeing the sliced meat, cheese, and vegetables laid out for supper, Adrienne had knelt and closed eyes to say grace, her long hair falling around her like a veil. She'd been eating nothing but potatoes and bread and lard for too long, she said. She'd gained so much weight recently . . .

To the left of the road rose two pillars—bumpy rectangles made of gray stones and festooned with honeysuckle—but I saw no castle beyond. Every acre of Galway held so many old gates and walls; this might be the gate to the castle, or it might lead to an ancient cemetery or modern mansion. To the right, a pair of indistinct ruts wound up the side of the hill. The way to John's house? I turned up it, my heart pounding from more than just the walk.

What if the door was opened by an American girl—or two? What if John was angry with me for bringing the letter? How would I even know it was he and not another cousin wanting to learn John's long-distance secrets? Behind me, I heard the slow groans of an old bicycle. A stout woman was peddling determinedly up the Skye Road, plastic shopping bags nestled on either side of the rear wheel. "Excuse me," I called, trotting back down the ruts.

She hopped off, looking helpful.

"Is this where John Sayers lives?"

"Oh, yes." She squinted up the way I'd been walking. "That'll be his car in the drive."

For the first time I noticed a small dwelling near the top of the hill. "Thanks," I said.

"No bother," she said, and remounted, probably off to tell her neighbors about the tourist woman seeking John.

His Fiat was shabby—nothing a typical American would cheerfully drive—but it looked fine in the dirt-and-thistle driveway. The one-story cottage was small, with deep windows and a red door. I liked the door. A dewy bottle of milk rested on the stoop, and a cat disappeared around a corner as I crunched over the stones. "Good morning," I called, rapping on the door.

No answer. After a few seconds the cat came back and leapt onto a fence post to eye me. A donkey behind some barbed wire sneezed. I wished I had an apple to offer it, a gesture of international, interspecies goodwill. Would John receive the letter like a goodwill apple, or a baited trap?

He must be home, I thought. It was almost 8 a.m.; surely a "wee bit of a farmer" wouldn't still be sleeping. Maybe he was in the shower, if the cottage had one. I knocked again, more assertively. Still no answer. I waited several minutes, getting my breath back. My heart was pumping irrationally fast. Although I was only delivering a letter, I was unable to shake a sense of adventure. He couldn't have gone out on foot, I reasoned, because if he had, he would have brought in the milk.

What a sleuth I was, on the trail of love. Maybe there was a back entrance. It seemed presumptuous to walk through the side yard of a person I didn't know, but I hadn't come five thousand miles, the last two on foot, to be deterred by a man ignoring my knock.

Sidling past the cat, I minced along the path of half-buried stones. There were no windows on the side of the cottage. Not wanting to surprise John taking a wash or a whiz in his backyard, I called, "Hello? Hello?"

From inside, a querulous voice echoed, "Hello? Is someone saying 'hello'?"

The back door stood open, and inside the dark room beside a neat fire, somebody's grandfather sat smoking a pipe: too old to be John, unless the poet-farmer had led an excruciating life. Then another figure blocked my view—a fortyish man, fat, with brown hair and, yes, deep eyes, perturbed and nervous.

"Are you John?" I asked. "John Sayers?"

Though he looked as if he wanted to deny it, the man nodded. I wondered if his cousin had somehow told him about me already.

"I'm Jill Kendall, I said, "a friend of Adrienne Hackney, in America."

At her name, John stepped outside and closed the door behind him, shutting off the old man from the light. Then he walked me away from the house, toward the lane.

"I have a letter from her," I said. "She thought you might want to know about Steve—Seamus."

He seemed to recognize his son's name.

"You know?" I said.

"Oh, yes," he said, but noncommittally. Perhaps he *had* received the other letters, in which case this one might be redundant and unwanted. I held out the envelope, which he snatched and folded into a pocket. "Very kind of you." He spoke quickly, even faster than most Irish people did. "You're here on holiday, are you? On vacation? Traveling round?"

I got the impression he had asked the same of thousands of women. "That's right," I said slowly. "We landed in Dublin a couple of weeks ago."

"With your husband, are you? Or boyfriend?"

What possible difference could it make to him who I was with? "Girlfriend," I said, and saw the question on his face, but I did nothing to answer it. My lover, Amber, was expecting me to arrive in County Clare that afternoon on the bus.

John shifted his gaze, evidently unsure how to continue. "So, you like the countryside, do you? Find it pleasant?"

"Oh, yes," I gushed, glad for an icebreaker. Soon we would get to the subject of Adrienne and Steve. "It just keeps getting prettier the further north we come. We went to Scattery Island—"

"People think it must be grand, living here," John interrupted. The statement sounded rehearsed, like the beginning of speech he'd given in many a pub to many a lady stranger. "And it is grand, remote and beautiful. But it does strange things to a person. It makes you face yourself in a way you don't have to in most places. You can't run away from yourself here."

As if considering his ideas, I gazed west to the sea, flat and hazy over the treetops, and thought, *Yeah, right. Those of us from the suburbs never engage in self-reflection.*

"A lot of people can't take it," he said. "When they're young, a lot of people run off. They have to get away from this for a while. They go to London, or Dublin, and try to hide."

Yes, Dublin. Was he explaining his own escapades?

"But once you get all that out of your system, you have to come back to this. At least I did. I couldn't live anywhere else. You know?"

Remembering that Adrienne would want to know every detail, I studied John. He had not aged well, after all, though he and Adrienne would still have made a nice couple. His belly was great with Guinness, and there were deep lines around his mouth, but his face was clear and tanned. The famous beard was gone, leaving only a heavy black stubble.

He was a middle-aged man who lived with his father, afraid of what his neighbors thought. Suddenly sorry for him, I turned to the donkey, which was meandering in our direction. "What a nice creature," I said. "He seems very happy." Like all the Irish animals I had seen, the donkey was full-bellied and smooth-furred, having plenty of room to roam in and lush greens to eat. It bent down to nibble something near my feet, then put its neck over the wire fence.

Stroking the coarse, gray mane, I murmured endearments: "Good boy. You're a pretty boy, yes you are. You're so good . . ."

"That donkey was mad," said John. "I had to have him gelded last year. Had to take him to the vet and have the operation. He was running mad—getting out of the pen, wandering up and down the road. I'd never know where he was one day to the next. I hated to geld him, but it had to be done."

"He seems gentle enough now," I said. As if to demonstrate, the donkey nuzzled my palm.

"Oh, he's all right now I've had him gelded. But he was running mad, he was. He'd go everywhere, you know. He'd be off at the neighbor's horse pen, trying to get up on the horses. Mad."

A poet's allusion to his own days of hormonal madness? I decided to stretch the metaphor and perhaps find out. "Maybe he wanted to make little mules," I said.

"Sure, that's natural enough, but he was acting mad with it—fighting and running about. Had to geld him, poor creature."

The animal moved away from my caress, and John shifted, apparently impatient for me to go. "You'll be about for a few days, will you?" he asked.

"No, unfortunately I'm leaving this morning." In fact, I would have to hustle to make my bus. "Did you . . . want to hear about Adrienne?"

"I'll read the letter," he said, touching the pocket of his jacket. "Very good of you to have come out of your way. Thanks. Have a good holiday."

"You should write to her," I said, suddenly desperate. "She'd like to hear from you."

"That I will," he said, nodding hard. "Sure I will."

The Skye Road was easier with gravity in my favor, and I nearly skipped toward town and my bus and my girlfriend, who was twenty-five years old and lovely. We'd never lied or let each other down, we had yet to break each other's hearts, and neither of us would ever unintentionally get the other pregnant.

That was all, except that as I came around the last bend to where the Skye Road straightened and flattened out, and the white hostel and the first pubs leaned against one another, I passed a couple heading up the hill. They were young, maybe in their late teens. He— another Sayers cousin, perhaps—had a black ponytail and carried a round wicker basket full of the day's groceries. She—his girlfriend, his sweetheart, his someone—came barely up to his shoulder, but she matched his steps, and he bent his head to listen to what she was saying. And I wasn't surprised that she had long red hair. They nodded to me but didn't say hello, caught up in their discussion. Earnest and serious, they looked almost like married adults, like people who planned to stay together their whole lives long.

Coyote Autumn

JOURDAN IMANI KEITH

In autumn, Yellowstone blinks her eyes and the scene changes. The waves of heat and summer tourists that tortured the pock-marked face of road across the brows and cheeks of this side of the earth thin out. Yellowstone throws her head back and laughs, shakes the strands of rivers, boiling and cooled until the mist strolls in like a sighing man or woman. It is time to mate, and the cry of bugling elk charges the cool, navy-blue night air with its demands.

This is where I was reborn, a Philly girl, traveling across the continent on a Greyhound bus, carrying concrete and my father's bones in my memory and in the slowing stride of my hip. This is the place where my baby bones, still soft, were cast into the river. I was a Philly girl floating in the grief of my father's passing and the malignant demise of a three-year relationship. I was a new Moses waiting to be lifted into the arms of night falling behind the Gallatin Mountain Range of Montana and the endless eyes of the Wyoming stars as I ran my fingers along new thighs. The warble of air and water passing over rock wove a river's tale around me; the long red fingers of earth rising in spires cradled me and placed my tongue in a basket of brightly colored purple lupine and the red of Indian paintbrush.

Florida seems an unlikely place to remember the story of my time in Wyoming. The sunset and swelling of the water, visible from my hotel window, seems an unlikely scene to remind me of the rugged blackness of a one-ton bison's shoulders or the canvas of wheat-colored grass that rose and curved like a woman laying on her side, my woman, at the time. Linda, her name, means "beautiful" in Spanish. These are the visions that reach around me, stalking the peace of other sceneries with coyote footsteps and the howl of missing her landscape.

In the summer of 1993, I arrived in the gravel parking lot of my seasonal employer, one of the two concessionaires who harvested the benefit of private amenities on public land through its outcroppings of three-star restaurants, hotels, and gift shops. Outside of the pristine beauty of Yellowstone, the nation's first national park, new employees were arriving from all parts of the country to be given name badges and polyester uniforms. I disembarked from the white school bus that had carried us from our pickup point in Livingston, Montana, through the spectacular scenery of jagged mountain peaks and the wild dancing of the Gallatin River along its right side.

I stood in the warmth of early July, at the employee entrance in the Old West town of Gardiner, Montana, looking at the stone arch that marked the territorial line of my future. My intention was to be an employee for just one season, to see the majesty of mountains whose photo had been tacked to the wall, like an unfamiliar prescription, posted in the dinge of the Philadelphia unemployment office. Healing had seemed only footsteps away. I filled out the simple application form, crossed out the box for "Black" and wrote in "African American." I checked the box for restaurant help, the generic term that signaled to the personnel office that I was willing to do dishes, do anything—except clean rooms—to work there.

I cannot remember meeting Linda. She was like a wind that penetrated my exterior. The man who loved her called her Little Whirlwind—Hu-tu! Dea Kaa-ta!—because she danced with all her heart, spinning in circles at the powwow. Little Whirlwind. I called her her name in Spanish, Linda, beautiful. Linda, Andrea, coyotes, the Gardiner River, Montana, the Boiling River, the Grand Tetons, alligators, Florida, car crashes—all shout like ghosts from Christmas past with their particular tales that sealed our future.

Still, I cannot remember meeting Linda. Perhaps it was during one of her wait shifts; I would have been in the kitchen, in the back of the house, at Roosevelt Lodge, where I was a dish dog, the name we affectionately called all the dishwashers. Perhaps I met her for the first time on the path to the shower house where employees and guests without indoor plumbing crossed paths in towels and uniforms. Perhaps Andrea had introduced us on the porch of the lodge while I sat in one of the carved rocking chairs or outside our cabin that was perched by the creek. It had all begun with Andrea, who had spoken Linda's name into the umbilical cord of the phone line that stretched from the outdoor telephone among the evergreens to my voice waiting to accept another collect call on the carpet of my Philadelphia apartment. Andrea, with her wooly curls, green eyes, and light skin, who had climbed out of the birth canal of Philadelphia to arrive in Yellowstone six weeks before me. We had become twins from different mothers, born in the mourning of failed relationships, the call of wild places, and organizing Philadelphia's memorial for Audre Lorde. Andrea's collect calls were breath and water, traveling through the tangled curl of my blue telephone cord to nourish me with tales of sawdust floors and barn dances, used cowboy boots and roaming bison, and Linda, a new sister friend.

What I do remember is the wooden beams of Roosevelt Lodge, the only rustic location in the park, which meant the small employee cabins did not have running water, toilets, or heat, except for what was generated by the wood-burning stove we stoked at night with logs made from pressed particles of wood. What I do remember is the night Linda and I climbed the curve of Sagebrush Hill on the side of the employee cabins and sat in the pitch dark and cold with the other employees, so that we could look at the untold number of stars and talk. We sat a few steps away from the others and whispered in low voices, shivering from the cold air of the night and the excitement. I moved closer to her. Chill was the perfect reason to put my thigh next to hers on the makeshift wooden bench. Suddenly, in spite of my adulthood and my work as poet, I found myself saying, "I like you."

She responded simply and warmly, "I like you, too."

Her words came too easily to carry the weight of my intentions, so I said, to my horror, "No, I like you, like you." What could be clearer or more embarrassing than that for anyone over the age of twelve?

She replied, "Oh, well, I don't like you, like you."

Linda was a small woman, petite and strong, with thin, light brown hair, a small pockmark near the curve of her brow and hairline. She wore pink whenever she wanted to and drove a huge old pickup truck. They didn't have girls like her in Philly.

I imagined picking her up in one arm, something I was fond of doing, but had been unable to do with my last lover. In my fantasies, Linda was a real Montana woman, with strong, lean muscles that pushed against the seams of her dungarees, which she wore with an "I can do it myself" attitude that often perturbed other people. The firmness of her voice left no room for maneuvering, but I had sensed her watching me or imagined her looking at me through her soft hazel eyes. I sat shivering among the sage plants on the hill, holding her rejection for a moment. I was more determined than before to make her "like me, like me."

The challenge was on. Before coming to Yellowstone, I had been riding my hybrid mountain bike for months and had slimmed down enough to know that my white overalls with only a sports bra would be the perfect outfit for our adventure the next week. She was an outdoor woman, and I needed to show her my stuff. We were going on a mountain-bike ride in the hills of Cooke City, the small town with a winter population of a hundred or so, just outside the boundaries of the park. There was one bar, one bike shop, one nice, café-style restaurant, one greasy spoon, one gas station, and only one road out, which lead to the winding elevations and drop-off edges of the Beartooth Highway at the "top of the world." The drive into town from Yellowstone through the La Mar Valley was peppered with buffalo, which is what many people called the bison, and it was filled with coyotes, which were invisible during the day. Soon wolves would be reintroduced to the valley, and pointing tourists hovering near the open doors of their vehicles would clutter the undisturbed scenery. But for now, the road to the park exit was only decorated by boulder fields and moose sightings by the river. Everything about it was majestic, especially to be in the truck, alone with her.

Fortuitously, the delivery truck had crushed the bicycle I had shipped from Philadelphia, and so it was only a vehicle for bringing us on our first date. The guys at the bike shop pronounced it "unsafe" to ride, since to fix it the frame would have to be unbent, which would weaken the metal. We abandoned the biking adventure for an outdoor lunch on the wooden deck of the Beartooth Café and a walk through the hills that caressed the town and made it impassable in the winter snow. During lunch, I steered our conversation toward the man who I had been fooling around with, making sure to mention that he knew I didn't "like him, like him" because I was a lesbian. I paused to smile, to let her know I wasn't taking myself too seriously. I casually looked at the afternoon thunderheads that threatened our outdoor excursion and then deliberately looked away and added, "Well, I like you, but you don't like me."

"Yes, actually I do like you," she jumped in without bubbling over.

I smiled, knowing the seduction had begun; my snug white overalls and bare arms had done the trick.

Through that first summer that moved toward the autumn air, which came suddenly and permanently to the landscape, I learned to love Linda. We opened our mouths to kissing and to howling by the rivers, to counting disappointments and dreams with the innumerable white clusters of stars. Her topography was as different to me as the Philadelphia streets were to the aspen-crested hills that had been scorched by the great fires of Yellowstone, but we found ourselves in the dark, answering the coyotes' song with our own voices.

Wind

TZIVIA GOVER

I woke to the sound of wind. Wind groaning. Wind whooping. Wind pushing riderless bicycles down narrow streets, twirling Styrofoam coolers and tossing flower pots from yard to yard. It was because of the wind that I woke that morning on a futon in the spare room of Chisao and Kan-chan's apartment. It was the wind's fault that I was stranded, although not unhappily, thirteen miles across the sea from my sister, the only native English speaker I knew there.

The spare room, outfitted with a low black table and rice-paper screens, was the only traditionally Japanese room in the apartment. The other rooms were defiantly modern. A blue oriental rug covered the polished living room floor. A three-foot-square television set, laser-disk player, karaoke machine, and CD player were arranged on shelves against one wall. A massive black armoire displayed a solitary red vase. But most striking was the view of the Inland Sea through the enormous windows that spanned the far wall. Because typhoons dance across the sea with reliable frequency, this architectural choice elicited comment and tongue-clucking from visitors who'd sit on the plush, charcoal couch facing the view. But what did anyone expect? Kan-chan and Chisao had set their entire lives facing into the wind.

My sister, Joanne, had met the two on her first trip to Japan. On that visit, Joanne had come to marry Saku, Chisao's cousin. "I think Saku's cousin may be a lesbian," she had written to me on a sheet of weightless air-mail paper. But given Joanne's rudimentary Japanese, and the fact that her husband and his family spoke even less English, she was left to guess.

My brother-in-law Saku was one of the few members of his extended family to move away from the fishing island on which they'd been raised. He made it all the way to America. Chisao had traveled a different kind of distance, moving to a nearby town to open a restaurant that served international foods and run it with her live-in partner.

When I first arrived at the Osaka Airport with my sister and brother-in-law, I was struck by the orderly aesthetics of the Japanese women I encountered. Their perfect black hair slid silently across slender backs, hypnotic as sea-waves at night. Their clothes were prim and pleated; round-brimmed hats sat obediently on their heads. They weren't trailing two steps behind their husbands, but I could see how they might. "Country people," Saku explained. This wasn't Tokyo; that was for sure. And in the next twenty-four hours, as we traveled farther and farther south to the seaside village where we would meet Chisao and Kan-chan before taking the ferry to the island village of Saku's birth, the sense of being on the outskirts only intensified.

We reached their restaurant at lunchtime the following day. Chisao emerged from the stainless steel kitchen, a cigarette pressed between her lips, her palazzo pants making a businesslike swish as she crossed the room to meet us. Her short hair accentuated the sharp angles of her pale face. As she greeted us, Kan-chan rushed past, wiping her hands on a clean towel as her long skirt tangled around her ankles. Her lipsticked smile burst across her face as she said, "*Hagemai mashtai gozaimsu.*" I said it was nice to meet her, too.

When they left my sister and me alone at a table with a plate of french fries and waffles between us, I nodded toward the kitchen and whispered, "Of course they are," answering the question that had hung between continents for two years. I could easily picture these two women strolling arm in arm through the East Village.

The restaurant, constructed of oversized glazed cement brick, had a pleasantly muted feeling. The sound of pop music in German,

French, and English infused the dining room with an air of unspecified foreignness in a region so homogeneous many of the children had never seen a Caucasian before my sister's first visit. The eclectic menu introduced chicken entrées, pasta, and pastry to diners in a small town where varieties of raw or cooked fish with tofu or rice were served for breakfast, lunch, and dinner. I looked around at the young, hip Japanese people gathered around the crescent-shaped counter, eating with forks, not chopsticks, and reading newspapers.

I left the restaurant with my sister and brother-in-law to catch the ferry to Hotojima, where I would meet the rest of Saku's family. For days I would eat eel, squid, and salmon in various forms and watch women bundle seaweed into bales or crawl through the sea's shallows searching for abalone. At night, from the shore, we could see the far-off lights of fishing boats on which the village's men made their livings.

We returned to the restaurant several days later, on our way back from a visit to the sulfur baths in Beppu. My sister and I told Saku what I'd determined about his cousin and told him he should tell her that I was with a woman, too. Again, my sister and I were left alone at a table, this time eating plates of spaghetti, while Saku conferred with Chisao and Kan-chan in the kitchen. After his conversation he reported back that they had invited me to stay the night as their guest. They'd take me to the ferry in the morning, they assured my sister.

Left alone with Chisao and Kan-chan, it became instantly obvious that for all we had in common, we lacked a language with which to discuss it. It also became clear that my stay would be extended. The television weather reports showed a massive green circle moving over the digital map of Kyushu, heading toward our peninsula, shaped like a finger pointing the way out to sea.

I sat at the lunch counter in the restaurant most of the day, reading a novel and waiting until three, when my hostesses would have their break. We climbed the stairs to the apartment and Kan-chan handed me a glass of soda. I noticed a gold band on her finger. It had a flat blue stone embedded in the front, just like the one Chisao wore. "They're beautiful," I said, pointing from one to the other.

Chisao twisted the ring with her thumb, as if to cover the tell-tale stone. Kan-chan's hands flew behind her back, as she lowered her head and said, "Thank you." I have often met lesbians who've had to hide the true makeup of their lives for decades, and who never completely let down their defenses. But I was now confronting what seemed to be an intractable closet door. That night we went to a karaoke bar, where I found myself singing "California Dreaming" to a room full of strangers. I thought the subject of their relationship would never again be broached.

The next day the rain swept in. "Typhoo, typhoo," Kan-chan said, pointing across the sea. The typhoon was approaching. The sea was empty of boats, and there would be no ferries that day. Kan-chan and Chisao closed the restaurant early, and we retreated upstairs, where the window glass was already shivering in its casings. Kan-chan cast a worried glance at the windows, or the sea beyond, I couldn't tell which. She twisted her hands and spoke in a rapid-fire staccato to Chisao, who leaned against the kitchen counter and took a slow drag on her cigarette.

We settled in around the coffee table with cans of soda. Despite the western couches and chairs, we sat on the floor, Japanese-style. Chisao said something to Kan-chan, who ducked into the bedroom and emerged with a pile of books and a pad of paper. She had taken an English class, and now she lowered an armload of Japanese-English dictionaries and phrase books onto the table. One was an English textbook geared to high school students. I thumbed through and found a chapter about Madonna and another about women's liberation. I pulled out my pocket dictionary, and we began our conversation, slowly eking out phrases.

"Why aren't you married?" Kan-chan asked.

A bold opening sally, I thought. My answer, pared back to the fewest number of syllables possible, was no match. "Because I don't want to." I flipped through the pages of my dictionary: "Why aren't you?" I asked.

For a moment I doubted myself. Maybe they really were just business partners and I'd jumped to conclusions. I realized then that

I hadn't seen them go to bed together. They had stayed up in the living room until after I went to sleep the night before, and both were awake and dressed by the time I was up in the morning. Maybe what I thought was the spare room was really Kan-chan's room, and the bedroom was for Chisao. I'll just ask them, I decided. But my slim dictionary did not include the word "lesbian." Anyway, remembering their reaction to my comment about their rings, I feared translating the term directly might be disastrous.

Meanwhile, Kan-chan had amassed enough vocabulary for her next statement. She said that Japanese men are difficult to get along with, but unmarried women are considered strange. Chisao added something in Japanese, and Kan-chan nodded and looked up a series of words. They knew only two other women who lived together, she told me. "It is hard to be different in Japan," she said. "Japanese women [she pronounced the word "oo-man"] are very . . ." she paged through her dictionary, then held her thumb under a word and puzzled over the pronunciation. She handed the book to me.

"Restricted," I read aloud.

Kan-chan nodded. "Restricted," she repeated. "Very restricted." She repeated the phrase in Japanese, and Chisao let out a tired laugh, then moved to the kitchen to smoke another cigarette. Above her, rain crashed down over the skylight.

I had an urge to pack their suitcases for them and rush them through the storm to the airport. I would bring them to Northampton, Massachusetts, where I lived, and where lesbians can go out for a romantic dinner and hold hands across the table; where two women can go to the jewelers and purchase matching rings without attracting attention. Even the straight merchants hang rainbow-colored flags on Pride Day, I wanted to tell them. The very fact that we had an annual Pride march and celebration would surely awe them. The language barrier, which had just been frustrating until now, was becoming infuriating. It was as if it had been constructed intentionally to keep these two women locked in isolation.

We needed a translator, I thought. We could call Uni, the young woman we had met at the karaoke bar, and who had told me in flawless English that she was married to an American pilot and had lived in New Jersey for ten years. But of course that would be impossible. We couldn't discuss this in the presence of anyone else. I doubted they'd feel free to speak even in front of my sister or brother-in-law. In this part of Japan, I had noticed, not even straight couples touch in public. Private lives were very private here.

I reached for the pad of paper and drew a picture of a house. Inside it I made two stick figures wearing triangular dresses. I pointed to myself and then to one of the cartoon women: "Me," I said. Then, pointing to the other, "My girlfriend, Chris." Then I covered the page with more little houses, and for every five or six, I put two women under one pointed roof. "My city," I said. "Many women live together." Kan-chan waved Chisao closer. They hovered above my picture, nodding and smiling.

For the rest of the night we exchanged questions. Was my lover thin or fat? Short or tall? Did we ever argue? What kind of work do the other women we know do? Kan-chan told me that she and Chisao had been together for fifteen years. They fought sometimes, she said. It wasn't always easy.

At three in the morning we were still filling pages of paper with drawings and words, trying to understand each other. "You go to bed now," Kan-chan finally ordered. Again, she and Chisao stayed in the kitchen, making long work of washing the glasses and ashtray and wiping down the counters and table. They stayed up chatting and tidying until after I had fallen asleep.

Kan-chan had been to Tokyo once, Chisao, never. They didn't have a computer or a modem, nor had I seen one in any of the other homes I visited in Tsukumi or Hotojima. There was television, of course, but I doubted there'd be anything broadcast that could help them out of their isolation. I began making a mental list of the books and CDs I could send them from the gay gift shops back home — then remembered how their relatives wandered in and out of their apartment unannounced and made themselves at home. What, I wondered, would be appropriate to introduce into their tightly regulated lives?

In the morning there was no time to continue our conversation. Wind slapped rain against the windows. The sea and sky had darkened into matching shades of gray. Kan-chan and Chisao hustled me out of the apartment as soon as I opened my eyes. "Come," they urged. Dressed and alert, they'd been too polite to wake me, even if that meant standing by as the typhoon crashed through the living room while I slept.

I followed them downstairs and through the deserted restaurant. Chisao went to the door and scouted the scene. Debris flew past as Kan-chan chattered excitedly in Japanese. For a second the wind quieted, and Kan-chan called out orders. We ran straight across the street to a cement building whose windows and doors were shuttered. As soon as Chisao knocked, the metal door slid open and shut again as soon as we were inside. Two small children were seated on the floor with their father in the living room. Their mother offered us tea, and we settled in.

The seven-year-old girl was excited to have a "geijin," or foreigner, in the house. She pulled English flashcards from her school bag and engaged me as her tutor for the duration of the storm. I practiced the Japanese words as she practiced the English. We repeated "*ohio*," "good morning"; "*arigato*," "thank you"; and "*inu*," "dog." My favorite word was "*hadoraku*," which meant "naughty child." Each time I said it, the girls giggled and jumped around.

As lunchtime approached the winds dulled. We returned to the apartment, which had endured without damage. Kan-chan shot a satisfied look toward the windows, which once again had weathered the typhoon. Within minutes of our return, one of Chisao's sisters arrived with her children. She was talking excitedly and pointing her raised chin toward the clouds hovering outside. I couldn't understand the words she was saying, but it was clear that she was reprimanding Chisao for insisting on that vast span of glass overlooking the sea. But for all of her berating, the fact was that the glass was intact. And after all these years, it was clear that Kan-chan and Chisao weren't about to change a thing.

Postcard

A Story

RUTHANN ROBSON

"You'll forget," Kiva accused.

As soon as I replied that I wouldn't, I was trapped.

Sure, it seemed as if I'd merely promised to send her a postcard. Millions of people take vacations only to spend their precious time purchasing rectangles emblazoned with a scenic panorama on one side and writing some version of "having-a-great-time-wish-you-were-here" on the other. And I'd have more time than most to accomplish my task. But I vowed to do it first thing.

One of the Caribbean's best beaches, surrounded by shimmering aqua seas.	
Dear Kiva:	Kiva Joseph
	612 Bellis Place
It really is this beautiful here with	Brooklyn,
colors that are amazingly beautiful.	New York 11235
~~Haven't been to the beach yet~~	U.S.A.

Even as I was writing out the postcard, sitting on the porch of our temporary apartment, I knew I couldn't send Kiva such typical tourist sentiments. Ah, the colors! How turquoise! How aqua! How the shades of water, vacillating between blue and green, stun the eyes. I had to say something more than it was as beautiful here as the postcard, lest I descend into the most torturous circle of hell, certainly designated for the sins of tourism, as Dante would have noted, if only he'd been as smart as Kiva.

I'd never confess to Kiva that I aspire to the status of tourist. To be a tourist means to possess privilege and wealth, and what's wrong with that? Kiva would instruct me that what's wrong with it is that most of the world's people don't have such opportunities. In fact, they leave the most beautiful lands and become immigrants to the ugliness from which I seek a "vacation." It's the postmodern version of Milton's *Paradise Lost,* according to Kiva.

Never mind that strictly speaking, I am not a tourist. No tourist would be staying in this apartment, although it's technically part of a "guesthouse" and does have a flush toilet and a porch. No tourist would be here for six entire weeks on a paying grant. Well, OK, the grant is Deirdre's, but I wouldn't be here without it. And no tourist would be driving a borrowed beat-up jeep on this less-populated side of the island, avoiding the donkeys and the goats and the chickens and the dogs that didn't seem to recognize the curving and steep road as dangerous. It wasn't more than two miles to the Calabash Boom School, where Deirdre was doing trainings about kids who'd been exposed to domestic violence, but it could take me almost an hour to get there. Usually I left so early that I had to wait for Deirdre, but last week I drove into an unusually heavy and sudden rain as I entered the Calabash Boom valley, only to find Deirdre huddled under the tamarind trees waiting for me.

"It's raining," Deirdre laughed as she struggled to open the rusted passenger side door of our borrowed jeep.

"Sorry," I'd apologized.

"So, it's your fault it's raining? Oh, goddess of rain!" Deirdre laughed. "The cisterns of the island worship you."

"No, my fault that I'm late and you had to wait in the rain."

"Oh, goddess that doesn't believe in the concept of island time! Oh, goddess that knew that my last appointment wouldn't show. Oh, goddess, does this mean that there's now a roof for the jeep?"

"No, the goddess has provided hats," I laughed, giving her a baseball cap that advertised Shipwreck Landing and navigating the jeep back onto Salt Pond Road, where I'd hoped there would be less rain, eventually, and we could go to Francis Bay beach this afternoon and look for turtles, swimming along the bottom of the bay, lazily eating seagrass, and peering at me with a disinterested caution as I drifted above them.

On my postcard to Kiva, I'd also lied about the beach, another sin I'd committed since coming to paradise. I had my feet in the water the very evening we arrived. It seemed nothing short of miraculous that we'd woken up in a snowy New York, and, after a typically harrowing taxi ride to the airport, long lines through security, a plane filled with screaming children, a taxi ride on the side of the road that would have been wrong that morning, a ferry ride past other islands, and a ride from the ferry terminal to our temporary apartment, we were sitting at a restaurant called Shipwreck Landing with the principal of Calabash Boom School and his family, including his mother (who owned the guesthouse) and his brother (who owned the jeep and was going off-island tomorrow) and his sister (who worked as a cook at the restaurant). Everyone laughed when I crossed the road to get to the water and take off my sandals (sandals!), but their laughter seemed to me generous and welcoming. Or at least not judgmental.

As Kiva's would have been.

No, I didn't wish Kiva were here at all.

Dear Kiva:

*These bright little birds are nosier than
you'd think, not just the thrumming of
their wings, but the sounds as they fight
over the flowers and the sugar in the*

*Kiva Joseph
612 Bellis Place
Brooklyn,
New York 11235*

U. S. A.

On our porch is a hummingbird feeder that we fill with one part sugar to four parts water, just like the principal's mother told me to do. We can sit in the broken cane chairs by the feeder and sooner or later the birds will dip their long beaks into the feeder's drilled holes. *Pit-chew, pit-chew, pit-chew,* their ricochet cries are combative. Who would have known that such tiny, lovely creatures were so aggressive? I'm close enough to be frightened once or twice as they whiz by, their beaks like swords. I can see not only the fluorescent green of their breasts but also a shimmering stripe of peacock blue.

And some of them do have little crests, like crowns, on their heads. I'd picked this postcard from the rack at the Starfish Market thinking it suitable for Kiva. Not that she liked birds, but she was her mother's daughter.

In the three years we'd lived together, Kiva somehow managed to be "indisposed" when her mother called every Sunday morning at precisely ten o'clock, so that I answered the phone to hear, "May I speak to my daughter, please." The please was perfunctory; her tone was commanding rather than questioning. When I complained about this to Kiva, she'd only said, "You can't expect less than imperiousness from a woman who named her only daughter after a queen."

Queen Kiva? It would always take me a moment to recall that Kiva's given name was Catherine, although it appeared on our lease and on her student loan repayment bills. Besides, weren't thousands of regular women named Catherine? Who thought of Catherine the

Great anymore? Although perhaps this island had once been her colony; it seemed to have belonged to every other imperial power at one time or another. Just as the hummingbirds do, the Europeans had a craving for sweetness that could only be satisfied by sugar.

I'd gotten my fill of this rotten history at the ruins of the sugar mill and plantation. It wasn't the altitude that made me dizzy, it was the brochure full of the details of slavery, molasses, rum, and revolts. The principal, a direct descendant of those who'd survived the unsurvivable, suggested it was worth seeing even as he intimated that many didn't approve its historical preservation. He looked at me rather than Deirdre then, assessing my background, I knew. For a moment, I thought I could hear the word "mulatto" or even "quadroon" ricochet around in his mouth. For unlike most of the "blacks" on island, I was a typical "black" of the Northeast Corridor of the United States: more brown than black and probably more European than African. Here, most people looked at me as if I were merely tan with unfortunate hair—although a few tourists at the ruins did seem inordinately uncomfortable in my presence.

Deirdre was blonde and blue-eyed and now so cooked-lobster-red that the volunteer guide at the ruins made it a point to tell her to stay out of the sun. Kiva had once screamed at me that Deirdre was "just another white girl." At the time I hadn't the quickness to respond that Kiva met the same standard.

It wasn't that I'd left Kiva for Deirdre, although I could understand how it might have seemed that way to Kiva at the time. I'd met Deirdre right after I moved out, letting Kiva keep the rent-stabilized Brooklyn apartment, the toaster, and anything else she said rightly belonged to her. I'd spent a long weekend in my new, empty apartment, cursing the fact that I was the type of person who'd have the phone connected before I moved in, because Kiva called every five minutes, even after I stopped answering and then, I'm sure, even after I'd unplugged the phone. I'd abandoned her, betrayed her, ineluctably destroyed her faith in lesbians and all of humanity. My new neighbors got to hear what a terrible person I was, because by Sunday night, Kiva had traced me to my new apartment (I thought I was so reasonable in providing her with my new phone number but not my address, but I guess I shouldn't have unplugged the phone). I finally answered the door when the cops arrived; I didn't want her arrested.

Two things happened that Monday, when to my relief I was back at work at PS 103 in the office. First, I met Deirdre. She was dripping scarves and beads but still managed to look tough and competent. She stood at the desk until I acknowledged her, and she then said "hi" in the sexiest voice I'd ever heard, though I'm sure it was just a normal "hi." She had an appointment with the principal and would be at the school for a few weeks on a specific project about kids who'd been witnesses in criminal trials involving their parents. It wasn't as rare an occurrence at the school as it had once been; we secretaries didn't even gossip about it anymore.

"Then I guess we'll have a chance to go to lunch," I said, before I could be shocked by my assertiveness, maybe even aggressiveness.

"Tomorrow would be great," she smiled.

The second thing that happened was that Kiva called me at work to tell me she'd just been diagnosed with brain cancer.

Snorkeling the colorful reefs is one of the countless pleasures of the Caribbean.	
Dear Kiva—Remember that aquarium at the Thai restaurant on Flatbush? ~~Snorkling~~ Snorkeling ~~is like being inside it~~	Kiva Joseph 612 Bellis Place Brooklyn, New York 11235 U.S.A.

Of course, I tear up this postcard also. I mean, I shouldn't remind her of the days when we were together and she was well enough to go to restaurants. At least on a regular basis, anyway, since Deirdre and I did see her at another Thai place, the night Deirdre and I went out to celebrate the news that she'd gotten the grant to come here and we began to seriously plot how I could join her.

"Kiva looks amazingly well," Deirdre had said, the pad thai noodles languishing on her fork.

I think I'd agreed, although I was calculating the vacation days I had from the school board. I'd meant to note whether or not Kiva was wearing one of the hats I had gotten her; she'd need to cover her head if she were losing her hair from the treatments.

"The woman she's with looks together. And she's black. Maybe that means Kiva will get over her infatuation with you."

I don't remember what I'd replied. I was probably thinking about how much I could fit into my blue suitcase.

But now that I'm here, I mean, really, how can I write someone about how much I love snorkeling, knowing she will never be able to do it?

I'm surprised by how easy it is. Some breathing and some swimming; some confidence and some looking—looking until one could really see. I splurge on a professional-level reef-identification manual, and while I'm not so nerdy as to be filling out the "Personal Record of Fish Sightings" chart that occupies the final twenty or so pages, Deirdre and I both consult the book regularly before and after our expeditions, weaving our sightings into our discussions.

"Do you think that was a spotted burrfish or a porcupine fish?"

"Well, it's hard to tell, since I couldn't see whether or not it was inflated. The book says they look the same when the porcupine fish is threatened."

"It was so cute. It looked like a miniature manatee."

"We're lucky to have seen it. It was silty near those rocks, and the book says they're shy."

Maybe that's why I like this fish. Sure, I love the blue tang, with their shifting hues, from baby blue to the deepest purple, often looking like luminous Frisbees that some goddess had tossed into the sea for amusement. I liked to float on top of them, and then dive down into their midst, swimming along and pretending that I was just another blue tang, even if I was about a million times their size and wearing a red bathing suit. A fantasy of belonging. Even if I were a fish, I probably wouldn't be a beautiful blue tang, because they traveled in large schools, shifting this way and that almost as if they possessed one mind.

No, I was more likely to be some shy fish. A yellowbelly or yellowtail or indigo hamlet. Or a big-lipped strawberry grouper hiding under the rocks. Or a scrawled cowfish, with sharp spines protruding over each eye, looking more like an aqua-and-yellow billy goat than a cow, I thought. Or a porcupine fish, which inflated and stuck out sharp sticks whenever others threatened to get too close.

That's what Kiva always said about me, only in more therapeutic terms that included phrases such as "incapable of intimacy." She diagnosed my failures as being attributable to my mother's death when I was thirteen, when my mother finally succumbed—the word they always used—after mostly being bald and in bed since I was nine.

But maybe it's Kiva, and not me, who is "incapable of intimacy." I was hopeful every time she told me she'd "met someone." Hopeful that the dramatic interruptions of my life would stop, that Kiva would find someone to support her in her medical travails that seemed to ebb and flow. But the "someone" always seemed to give Kiva even more reasons to call me, usually at first to sing "someone's" praises, inclusive of sexual suggestions, and later to complain about "someone's" lack of emotional depth.

I understood my role as simply listening. If I flattered Kiva on the features of her newest lover, I was treated to comparisons in which I was insulted. If I commiserated with Kiva about her soon-to-be-ex-lover's shallowness, I was dismissed with references to the "perfect Deirdre."

I never mentioned Deirdre to Kiva unless I absolutely had to, but Kiva had realized she was perfect nonetheless. Not really perfect, of course. We've been together too many years for either of us to still believe the other is perfect. Deirdre is both superstitious and sentimental. She screams at the radio during presidential addresses, although she insists on listening to them. She brings her work home too often, including the occasional flesh-and-blood child who has slept on our couch for a few nights. She drives too fast and is a lousy cook.

But Deirdre is trustworthy. If she says it's raining, it is—she's not saying it because she wants me to look out the window for some other reason, to worry about whether or not she'll get wet, or to postpone a walk with a friend. It's just raining. She might be laughing about it. Or she might be pissed about it, but I never think it's somehow my fault.

It's somehow my fault when Kiva's newest "someone" disappears. Once in a while, "someone" will be quickly replaced by "someone new," but usually there is an intervening period of despondency and anger, filled with late-night messages suggesting that a hospitalization is imminent. It was during one of these rants that Kiva told me she regretted being a lesbian: "I'm sick of lesbians. All of them have issues with their former lovers. Or their mothers. Or both!"

I have to admit I laughed, even though I felt a tidal wave of recognition.

After all these years, why do I still talk to Kiva?

My mother would not have liked Kiva, I've no doubts. She would like Deirdre, definitely. And she would have liked snorkeling, I think. Though I don't know why I think that. But certainly she would have liked the fact that I liked it. She would have taken pleasure in my happiness, I'm sure. I would send her one of the foureye butterflyfish magnets, bright yellow, that they sell in the gift shop next to Shipwreck Island. Perfect for her refrigerator. I would send her a million postcards.

The Queen Conch or Pink Conch (Strombus gigas) is found in warm shallow waters in grassbeds of the Caribbean Sea. Its meat is used for traditional fritters and its shell for jewelry and conch trumpets.	
Dear Kiva: *I've found the most lovely shell! Well, maybe "find" isn't exactly the right word, since it involved a long hike over*	*Kiva Joseph* *612 Bellis Place* *Brooklyn,* *New York 11235* *U.S.A.*

Deirdre and I agree we can't kill a conch, though I covet their shells in the shallow bay where they congregated inside them, slimy and living and breathing. The shells are dully colored among the silt and grass of the flat cove, but I know that with a little polishing I could render their insides as coral as a postcard, although that isn't worth murdering them. I have neither the stomach nor the politics for that, even though I have conch fritters with a lime 'n' coconut at Shipwreck Landing whenever I can. And I guess I could forgo the fritters and frozen drink a few times and buy a polished conch shell at the gift shop next to Shipwreck Landing, but the shell seems too encased in acrylic or some sort of lacquer to me, plus it's pretty expensive.

But then I hear (over lime and coconut drinks, in fact), that there's another bay fringed with mangroves, only a short hike over a few hills, frequented by the locals, who hunt for conch for their fritters. Since they wanted only the conch, they left the shells in mountains on the beach. I could spare my conscience and have my prize!

Deirdre is easy to convince, only insisting that we go in the morning before it gets too hot to hike, so we wait for a day she doesn't have appointments at Calabash Boom and set off on the Brown Bay Trail.

It is steep and rocky, but wide in most places, and I'm not worried about getting lost, just losing my breath and embarrassing myself. A few other hikers pass us, sturdy white couples who looked to me as if they'd made a wrong turn out of the Alps. They're not yodeling, but they are talking in sing-song voices and wearing those thick heather-colored socks and lace-up boots. At one point, I'm ready to be mortified when a woman on crutches passes me, until I figure out that her "crutches" were metal walking sticks. I don't think the principal or his family own such sticks or socks, so I try to act indigenous in my sport sandals and island-print skirt and darkening skin, scrambling up the path, back down, and twisting until we left the prickly ketch 'n' keep bushes behind and landed on a beach.

Sure enough, there were conch shells in the brush. Not the "mountain" that had been boasted, but enough so that I had some choices to make. They all had a split between the second and third whorls from the tip, probably made by the claw of a hammer so that a knife could be inserted to cut the conch's muscle from the shell for easier removal. Or at least that's the way I'd heard gathering conch described. It sounded gruesome, even without the detail of the mollusk's two tentacle eyes peering out from the lip of the shell, before the creature was knifed and yanked from life.

But I am only scavenging for corpses. I choose one that is large, but not the largest, and in pretty good condition. I have to resist the urge not to take two. I could bring one back for Kiva. Though the claw hammer split on the shell's head might be too much of a reminder of her own ordeals.

I'd avoided Kiva since I saw her in the Thai restaurant, but somehow she'd heard that I'd be away for a while, and she'd been leaving me messages that it was urgent that she see me before I left New York. When I said I'd drop by sometime in the next few days, I learned it wasn't so urgent that I shouldn't telephone first. Kiva needed to make herself presentable before I arrived.

"I hate dykes in lipstick," I joked.

But then she reminded me that she'd always worn lipstick, even when we'd been lovers, proving again that I'd never truly loved her, I suppose, and that my betrayals were as inevitable as they were incessant. I could never atone, no matter how much I tried.

Her "Coral Glow" lips trembled as she told me about her upcoming brain surgery, scheduled to occur while I was away. She hadn't wanted to tell me, she'd said, and ruin my trip, but given the possibility that she "might not be here" when I returned, she'd thought it only fair to let me know.

"What do the doctors think about your chances?"

"Fifty-fifty."

A broken queen conch shell or the perfect postcard could not improve Kiva's chances, but since Kiva told me the hospital wouldn't accept flowers or even visitors, it seemed a small effort to make on her behalf.

After all, I was Kiva's longest lasting relationship, even if she wasn't mine. Not even by half.

Local donkeys, originally brought by the Spanish, roam
wild and free, sometimes blocking the mountain roads.

Dear Kiva:

Although they don't wear hats! Just
something to make you laugh a little as
you recover. See you soon!

Kiva Joseph
612 Bellis Place
Brooklyn,
New York 11235

U. S. A.

The drawback to Honeymoon Beach is not the honeymooners or the moderate hike it takes to get there, but that it is easily approachable by water from the big resort-mottled island to the west. We've had about a half hour alone on the beach, except for an occasional donkey, when a yacht-sized boat moors itself just beyond the markings for the reef and starts discharging its passengers by dinghy. Some land on the beach holding their snorkel equipment above their heads, as if it weren't meant to get wet; most don't seem to have any masks or fins at all. I find myself watching one woman I couldn't ever imagine getting wet as she dispenses food, blankets, towels, lotions, books, and even a chair. Her presumptive husband and three adolescent children surround her, claiming the items they need and fanning out across the beach. Unfortunately, the one who sits closest to us is the husband, settling into the chair and lighting a pungent cigar.

They never get to see the stand of elkhorn coral, a bright yellow, surrounded by yellow grunts that floated within its stalks and above it, as if they belonged to it. They never get to see the thousands of brilliantly colored parrot fish biting with their fish teeth on the reef and then discharging it as white sand. And they never get to see the large pompano or something I saw, swimming parallel to me, with an eye so huge it startled me into shrieking "Deirdre" into my snorkel, causing Deirdre to laugh and fill her mouth with water. Although she did agree the fish was amazingly huge.

They never get wet.

Or even, really, sandy.

And then, they are leaving.

The man next to us takes the cigar but leaves the chair. It's blue and white striped, a folding camp-type chair, and it would look very stylish on our temporary porch. I can see myself folding the aluminum legs and carrying it back up the Lind Point Trail to where our borrowed jeep waits for us. But the woman I'd been watching earlier soon ends my coveting by coming for the chair, folding it expertly, and putting it in a matching blue-and-white-striped bag. She hoists it on her shoulder, with five—I am counting them—other large canvas bags.

She teeters onto the dinghy, as another woman commiserates, "Wow, you're loaded down like a donkey."

"Like an ass." I say this more loudly than I'd intended.

Deirdre tells me I am bitchy.

"I guess. But what's with these straight women?" I don't mention that she's taking "our" chair.

"It's not just heterosexuality," Deirdre laughs. "Some people just have a hard time being loved."

This isn't the first time Deirdre has said this to me. The first time was the night of the day we'd met, after a dinner at an Italian restaurant, sipping coffees. We were talking about our former lovers, obliquely, without mentioning names. I'd applied Deirdre's comment to Kiva—who was probably dialing my phone or knocking at my door that very moment—wondering if that was her problem, that she couldn't accept the fact that I had loved her. And so she challenged me until she'd ground my love down.

Yet Deirdre's comment also pertained to me. As soon as I met her, I was already panicked that Deirdre would soon see me as a shallow, disappointing, mediocre woman, scarred with cellulite and messy memories. To let one's self be loved was to risk being an object, not just an "object of affection," but a thing. As inconsequential and flat as a postcard.

Seven years later, I'm no longer terrified.

Except sometimes.

That she'll know that I'm the kind of woman who goes off with her lover to paradise while a friend is dying.

"Kiva is having a risky brain surgery," I confess.

Deirdre asks me how I feel about that. As if I can label my emotions. Happy. Sad. Guilty. Love. Any maps of my inner topography seem as much of a deception as the sepia maps of the explorers. Greenland wasn't green at all, the New World wasn't new, and even this island on which we're standing is no part of India.

And on the island itself, Brown Bay isn't brown and Chocolate Hole isn't chocolate or even chocolate-colored. Coral Bay isn't filled with coral and never had been. The lambs on Little Lameshur Beach are not little, or lame, or even lambs, but goats, butting their horned heads against each other on the sheer dirt road.

"Let's go in the water," I answer, eager to identify another scrawled cowfish, another blue tang, another cute porcupine fish.

Masked and finned, we float along for a few minutes, wary of encountering the huge pompano again. In the shallows, Deirdre keeps pointing at some flat rocks, telling me to look, but I don't see anything.

Finally, she takes the snorkel out her mouth and tells me what she's pointing at.

I still can't see it. I look and look and look and even de-fog my mask with spit and look again, Deirdre all the while pointing to blank rocks. Until finally a shift, ever so slight, and I see the peacock flounder, blended into its bed of rocks, but as obvious as the sun in the sky overhead.

I'd like to say I know right then. That I have an instantaneous epiphany. That the sky opens up in a revelatory downpour and a bolt of thunder strikes me. But it isn't until later—the resort boats all gone for the day, with the clouds hugging the horizon, a few white-caps reaching up to blur the boundaries between sea and sky, and a surfeit of storm clouds, obscuring the setting sun—that I realize.

We're walking back up the Lind Point Trail when I ask Deirdre why she never told me that Kiva had been lying all these years. That she didn't have brain cancer for the last seven years, that she hadn't been hospitalized and wasn't now, that she had been making a fool out of me, and that I was stupid, stupid, even more stupid than stupid.

"Some things you have to see yourself," Deirdre says simply.

Goddess, how can she love such an ass?

There are no "jumbies," the West Indian word for ghosts, on Jumbie Beach—just beautiful aquamarine water, white sand, and palm trees. *Dear Kiva:*	 *Kiva Joseph* *612 Bellis Place* *Brooklyn,* *New York 11235* 　　　　　　　*U.S.A.*

I rip up my last postcard to Kiva.

Hot Springs, Montana

LORI SODERLIND

On the western side of the Flathead Indian Reservation in Montana, just off the main road that leads up to Kalispell, Glacier Park, and other vacation destinations, I stopped in a small, nearly vacant town called Hot Springs, to visit a woman named Wolf Crone. She had suggested that we meet at the springs themselves, on the edge of town. You couldn't miss them; it was a small town, and if you were unsure what road to take, you could just follow the sulfur smell, like rotten eggs, and that would lead you to the water.

"How will I recognize you?" I asked her.

"Oh, don't worry," she said. "Come early. There won't be anyone else there."

I discovered Wolf Crone in a newsletter that circulated at women's music festivals and other events back then—this was in the early 1990s, before the Internet caught on, when all sorts of information got passed around on stapled pages. She was listed in a section with travel contacts in every state.

I have family in Montana, so I had been west before, exploring my family history, but something about encountering Wolf Crone in that newsletter made me think I could find more than just my roots out there. Wolf Crone, like certain other women I knew who had grown up as Marys or Frans or something equally conventional, had discovered her true self and found her true name, and by changing her name she was announcing her truth. It was the sort of thing

I would never do, but I understood the urge to do it. In my early twenties I traveled mostly to consider who else I might be, if I lived in other places. There were parts of myself I wanted to shed, too. I wondered if there might be a Wolf Crone—or someone else—in me.

No other place seemed so far away and strange as Montana. It is on the way to nowhere, it is full of nothing, a place to live with unvarnished truth because really, faking served no purpose. For one thing, who would notice? I set off to meet people who lived there, and through them to find the authentic place I dreamed about. But I was not quite confident enough to leave those encounters to fate; I planned them all, just like I planned to meet Wolf Crone.

We found each other at the springs, on the end of a dirt path where a boardwalk leads over the mud to the water. She was a small woman in enormous dark glasses, with gray hair like dry, dead grass and skin dark as leather, from years out in the sun. The hot springs bubbled up in the ground around us; railroad ties had been used to make a pool, so that the water was deep enough to submerse yourself. We took a dip, and while we stood in the water, she told me the difference between the various pools, how some spots are hotter than others, and how the corn holes were named for the corns on your feet, which you soak in them, but they're deep enough that you can put your whole body in and stand there in the mud.

"Always come to the springs in the mornings, before the heat of the day makes the water too hot to stand in," she said, "and before the crowd trickles in."

"Crowd?" I said. "Hot Springs is practically a ghost town." There was nobody there. On the main road, none of the shops were open, and the goods in their windows were old. The gift shop offered sweatshirts whose fish and black bear decals had faded in the sun. The motel nearest the springs was boarded up and falling to the ground. I had gotten a room the night before at the Syms Hotel for just $10. I was the only guest, and it felt as if no one had stayed there for years, as if the innkeeper lived there alone, waiting. How marvelous it seemed to me that this tourist spot on those tribal lands had failed. That meant the real Hot Springs was still there for me, unspoiled.

"People do come, though," she said. "The tourists come for the water. Because the water heals."

I never questioned that the mud in Hot Springs was magic. I would have said that people came to have their hearts mended, and their souls, that they came to soothe the aches that I felt, at twenty-five, all the uncertainty about who I was and what my life would be like. Unexpected disappointments had started welling up. To me, healing meant forgiving all that.

But that's not what she meant: she meant arthritis and asthma. She meant that mud can help the body heal. Maybe that is why most of the people in Hot Springs were old, over sixty, like Wolf Crone; they had come to stop the physical effects of aging, not the emotional ones.

She said it was a holy place, too. Sometimes, you could find offerings left at the pools, sticks tied together in shapes, small bags of herbs or incense, feathers tied to rocks or twigs. These things resemble the gifts American Indians once left at holy sites, but the Flathead probably aren't the ones who leave them now. The local Flathead are mostly Catholic. The sticks and feathers are left by visitors, mostly. Wolf Crone said you have to leave stuff in the trees as an offering, to thank God for the healing, to help your asthma and such.

I went with Wolf Crone back to her house, which was tiny and contained, among other things, a little spotted puppy. Curtains made her one room into two. She tried to keep her home dark, she said, and outside she wore heavy sunglasses, because she had a problem with her eyes. She believed that the water could help her arthritis, but only darkness seemed to soothe her eyes. She lit a candle, then lay down to rest on a sofa-bed, hugging the puppy like it was a child and telling me about all the dogs that had come before, and how they died.

The black one—she showed me his picture—had died years ago. "He was hit by a truck when he was two years old," she said. She rubbed the picture frame with her sleeve, then handed it to me. Another dog traveled with her here from California, then eventually died of old age. Her candle flickered in the dim room. A retired teacher, she had moved to Hot Springs from California after she read about the water, and also about the low cost of living for seniors there. "Retirees are moving here," she said. "It's picking up." It seemed hard to believe.

She said people were coming back to Hot Springs, that maybe some of those boarded-up buildings I'd seen would get well soon, as if their health could be restored. She said this like it would be a good thing.

"I sort of hate that though," I told her. "Montana is changing." Since I'd first come in 1989, lots of people had been moving to Montana—people from California, most of all. I wanted Montana to be a sacred place, to be left alone. It's hard to be sacred when you're subdivided. When I first visited, there had not been a McDonald's in Bozeman, but lately more people were grasping for an authentic piece of Montana, so many that they'd started cutting up the land into ten-acre lots and building houses faster than you could count. They seemed to be missing the point. Hot Springs felt to me like real Montana, still: remote and unbothered. It could be lonely to live in a place like that, but to me, being lonely was part of the magic, part of the cure. It all depended on what you thought needed healing.

"Ah," Wolf Crone said, "but everything changes." She smiled, and her cheeks made accordion folds out toward her ears. "People are fickle. People change their minds about what they want all the time." How many places in Montana could we name where people had settled a town, then decided to leave? Just look at all the ghost towns. People change their minds.

Wolf Crone took me to lunch at the Hot Springs Senior Center, where the folding lunchroom tables were lined up across the room, and suddenly it seemed the town really was booming. All the tables were full. We sat with her friends Joe and Helen, who were so happy to see a new face that Helen offered to give me her plate of meatloaf.

"I didn't touch it yet; I'll get another," she said, and she was half-way across the room before she listened to Wolf Crone and turned around to come back.

"She's a vegetarian," Wolf Crone cried. "Helen, come back. She won't eat it."

Wolf Crone wondered where her other friend was, a woman over ninety, so old that she hardly left home at all anymore, except to buy groceries or to have lunch at the center. She still raised cattle, of course. "Of course," I concurred, uncomprehending. Joe and Helen told me they also raised cattle. If you grew up on the land as they had, then that was just what you did.

Helen told me she was Shoshoni, not Flathead, a distinction I did not understand. She smiled painfully wide and leaned into me when she was talking in a way that made her look as if she were always on the verge of saying something funny. Her eyes lit up and she smiled, and I waited, but the funny something never came. She didn't say much except when I asked questions. Her earrings were small and gold. She carried a white vinyl handbag full of papers and lipsticks and things.

"So you aren't a Flathead?"

"No."

"But you live on the Flathead Reservation?"

"Sure. Sure I do."

It seemed funny to me that Wolf Crone was a white woman from California but Helen, who had grown up on a reservation, was just Helen. I didn't say anything, but it seemed like they had sort of traded places.

Helen said that her father came to Montana from Canada, and because her father was Shoshoni, he could not get food or money or any kind of assistance on the Flathead reservation. "No, if you were Shoshoni, the Flathead wouldn't help you out."

"Then why would he come here?"

"Free land. The Indians wouldn't help us, but the government did," she said. "They gave away free land." Helen's family got land as homesteaders, just as my grandparents had.

I found this confusing, too. I had thought that it was all pretty simple, that the government had given land to white settlers and put Indians on reservations. On the Flathead Reservation, Indian families were the homesteaders, and tribes turned their backs on each other.

"Oh, the Flathead," she said. "There are not really any Flathead. No." She shook her head. Flathead is a name that lumps together Kootenai and Salish tribes. "White people called them Flatheads, a long time ago," she said. "It doesn't mean a thing. It's just a name."

Joe leaned his head forward. The brush of crew cut lunged toward me, and he mussed the bristles with one hand. "Flathead," he said. Then he smiled.

They started folding up the metal chairs at the senior center, and everyone was talking about heading off for naps. I did not want to lose Joe and Helen, and I asked if I could spend more time with them.

Joe smiled, and Helen said, "Oh," which came out like more of a noise than a word, loosened from her brightly colored mouth. Then she nodded vigorously. They wanted me to come over to their house. We stood there smiling and nodding at each other, excited to be making new friends.

That's when their friend Chuck came over, wearing his World War II–era veteran's cap, and he slapped Joe and Helen each on the back and said, "You want to know about the reservation, you're asking the right person. You ask Joe. He knows more than anyone."

I looked at Joe and asked, "Is that right?" But Joe just smiled.

"Hell," Chuck said, "we're all white Indians here anyhow. Know what I mean?"

I said I guess I did, but, it's not something I would feel comfortable to say, myself. Just as I thought "healing" implied something spiritual, I had a particular reverence for Native Americans. I almost felt unworthy of knowing them, and I felt shy there, on their land. They were still different from someone like me, weren't they? Was that wrong to say?

Chuck said, "Hell, missionaries took all the Indian out of the Flatheads. We're not Indians here." Then he leaned in to make sure I would hear. "We're Catholic."

"Oh," I said. I wanted to apologize for what the missionaries had done. Did Chuck want to be Catholic? Did he miss the parts they took away?

"Go see the big church in St. Ignatius," he said. "They didn't have to kill the Indians here. They just sent us all to church, wiped us out that way." On Sundays back a century ago, everyone who lived in that region, Indians and missionaries and white farmers alike, went to Mass at the church in St. Ignatius. The church is probably the biggest building on the reservation, and on its walls are paintings of Jesus and Mary. Jesus is wearing a headdress. Mary is wearing braids and beads.

"The missionaries, you know, they made us a church then they kicked us all out, made us pray in the basement," he said. "They couldn't stand the smell of buckskin." I looked at Joe, who was wearing a white T-shirt and overalls, nodding.

"Oh," said Helen, "I love the smell of buckskin, Chuck." She laughed a little.

Chuck started telling me that Vatican II had ruined the church but that he was still a good Catholic; he talked to me about the Latin Mass for awhile until Wolf Crone came by and said they'd be locking up the doors soon. I made a plan to see Joe and Helen later and then went off again with Wolf Crone.

Wolf Crone gave me a driving tour of Hot Springs. We rocked slowly through the hard-packed roads in a small car with poor suspension. Wolf Crone pointed out the old tourist inns that had once been loaded with white visitors stopped on the route between Missoula and Glacier National Park. Most of the hotels had been closed since the 1950s, when Montana was in its previous boom. One or two small inns had recently reopened, and the tourists were returning.

We rolled down Main Street and then up a small hill to a house set back in some pine trees. This was the home of a woman who made rattles and things like the ones I'd seen hanging on trees at the mud pits. Her porch was covered in dream catchers and clay pots. Inside, the front room was laid out with jewelry, incense, and tortoise shells full of pellets that rattled when they shook. There were paintings of horses and fields, and of women sitting beside teepees. All of it was for sale, and much of it was made by the woman who lived in the house, a white woman with braided hair and a sedate, pleasant face, who sat working behind a counter.

I wondered if Wolf Crone was secretly in love with the craft woman, because she seemed way too happy to be in that place, stepping through it with excitement, like everything she saw in there was precious. She was either in love with that woman or she really liked to shop. Or, I supposed, these rattles, earrings, and drums truly touched her.

Somehow, they bothered me. They didn't seem authentic, even though they were handmade. Wolf Crone pointed out the things in the shop as if she had made them herself, adoring whatever she set her eyes on. I bought a clay pot, hoping to please her. Then Wolf Crone drove me out deep into the reservation, past ranches of yellow grass and mountains and cows, back to the red house where Helen and Joe lived.

Helen was so excited to have company, she pulled me inside and nearly pushed me down onto her vinyl couch. Joe tagged along behind. Helen raced around, trying to show me everything, to tell me everything about herself, as if she'd had no one to tell for a very long time. She was not shy, as she had been at lunch. I didn't have to ask a thing. She took down every picture from the walls, one at a time, and brought each to me, talked about them, thoughts tumbling out over thoughts. From the porch through the kitchen and into the living room, their home was packed with things, aging, warping, dusty: tall stacks of yellowed newspapers, pens in holders, dolls, velvet paintings, statues, firewood, canned food, furnace parts, a rack of guns.

As a girl, Helen said, she went to the Indian school at St. Ignatius; she loved the nuns. She helped farm her mother's eighty acres; she picked beans for a penny a row, saving money slavishly until the day, when she was just a young teenager, that she had enough bean money to buy the thing she had always wanted: a pair of cowboy boots.

She brought me the boots. They were stashed in a cabinet, and she found them immediately, as if she had left them there yesterday. The boots were black and white leather with a pointed toe, and they were worn, but so clean they were shining. She set them on the floor next to the pictures she had taken down and went off to find more things to show me.

Joe is a Salish Indian, which makes him a true Flathead. He and Helen live on the same plot of land that his family had farmed for three generations, out east of Hot Springs in Perma. In the field beyond the bluebird boxes, his grandmother's plank home still stands, tipsily. That was his family's first home on the reservation, and he was born there in 1917.

Chuck had told me, "Joe could tell you a lot of stories." But Joe wasn't talking. He looked up at the dream catcher hanging in the window, and pointed at it by tipping his head.

"Know what that means?" he asked.

Midwestern tribes believe the web of a dream catcher holds away bad dreams; the pattern is sometimes formed of a dream or vision of the artist. The web is decorated with feathers or other found items. I knew this. But I told him, "No, I'm not sure," because I wanted him to tell me. He didn't. The commotion started again.

At the door, Joe's dog dropped a mouse. The dog's name is Sups, the Salish word for "tail." Sups's tail curls even as it wags. He brought the mouse; Helen brought a picture of Joe's father, a black-and-white photo like a poster for Buffalo Bill: see the red man in his own homeland! Helen turned it over; the picture was a souvenir postcard. "Oh, oh, look at that, a postcard!" She smiled, and went looking for another picture. I studied Joe's father in gunfighter days: a full-blooded Salish man, young, leather chaps and vest with stars, gun in holster, moccasins, black eyes staring deadly at the camera. His jaw is clenched beneath smooth skin, his long black hair tucked into his collar. Joe said his father died in 1919, shot by another Salish man, back when Indian men on reservations drank a lot and shot each other, often. That's all he said about it.

Joe pointed again at the dream catcher hanging in the window. "Know what that means?" he asked.

Helen seemed to be running out of things to show me, and that made her a little nervous, like I would be disappointed. I didn't want to cause her distress, so I stood up and told her that it was getting late, time to go.

Joe came over and took me by the shoulder and said it one more time, "Know what that means?" pointing at the dream catcher. Then he laughed out loud and said, "I don't!"

We went outside. He pointed at the sweat lodge he had built in his yard and said that this was where he prayed the rosary. *The best of both worlds,* I thought. Helen told me I should visit again, maybe every year. She seemed happy to make a friend who was so different from her: I was so much younger, and everyone else on the reservation seemed old. The young Flathead had been leaving in droves. A new school had opened to try to teach young people the Salish language, but the language too appeared to be leaving. I gave Joe and Helen each a kiss and said goodbye, then drove back to Hot Springs, where Wolf Crone dropped me off at my hotel.

The Syms Hotel was a big old art deco building, made of stucco and painted bright pink, with only a few rooms reopened. The innkeeper sat playing a flute on his car-seat sofa; he nodded hello without interrupting his tune. He had the lights off, and the lobby was glowing with candles. I went inside and drew myself a mineral bath in the deep tub in my room.

In Montana in the 1990s I sought to "find myself," as if there was one self to find, and if you looked in just the right place, there you would be. I wouldn't hope for the same thing if I went back now, not just because I'm older and more settled into myself but because Montana also is not exactly what it was. The place that once seemed to me to hold certain answers now seems always to be in the throes of some transition or another, booms and busts, migrants coming through to claim and reclaim the land. Hot Springs surely has been remade again in the past decade, become grander than it was when I was there. I think it would not seem as lonely and strange, which is what I loved, then, because it's how I felt: unsure of myself, longing for something, and also a little bit in love with that longing. By now Joe, Helen, and Wolf Crone are gone, and to know that place again, I'd have to start all over. But even so, I still think Montana remains somehow more real than other places, maybe because of the landscape; the mountains never go away. In New Jersey, most of what you see is manmade, full of people—and when people get involved, there appears to be no clarity.

I went back to the springs one morning before I left, to soak in the corn holes. I slipped into the ooze like a new skin, looking for a holy moment. Mud stirred around me, and I felt swallowed by the earth. I did this soak because it was a strange thing to do but also because I wanted to be made better than I was, somehow. I wanted to be healed, and they said the hot springs could do that. In the mud, my lungs stirred with menthol and licorice and sulfur, all the mingled smells in the air. Beyond the Mission Mountains past the distant edge of town, thunder rumbled in a morning storm. I stayed there, alone, swallowed in a pocket of the earth, for what felt like ages. I did not heal anything, or learn much, or change anything about myself perceptibly that day. I washed off that layer of mud and moved on, and kept trying.

Bashert

LESLÉA NEWMAN

---

*T*hese are amazing."

"Incredible."

"I've never seen such beautiful paintings."

"I've never seen such a beautiful model."

Susan just smiled and tried not to spill the glass of white wine she was holding, as an eager patron of the arts jostled her silk-clad arm in his haste to get a closer look at her work. And instead of sipping her wine, she drank in the moment many were calling her overnight success, though she knew it had begun with another moment over twenty years ago . . .

"You're going to Israel for a year, to work on a kibbutz," Susan's parents said to her the summer after she graduated from the State University of New York. "No need to thank us for this wonderful opportunity we're giving you. Just go, see, enjoy, and maybe you'll even learn something about yourself."

What Susan's parents didn't tell her was this: over a million Jewish men in this country and you couldn't find one to marry? What's wrong with you? Twenty-one years old you are, with no boyfriend, no career, just a B.S. in art history—that and a token will get you a ride on the subway—what else can we do but ship you off to the land of milk and honey and see what God has in mind for you to make of yourself?

And so Susan packed a few articles of clothing along with her charcoals, drawing pencils, and sketch pads, kissed her parents goodbye, and boarded an El Al jet that was filled with *sabres,* or native Israelis who spoke the language of her people, though Susan hardly understood a word. She knew, from reading a travel brochure, that a *sabre* was literally a fruit that was tough on the outside and sweet and tender on the inside, and she could understand why her fellow travelers were so dubbed, at least the outside part. They didn't talk as much as bark at each other, their words filled with the language's trademark guttural utterings, each one sounding like the beginning of a spit.

Susan leaned back in her seat and closed her eyes as the plane lifted into takeoff. She didn't mind being surrounded by people she couldn't communicate with; on the contrary, she found it strangely comforting. Susan often thought of her life as a movie, a foreign film with distorted sound and a grainy picture shown at an art house with creaky seats in need of repair. Going to the Jewish homeland was just the next scene in the film of her life that someone else was forever directing. Susan didn't try to protest, didn't try to rewrite the script, didn't ask for a different part. She didn't board the plane willingly or unwillingly; she took her seat and buckled up automatically, just as she had gone off to college, putting one flat foot in front of the other with a sigh and hoping for the best.

The flight, which lasted an entire day, was completely uneventful until the wheels of the plane touched ground. Then, as if on cue, the *sabres* burst into song: "Hatikva," the Israeli national anthem, whose title, Susan knew, meant "the hope." Even though Susan could have joined in—she knew the words and the melody from singing it in temple during the High Holy Days—she chose to remain silent and let the fervor and passion with which the Israelis sang envelop her. By the time the plane got to the gate, Susan's eyes were brimming with tears. The song ended just as the "Fasten Seat Belt" sign was turned off. Then the moment was broken and chaos ensued, with everyone jumping up to grab their carry-on luggage and dash off the plane.

Susan made her way over to a man standing at the gate flashing a hand-lettered sign that read "Kibbutz Volunteers." She showed him the letter she'd received assigning her to a medium-sized agricultural kibbutz located in the northern part of the tiny country, near a city called Haifa. Other people brandishing letters approached as well, and when a dozen of them had gathered, the man herded them out into a van and whisked them off into the night. Susan slept most of the bumpy ride and then, once delivered, let herself be led, stumbling, to the room she would call home for the next twelve months. She tried to be quiet, as three other girls were already sleeping in the small, crowded cubicle, but she couldn't help turning on the light for just a minute and she was forever glad that she did, for there on her mattress lay a spider, a huge brown, bristly-hairy spider that she was in no hurry to share her sleeping quarters with.

"Oh my God," Susan gasped in a stage whisper loud enough to wake the girl in the next bed.

"What is it?" the girl whispered back, her voice sleepy and annoyed.

"A spider. It's bigger than my fist. I've never seen—"

Susan's words were interrupted by a thwack! as the girl threw a shoe onto her bed, sending the spider scurrying away. "You'll get used to them," she murmured, rolling over and going back to sleep.

Susan didn't have much time to get used to anything, as the next morning she was woken up at five o'clock to get ready for work. She'd been assigned the orange fields, which the kibbutzniks called *Pardis,* meaning Paradise. Susan introduced herself to her new roommates: Rona, who hogged the bathroom, blow-drying her hair for a good half hour even though it frizzed up the minute she stepped outside; Yael, neé Janet, who though born and bred in Hoboken, New Jersey, now spoke English in short, broken sentences with a pseudo-Israeli accent; and Madeleine, who hailed from England and didn't understand why they had to wake up so early—it wasn't like the "bloody oranges" were going anywhere.

At six o'clock sharp, a small truck pulled up to pick up Susan and company. All the volunteers were dressed alike, in regulation kibbutz clothing: white T-shirts, khaki shorts, canvas work boots, and cotton hats. Susan, always sensitive to color or lack of it, thought they looked like a studio full of blank canvases waiting to be painted. But as soon as they were dropped off in the orange grove, sleepy as she was, Susan saw the beauty of the contrast between the volunteers' drab clothing and their colorful surroundings. No wonder it was called Paradise: the trees were lush with emerald green leaves that shone in the sun; the sky was a perfect cornflower blue, the likes of which Susan had never seen; and to top it all off, the sweet, intoxicating smell of oranges wafted through the air like the perfume of a beautiful woman who had just left the room. Susan felt a bit lightheaded, from the aroma, the early hour, and undoubtedly a severe case of jet lag.

She took a swig of water from the canteen hitched to her belt and tried to get ahold of herself as she listened to the instructions a man named Shlomo was yelling in her direction. But it was useless to pay attention; Susan couldn't even figure out what language Shlomo was screaming in, let alone understand what he was talking about.

Each volunteer was given a rickety wooden ladder, a white canvas bag, and a row of trees. Somehow Susan figured out that her mission was to drag the ladder to the start of her row, lean it up against the first tree, climb to the top rung despite her fear of heights, drop oranges into the canvas bag slung across her shoulder, climb down the ladder, walk to the end of her row, and dump the fruit into a crate the size of her new living quarters, all without injuring herself. This, she found out, was easier said than done—in Hebrew or any other language—because the more oranges she dropped into her bag, the heavier it grew, and the shakier her balance became. As Susan tried to shift her weight, the ladder beneath her shifted its weight as well. Several times she held on for dear life as the ladder threatened to topple; twice she even found herself praying to a God she didn't believe in, but, she reasoned once her safety was secured, if God wasn't here in Paradise, where else would He be?

To Susan's surprise, the skins of the oranges, even when they were ripe, were not orange in color, but rather a dark forest green. When she saw the other volunteers up in their treetops were snacking, she followed suit, digging her thumbnail into the thick rind of an orange and pulling it back to expose the pale orange pulp inside. Susan tore into a section with her teeth and as juice dripped down her chin, she marveled at how sweet the fruit tasted, much, much sweeter than any orange she had ever eaten at home. There were two ways to tell if these green-colored oranges were ripe: by whether they came off the tree easily (they had to be twisted by the stem, not yanked) and by their size. Shlomo, who Susan learned from Madeleine was from Argentina and therefore spoke Hebrew with a thick Spanish accent, handed Susan a measuring tool made of wire, shaped into a circle, like a child's oversized bubble wand. But instead of blowing bubbles through the circle, she was instructed to hold it up to orange after orange to see if the fruit was big enough to pluck. Of course, it didn't take long for one of the male volunteers to hold up his wand to a girl's bosom, first one breast and then the other, to see if either one was ripe. The girl merely giggled, as did several other volunteers; some of them even called for the boy to bring his wand over to see if they measured up. Susan just ignored him.

By eight o'clock, the sun was hot and orange-colored in the sky and a whistle was blown, signaling breakfast. All the volunteers clamored down from their ladders and made their way over to a cluster of picnic tables set up outside a cabinlike structure where Shlomo had prepared a feast Susan couldn't believe: fluffy omelets made with avocados grown on the kibbutz; huge bowls of creamy white yogurt topped with swirls of amber-colored honey; sandwiches made of challah and Nutella, a gooey chocolate spread with a thick, mudlike consistency; and for dessert, halvah, a sticky-sweet brick made of honey and ground sesame seeds. Susan, whose father was a dentist, wondered if she'd have any teeth left by the end of this "life experience" that her parents had given her. Still she chowed down with the best of them, passing the salt and pepper when motioned to, but mostly remaining silent as conversation and jokes in Hebrew,

Spanish, Danish, Russian, and English swirled around her. Susan sat with the English and American girls whom she could at least understand, but she felt distant from them, and distant from herself. Of course she was awfully far from home—halfway around the world!—but that really didn't matter. Susan always felt removed from whatever situation she found herself in, like she was underwater or behind a window made of thick, smoky glass.

After breakfast it was back to work until noon, and then it was quitting time. The intense heat of the sun forced everyone down from their ladders and back into the truck to be driven from the fields to the main dining hall in the center of the kibbutz. Lunch was served at exactly one o'clock and Susan, who barely ate breakfast at home—a cup of coffee and maybe half an English muffin—was surprised that despite her Paul Bunyan–sized breakfast, she was ravenous. The kibbutzniks ate their main meal of the day in the afternoon—vegetable soup, broiled chicken, baked potatoes, cooked carrots, and, of course, dessert, a sheet cake with chocolate frosting that set Susan's teeth on edge. Still, she filled her belly and then retired to her room for a much-needed nap.

Less than an hour after Susan's head hit the pillow, there was a knock on the door. "*Ulpan!* Fifteen minutes," someone called. "Ulpan" meant Hebrew school. Susan dragged herself out of a deep sleep and rapped on the bathroom door.

"Just a minute," called a disembodied voice she recognized as Rona's.

"She lives in there, love." Madeleine gestured with an open compact and then began powdering her nose. Madeleine was one of those women who tried her best to make any getup—even a bland kibbutz outfit—into a fashion statement. A great deal of cleavage showed above the neckline of her white cotton T-shirt, and she'd tied the bottom of it up in a knot, so that her belly button peeked out over the khaki shorts that tightly hugged her abundant thighs.

"Rona. Hair." Yael pointed to her own scalp and shook her head in disapproval. The curls of her short "Jew-fro" bounced up and down with the motion.

Finally, Rona emerged and Susan entered the bathroom, which contained a sink with a mirror hanging over it, a toilet, and, instead of a shower stall, a spigot with two faucets underneath mounted right into the wall. When Susan showered, the toilet and the sink got soaked, as did her clothing and towel. Not only that, a good two inches of water remained on the floor, until she figured out she had to push it all towards a drain in the corner with a rubber squeegee. The water moved slowly until Susan removed a glob of Rona's hair from the drain. Dorm life, Israeli style, she sighed as she hurried to get dressed and catch up with her roommates who were also headed out to Ulpan.

"*Shalom, shalom.*" Ze'ev, the Hebrew teacher, greeted his students with great enthusiasm and motioned for them to sit down at the large circular table in the middle of the room. Ze'ev's classroom was outfitted with a desk and a blackboard, above which hung green sheets of paper with the Hebrew alphabet printed in large, white letters. Susan, who had dropped out of Hebrew school after only one year and never had a bat mitzvah, stared up at the letters, but try as she might, she could not drag their sounds up from the dredges of her long-term memory bank.

"Ze'ev." Ze'ev pointed to himself and then pointed to Susan.

"Um . . ."

"He wants to know your name, love," Madeleine whispered.

"Susan."

"Shoshana." Ze'ev bestowed upon Susan the same Hebrew name she'd been given long ago by her childhood Hebrew school teacher. "*Ahnee* Ze'ev. *Aht* Shoshana." He pointed to Madeleine. "*He* Malka." Then Ze'ev turned to the class and asked "*Me* Malka?" They answered in response, pointing to Madeleine, "*He* Malka."

Susan was utterly confused until Madeleine explained in a whisper that *he* meant "she," *me* meant "who," and *who* meant "he." Other than Madeleine's explanatory whisperings, not a word of English was spoken during the entire lesson, and by the time the hour and a half was over, Susan's head was spinning.

From four-thirty to six-thirty, the volunteers had free time. Susan, not knowing what else to do, went back to her room and unpacked her things. There were no dressers or bureaus for the volunteers; instead each room had four metal, high school–like lockers installed along one wall. Susan opened the door of the only locker without a lock on it (she'd have to ask someone where to get one) and was touched to see a "welcome" packet inside. The packet consisted of a brochure explaining the history of the kibbutz, a chocolate bar, a package of cookies, and a pair of socks with the kibbutz's logo on it.

After Susan unpacked, she grabbed her sketch pad and went outside to sit on the grass outside the volunteers' residence hall. She'd promised herself she'd draw every day, even if only for ten or fifteen minutes. A real artist has to be disciplined, she reminded herself, though she knew she wasn't a real artist. Real artists were passionate. Real artists were creative. Real artists were driven. Susan knew she wasn't any of these things.

Oh, she could render a passable likeness of a flower, a table, a rock, or anything else that was placed smack dab in front of her. But her drawings were wooden; they lacked any kind of feeling or emotion. They didn't really express anything. That's what her college professors said anyway. They kept telling her to loosen up.

"Your still lifes have no life in them," one of them had said. "Just let your fingers go," said another, taking her wrist in his big, hairy hand and shaking it up and down until her arm flopped like a rag doll's. "That's it," he nodded approval. "Now try and draw." She didn't think it made a bit of difference, and even though the teacher had said, "That's better," she could tell he didn't mean it.

Susan squinted her eyes against the bright sun and decided to draw some of the low, flat buildings around her. She needed to work on her perspective anyway. But as soon as she put charcoal to paper, she was interrupted.

"Drawing, eh? I'm Jeremy, from Canada. You're new here, eh?" Jeremy flopped down cross-legged, right next to her.

"Yes," Susan said, reluctant to introduce herself.

"Susan, right? I sat across from you at *ulpan*. Which do you prefer, Susan or Shoshana? They call me Jacob, but I can't get used to it."

Susan continued to draw without answering Jeremy, but that didn't stop him from keeping up a running conversation.

"I've been here about a month. It's all right, don't know how long I'll stay. They've already asked me about making *aliyah*, but I don't think I'll go that far, what about you, eh?"

"What's 'aliyah'?" Susan asked as she shaded in the side of a building.

"Oh, you know, moving here. Permanently. Becoming an Israeli citizen. You've heard of the Law of Return, haven't you?" Susan shook her head so Jeremy explained. "It means every Jew can become a citizen, no questions asked. They'll be bothering you about it before long, so you better start thinking about it. Hey, want to take a walk after dinner?" Jeremy abruptly changed the subject. "The nights here are very beautiful."

Was he asking her out on a date? "Thanks, but I'm really tired. Still jet-lagged. Sorry."

"All right. Maybe another time, eh?" Jeremy scrambled to his feet and stood over Susan for a moment with his arms folded, casting a long shadow over her work-in-progress. "I don't think you've got it quite right," he finally pronounced before turning on his heel and walking away.

"I think Jeremy fancies you," Madeleine said later as she and Susan walked to the dining hall for dinner. "He's cute. Do you fancy him as well?"

"Oh, I don't know. He was just being friendly," Susan said.

"Since when have you known a bloke to just be friendly?" Madeleine shook her head and stuck her fists on her hips. "Watch out for the kibbutzniks, love, especially the married ones. They've heard you American girls are easy." She winked as she handed Susan a tray.

Dinner was a light meal, much to Susan's relief: plain yogurt with tomato and cucumber salad, matzo, and challah with several types of mild cheeses, and fresh fruit for dessert. After dinner, Madeleine, who'd appointed herself as Susan's personal welcome wagon, escorted her into the canteen, where the volunteers, as well as some of the young Israelis, gathered to drink coffee, eat sweets, and, as Madeleine informed Susan in case she couldn't see for herself, pair off to take a walk in the woods and smooch.

"You see him over there?" Madeleine pointed with her cup as she and Susan waited in the coffee line. "That's Mike. He's lovely, isn't he? But he knows it, thinks he's God's gift to women. He's from California, a real playboy type; he's been here about two months, and he's already been with several girls. Last week he was with her," Madeleine indicated one of the volunteers from Holland, who was tall and slim and had brown wavy hair down to her waist, "and now he's with her." She nodded toward a woman who could have been a carbon copy of the first one she'd pointed to, only her hair was flaming red. "Now Jeremy, he was with Yael for a while, but she dumped him for that handsome *sabre.*" Madeleine pointed across the room.

"I fancy Stuart," Madeleine, who had been whispering all this time, dropped her voice even lower. "But he won't give me the time of day. Maybe you could talk to him for me, love, what do you say?"

"Oh, I don't know." Susan and Madeleine reached the front of the line and Madeleine showed Susan how to make coffee the Israeli way: drop a spoonful of instant espresso into your cup, add five packets of sugar and then about a tablespoon of hot water. Mix that up into a gooey paste, add another half a cup of boiling water, and then top it all off with half a cup of milk. Susan's lips actually curled as she drank her concoction, but she forced herself to swallow, reminding herself: when in Rome . . .

"Here comes Jeremy." Madeleine raised her cup to him in greeting and then started to sidle off, but Susan grabbed her arm.

"Hello ladies," Jeremy said, though it was clear he was speaking to Susan. "*Mah-nish ma?*"

"*B'seder.*" Madeleine answered.

"How's everything? Fine." Jeremy translated for Susan. "Maybe I could be your tutor."

"Ooh, I bet he could teach you a thing or two." Madeleine nudged Susan's arm. "Go on, you two. *Lila tov.*"

"*Lila tov.* Good night," Jeremy replied.

"Uh, I'm really tired. I'm going to bed. Excuse me." Susan hurried out of the canteen and headed back to her dorm room. She wasn't interested in Jeremy, and she hoped he'd get the message soon. As she walked down the path lit only by moonlight, she caught sight of several couples strolling arm in arm, and several others standing perfectly still, not strolling at all.

Susan hurried along, trying to make herself invisible and not disturb anyone. She wasn't particularly interested in romance, and she hoped the kibbutz wasn't going to be a repeat of college, which had basically been a repeat of high school. Girls getting all giggly and googly-eyed over boys who thought they were good for one thing and one thing only: wham, bam, thank you, ma'am.

Not that Susan was a prude or anything. She'd had her share of sexual experiences; after all, it was the seventies, the height of the sexual revolution, and everyone was screwing around. But for some reason, the boys who "scored" with a different girl every night were revered as studs and the girls who brought home a different guy every night were degraded as sluts. And what, Susan wondered, was so revolutionary about that?

Susan didn't think romance was all that important, anyway. Her art was what was important, and of the few boyfriends Susan had had, none of them had taken her work seriously. Carl, a boy whom she saw on and off during her sophomore year, had shown interest at first, but as time went on, Susan saw the real reason for his curiosity: he was hoping she would draw him. Even though, as Susan pointed out, she didn't do portraits, she did still lifes and landscapes. She tried explaining to Carl that portraits were tricky, and most of the time, the subject was disappointed with the finished product, even when the artist was a pro, which Susan was not. She'd only taken one figure-drawing class, which was required for her major, and then went back to inanimate objects, which were much safer—they didn't argue with you about what they looked like. A portrait artist needed to have that special something to capture a person's essence on canvas, and whatever that special something was, Susan knew she did not have it.

"Just try," Carl kept insisting despite Susan's protests, and so one day she did, mostly to shut him up. They'd spent the better part of the afternoon making love, and then Carl was lounging on the single bed in her dorm room, his leather belt looped around the doorknob as a sign for her roommate who was due back from her chemistry class any minute.

Susan took out her art supplies and tried her best, but even Carl had to admit her sketches weren't very good. When he actually said, "Oh well, back to the drawing board," Susan knew their affair was over.

There had been a few other boys on and off throughout the rest of her college years, but none of her affairs (calling them relationships would be stretching it) lasted more than three or four months. Susan never had trouble attracting boyfriends—she was of average height and weight with dark brown hair and eyes, someone a boy wouldn't necessarily notice in a crowd, but someone he wouldn't be ashamed to show off to his buddies, either. She was the kind of girl a guy would ask out when he didn't have the nerve to approach the girl he really wanted to be with: the curvy blonde bombshell who wouldn't give him the time of day unless he was the school's star football player. Susan didn't mind though. She only dated because she thought it was expected of her. And she didn't want her friends to think there was something wrong with her.

And she liked sex. She liked the things her body did, the way it seemed to rise and expand like a loaf of challah baking in the oven before her orgasm exploded, sending little zings of energy everywhere: to her hands, her feet, the nape of her neck, the small of her back, the insides of her thighs. Afterward, Susan felt like she sparkled, and she loved to look at herself in the mirror then, to see the red flush spread across her chest and neck all the way up to her cheeks. It was the only time she ever felt truly beautiful. But the truth was, she didn't always come when she was with a boy, though she never had any trouble by herself. By herself it was more intense. She could take her time, and not have to worry about what somebody else was thinking or what somebody else wanted. And best of all, afterward she could just lay in bed naked with the covers pulled up to her chin and smile. She didn't have to wrap her arms around some sweaty, smelly boy and tell him what a wonderful lover he was. She didn't have to dodge the wet spot. She didn't have to wonder when whoever was sharing her bed would leave already so she could get back to her latest painting, waiting patiently for her over in the art building, propped up on its wobbly easel.

Susan got undressed and crawled into her tiny bed, first making sure there were no spiders under the thin, cotton blanket. She slept well, not even hearing her roommates come in, until the five o'clock alarm woke her to get ready for work again.

So the weeks went on: Pardis in the morning, *ulpan* in the afternoon, socializing in the evenings. Susan found she enjoyed working in the orange groves. She liked the color her skin was turning: a golden brown similar to the blond oak table in her parents' dining room. She liked the muscles that formed in her upper arms and the backs of her calves. She liked the feeling of accomplishment that came when she got to the end of her row and started up the other side. And she was making slow, but steady, progress with her Hebrew. She could actually hold a simple conversation about the weather or the time, though she still had trouble reading and writing. She managed to draw a little bit every day, too, though more often than not some boy, either a volunteer or kibbutznik, interrupted her, wanting to take her for a walk or better yet, back to his room. Susan was continuously shocked at the bluntness of these offers and always declined politely, as she did in the evenings at the canteen with Madeleine at her side wistfully staring at the "blokes" she fancied, most of whom ignored her.

Summer melded seamlessly into autumn. The days were still hot but not as fiercely so; some nights Susan even had to wear a light sweater to walk back to her room from the canteen. Rosh Hashanah came and went, as did Yom Kippur. Susan was shocked to see that the kibbutzniks celebrated the Day of Atonement by having a picnic instead of fasting, and no one even mentioned going to synagogue.

There were also field trips for the volunteers on Shabbos, the only day of the week they didn't work. Once they went to the Dead Sea, and Susan saw what she'd always heard was true: you could float on your back and read the newspaper; there was so much salt in the water it was impossible to sink. Another time, they went to Jerusalem to shop at the *shuk* and visit the Wailing Wall. Susan bought some earrings made of silver and turquoise-colored Elat stones from an Arab who cut the price in half. "For your eyes," he said, "your beautiful eyes." She stood at a distance from the Wailing Wall for a long time, watching men and women approach the ancient structure, pushing tiny pieces of paper between its cracks before she knew what she wanted her "letter to God" to say: please keep my parents safe, well, and happy. Susan, though not exactly happy herself, was not exactly unhappy either. She grew used to life on the kibbutz; she was in a holding pattern, but just as she began to relax into her days, everything changed.

It began with the weather. The rainy season arrived, and the words "soaked to the skin" took on a whole new meaning for Susan, who had never experienced such torrential downpours before. The rain came down in absolute sheets, and even when it wasn't raining, the air was cold and clammy. The first day the rains began, Susan ran out to the porch to take in a few pieces of laundry she had hung over the railing to dry. When she lifted a navy blue pullover, a dozen buttons clattered to the porch's wooden floor, making a small, tinny racket. Susan was puzzled: how did all those buttons come loose at once? She knelt down to scoop them up and then realized, to her horror, they weren't buttons at all; they were hard-shelled black beetles holed up for shelter. Susan dropped the sweater with a shriek; it poured over the railing into the mud, where it stayed for several months before someone else picked it up and removed it.

Working in Pardis was out of the question. First Susan was reassigned to the laundry, which she hated, then she worked briefly in the kibbutz's equivalent of a day care center, but she didn't fare well there either. She was intrigued with the way children were raised on the kibbutz. From the time the children were six months old until they turned eighteen and went into the army, they lived away from their parents in a large building called the children's house. Each section of the children's house had about six kids in it, who grew as close as siblings to each other. Children saw their parents for three hours a day during the week and all day on Shabbos. Susan tried her best, but it was difficult for her to work in the children's house because even though her language skills were slowly improving, she still spoke less Hebrew than a typical two-year-old, making it impossible for her to have any control over her pint-sized charges. That left the kitchen. Madeleine cringed visibly when Susan told her of her new work assignment.

"What's so bad about the kitchen?" Susan asked as she enjoyed what the volunteers considered a special treat: pieces of bread toasted on the metal safety grates of the small kerosene heater that tried in vain to take the dampness and chill out of their room.

"Norit," chorused Madeleine, Yael, and Rona together, pretending to shake in fright.

"Who's Norit?" Susan asked.

"I'm sure you've seen her, love, sitting by herself in the back of the dining room in white trousers and a big white hat?" Madeleine licked butter from the tips of her fingers.

"Tall. Grand. *Gadol*," Yael said, holding up her arms in a wide circle, indicating girth.

"She eats girls like you for breakfast," Rona warned, as she knelt in front of the heater to turn her toast with one hand, the other keeping her long, straightened hair out of danger.

"It's because she never married," Madeleine explained. "And she has to be, what? Thirty, thirty-five? She's probably never even had a chap."

"Old maid. No good." Yael tsk-tsked.

"This one girl, Andrea, from Massachusetts?" Rona said. "She told me Norit goes into the chicken house, picks out a bird, cuts its head off with a cleaver and laughs as the poor, headless body runs around the coop."

"Ewww!" Madeleine pretended to gag on her toast.

"No true," said Yael. She crossed both her hands around her own throat in protection and then looked at Susan with sympathy. "Mazel tov, Shoshana. Good luck."

Susan wasn't too worried about working with "Norit the Nazi" as some of the volunteers called her behind her back (though not within hearing range of the kibbutzniks, many of whom were Holocaust survivors). Surely the stories about her were exaggerations, and if Susan just stayed out of her way and did what she was told, she'd be fine. But it was impossible to stay out of Norit's way. The woman was enormous, and her bulk took up most of the narrow, crowded kitchen where Susan worked, peeling cucumbers, slicing tomatoes, and digging the eyes out of potato after potato. Try as she might, Susan couldn't work fast enough for Norit, who didn't say much— she didn't have to; a silent scowl was enough to inspire Susan to double her efforts and pick up her pace even though her arms ached from scraping pounds of carrots against a grater that was in dire need of sharpening.

Norit flew about her domain, barking orders, brandishing knives, reaching for oversized pots and pans that hung on huge hooks above her head and banging them down onto the stove with a clatter. Her hair was a mass of sand-colored curls; try as she might, they would not stay contained beneath the white chef's hat that stood upright upon her head, adding to her already impressive height and stature. Susan guessed Norit was over six feet tall and weighed at least two-hundred-and-fifty pounds. Yet she was all speed and muscle, lifting enormous vats of soup off the stove, pummeling mountains of raw challah dough into submission with her enormous, bare hands, hauling in yet another fifty-pound bag of carrots for Susan to peel and grate. Susan was a bit afraid of her, like everyone else; but she was fascinated, too, and she couldn't help staring at Norit, though she quickly averted her eyes and went back to work whenever the woman so much as glanced her way. Norit was a mad, whirling dervish of energy. Unlike the other Israeli women, she didn't turn all coy and giggly when a man entered the room. She had no patience for anyone—man, woman, or child—who got in her way or prevented her from completing whatever job was currently at hand. Norit meant business, and Susan admired that. Still, did she have to be such a stern taskmaster? By the time they broke for breakfast, Susan was in a sweat; by the time lunch came around, she was beyond exhausted. She noticed no one sat with Norit at either meal. The kibbutzniks ate on one side of the dining hall, the volunteers on the other, and Norit just sat in the back at a little folding table, sipping a cup of tea and munching on a dry piece of matzo.

After work, Susan went back to her room and drew whatever she found there: Yael's tired, muddy, Van Gogh–like boots slouched against each other in the corner; Rona's ragged, stuffed teddy bear lying sideways on her pillow; Madeleine's lipstick, compact, and black lace bra. But one day, weeks into the rainy season, Susan was seized with cabin fever. There was an hour or so before *ulpan*, and she decided to take a walk. There was actually a break in the rain, though it was far from sunny—it was foggy and misty, almost like Susan was walking through a cloud. She donned a yellow slicker, jammed a pencil and a small sketch pad into her pocket, and started on her way.

She walked down the path to the canteen, around the dining hall, and past the small, square homes of the kibbutzniks, each one of them built exactly alike. Susan didn't have a particular destination in mind, she just wanted to go somewhere she hadn't been before, and walked wherever her feet decided to take her. After a while though, she realized she was headed toward something: a sound that was very faint at first, but grew louder and stronger with every step. Someone was singing. Susan couldn't make out the words, as they weren't in English, but the melody was lively; she could imagine it being sung by a barful of men clinking beer steins and chugging their brew down in one long, uninterrupted swallow. Except the person singing the song was a woman, her voice round, lusty, and full. Her song put a bounce in Susan's step and a smile on her face, though she didn't know why—maybe because Susan herself would never sing a song like that, so lively and full of joie de vivre. Susan was curious to see who was singing, even though she imagined the woman wouldn't want to be disturbed, in the same way Susan hated to be bothered when she was trying to sketch or draw. Still, she put one foot in front of the other until she turned a corner and stopped dead in her tracks, unable to believe what she saw.

It was Norit. Enormous, intimidating, gruff, no-nonsense Norit was singing at the top of her lungs. And not only that. She was stark naked, standing underneath an outdoor shower rigged to the side of what must have been her living quarters. Susan knew a decent person would turn and walk away immediately, but she just couldn't move; the sight before her was too mesmerizing. It was as if someone put a spell on Susan, changing her legs into two slim tree trunks rooted into the ground.

Norit, underneath her dirty white uniform smeared with butter, flour, and cooking grease, was beautiful. More than beautiful. Stunning. Magnificent. Dazzling. Her body was massive, full of curves and crevices, simultaneously hard and soft, sturdy and delicate, completely unlike Susan's body, which had always seemed fine before but now seemed wholly inadequate compared to the work of art that was Norit. As she turned this way and that, soaping herself up, rinsing herself off and singing all the while, Susan continued to stare at Norit's flesh-covered form, a feast for the eyes, a true masterpiece. How her plump arms shimmered, how her rounded belly curved, how alluring were the two sweet folds of flesh above her waist, how dainty were her tiny feet, how abundant her dimpled thighs! And as if all this wasn't enough—(*dayenu,* as the Passover song goes)—when Norit finally spotted Susan, she didn't shriek and rush to cover herself or yell at Susan to run away. Instead she opened her arms wide and smiled, as if to say, *Look at me. Aren't I fabulous?* and then motioned impatiently to Susan to come join her, as if she'd been waiting for this moment all her life, and what in the world was taking her so long?

And Susan, who had been surprised at everything that had happened to her thus far in this strange yet familiar land, wasn't surprised at all. Finally, she was wide awake, no longer sleepwalking through what she knew hadn't been much of a life. Finally, the movie of her existence was reaching its climax; at last the director who lived rent-free in her brain was calling for action. And Susan complied: she took off her raincoat, her rain hat, her rubber boots, all the clothing she'd been wearing for weeks in order to stay dry, and dashed into the water. She wanted to be like Norit, drenched, soaked, saturated. The wetter the better. Norit soaped her up, scrubbed her down, singing all the while.

And for the rest of that afternoon, and many days that followed, Susan at long last learned the subtle nuances of Norit's foreign tongue and discovered just how sweet and tender on the inside a tough, gruff *sabre* could be.

Of course Susan and Norit didn't live happily ever after, though they did live quite happily for the rest of the year, until Susan's time in the Holy Land drew to a close. Of course there were many tears shed and many promises made, all of which were eventually broken. Susan never did go back to Israel, and Norit never did come to the States for a visit. Their tearful, once-a-month phone calls dribbled to an end, and their letters dwindled down to birthday and Chanukah cards. One day a letter Susan had sent to Norit came back stamped "No longer at this address," and that, she concluded, was the end of that.

Until the year that Susan turned forty and, right on schedule, had her midlife crisis. After she had returned from Israel (with no boyfriend in tow, much to her parents' dismay) she'd gone back to school for her teaching certificate and made peace with the fact that while she would never be a great artist, she could still have art at the center of her life. She taught drawing and painting at a community college in upstate New York, where she had settled down; she also volunteered her time at a nursing home, helping the residents work with soft modeling clay, which was good for their gnarled, arthritic hands. She'd had a serious relationship that had lasted the better part of a decade, and though it hadn't worked out in the end, Susan and her ex-lover remained the best of friends. And now Susan had a brand-new lover, a round, ripe, luscious woman named Beverly, who made the short hairs at the back of her neck stand on end every time she walked into the room. Life was good—better than good—but still, there was something missing. Susan, on the brink of turning forty, was feeling nostalgic, but nostalgic for what? She didn't have a clue.

As part of entering a new decade of life, Susan decided to clean out the large shed she had built behind the house to use as a studio. She'd recently read a book on feng shui, and was intrigued with the notion of creating beauty and peace in one's life by making one's living space and work space as beautiful and peaceful as possible. To do this, Susan learned, she needed to hold up every object she owned and put it to the test: did she feel good about the object? Did it reflect whom she was today? Did it add to her feeling of well-being or detract from it? Susan was sitting on the floor in the middle of her studio surrounded by piles: things to keep, things to box up and store, things to give away, things she wasn't sure about. She had just come to her old sketch pads from her trip to Israel and was flipping through the pages when there was a knock at the door.

"It's open," Susan called, knowing whom it was.

"Want some company?" Beverly poked one foot cautiously into the room. She knew Susan's studio was sacred space and never entered before permission was granted.

Susan looked up and smiled. "C'mon in."

"What are you doing?" Beverly stepped carefully around the piles, knelt down beside Susan, and kissed the top of her head.

"Just sorting through my things. In with the old, out with the new, you know, trying to deal with turning forty."

"The best is yet to come, honey. You'll see." Beverly, having crossed the great divide into middle age several years ago, spoke with authority. "Hey!" She looked down at the sketch pad Susan was holding. "I thought you didn't do portraits."

"I don't," Susan said, despite the hard and fast evidence to the contrary spread across her lap. "I just did these as a favor for someone."

"Who's the model?" Beverly squinted her eyes for a better look.

Susan felt her face grow red and knew this wasn't her first hot flash. "Norit," she whispered softly.

"Wow, she's a looker. Should I be jealous?" Beverly teased.

"No." Susan wasn't in a teasing mood. "You should be grateful. If it wasn't for her I wouldn't be with you."

"Is that so?" Beverly looked from the drawing to Susan.

"She changed my life," Susan said and then told Beverly the story of Norit, hunting up the one photo she had of her in addition to the sketches.

"Wow," Beverly said when Susan was done. "What a risky thing to do, to seduce you like that. And how brave of you to just dive in."

"Norit said it was *bashert*," Susan said with a faraway look.

"What does 'bashert' mean?" Beverly asked.

"It's hard to translate, but it means fate, meant to be, kismet, something like that." Susan grew silent for a minute, not telling Beverly that "bashert" had another meaning: Norit had called Susan "bashert" as an endearment, meaning "my destiny," and Susan had called Norit "bashert" as well.

"Wow," Beverly said again, still studying the sketches. "I guess I owe her big time."

"So do I," Susan said, closing the sketch pad and putting it on top of the "I don't know" pile.

"Were the drawings for her?" Beverly asked, studying the photo of Norit.

Susan nodded. "She liked them a lot, but I don't know. I never did anything with them." Susan shut her eyes for a minute, remembering the endless arguments she'd had with Norit, who, like Carl, had longed to pose for her. First she'd teased her: "Am I not beautiful enough for you?" she asked, putting one hand on her hip, the other behind her neck, and then throwing her head back in a fashion model's pose. Susan laughed and tried to explain that it wasn't Norit's lack of beauty; it was her own lack of talent. But Norit didn't buy that. "*Lama lo? Lama lo?* Why not? Why not?" she kept asking, her impatient voice growing louder and louder until one day Susan shrieked, "Because I'm no damn good!" and then to her horror, burst into tears. Norit held her and stroked her and then abruptly pushed her away. She disappeared into the bathroom for a moment and then returned without a stitch of clothing on. Susan reached up to undo the top button of her own blouse but Norit did not want to make love. Norit wanted Susan to draw her and demanded she do so in a voice that would not take no for an answer. Susan dried her eyes, glared at Norit, and drew.

"*Tov. Yoffi.* Good. Pretty." Norit had been pleased but Susan, always the perfectionist, saw only the flaws in her sketches. She put them away and, though Norit continued to ask, plead, and demand, never drew her again.

"I know how you can pay her back," Beverly's words cut through Susan's thoughts. "May I?" She reached for the pad after Susan nodded. "You can work on these."

"What do you mean?"

"I mean, these are gorgeous. Look at the lines, the shapes, the shadows. These drawings have something those don't." Beverly waved a plump arm at the studies of fruit and furniture hanging on the wall. "I may be going out on a limb here, Susan, but these drawings have . . . I don't know . . . heart. They have your heart. And soul. They're alive. Your other paintings . . . I mean they're good and everything, but they don't . . . they don't move me like these do. Even unfinished, these sketches have a life to them your other work doesn't have. Oh God." Beverly looked down at her hands. "Me and my big mouth. Did I go too far? Are you going to break up with me?"

"No," Susan said slowly, looking from the sketch pad to the wall and back again. "Only because I know you're right. But I don't know if I can do it."

"Why not?"

"I don't know." Susan flipped through the sketches. "They're so . . . so out there. I'm afraid of exposing Norit like that."

"I think," Beverly stayed Susan's hand with her own, "you're afraid of exposing yourself like that."

"But all I have are these sketches and this one photo," Susan whined. Knowing she'd been found out, she looked for any excuse. "You know I need to have something in front of me in order to draw it."

Beverly threw her a look that said *I'll love you whether you rise to the occasion or not, but both of us know what's really going on here* and then got to her feet. "I'll come by later, okay?" she said. Then she tiptoed out of the studio, shutting the door behind her.

For the rest of that afternoon, Susan drew. She drew from memory; she drew from experience; she drew from deep inside her. And when Beverly came back later that evening with take-out Chinese food to share, she didn't have to say what Susan already knew: that afternoon's work was the best she'd ever done.

Susan hadn't submitted her work to galleries for years, but with Beverly's coaxing, which grew into insistence ("It's not for nothing you're dating a pushy broad!"), she took slides of her work and sent them out. First she was accepted to group exhibits, then she sold a painting or two, and at last a New York gallery offered her a one-woman show. When the letter came, Beverly grabbed both of Susan's hands and whirled her around the room. "You did it!" she shrieked, engulfing her lover in a big bear hug.

"Yes, but I would never have done those paintings if it wasn't for you," Susan pointed out, eager to share the glory.

"I didn't do anything," Beverly shot back. "It was *bashert*. Meant to be."

———

Susan looked up at her paintings framed so beautifully and hung so expertly on the gallery's walls. She'd obscured Norit's face for the most part, with a raised arm or a turn of the head, just to be on the safe side, even though twenty years had passed and she was sure that Norit, like herself, had changed over time. Still, Susan wanted to be sure that Norit remained unrecognizable, in order to protect her privacy. It was a small world, and one never knew—perhaps somehow, someday Norit would stumble across her paintings. Susan wondered what Norit would think of them. The woman had no shame when it came to her body, and Susan imagined she'd be flattered, proud, pleased. At least she hoped so. She closed her eyes for a moment and whispered to Norit, *toda raba,* thank you so much. For everything.

For teaching me to love you and therefore love myself. For holding me tight and letting me go. For inspiring me and believing in me. For this moment that I've waited for all my life. And even though the room was noisy with the oohs and aahs of the crowd, Susan could swear she heard Norit's voice close to her ear, whispering *vah-kah-sha,* Bashert. You're very, very welcome.

Fruits at the Border

LUCY JANE BLEDSOE

———

*P*at negotiated a great deal for the car in Punta Arenas, with the only hitch being that if we took it into Argentina, we'd pay a huge daily tariff. Not a big problem since our destination was Lago Blanco, the biggest body of water in Chilean Tierra del Fuego. Of more immediate concern was the condition of the car itself: the tires were toy-sized, the body was trimmed in rust, and the windshield was a spiderweb of cracks. The rental car agent, Miriam, who wore tight black pants with flared legs and spiked heels, stepped carefully around the wreck parked on the dirt and stone lot, telling us that the busted windshield was our good fortune since she wouldn't charge us anything at all if we completely shattered what remained of the glass. We carefully documented with Miriam the dents, gouges, and scraped paint all over the body of the car; took the keys; and spent an hour trying to find our way out of town.

I had expected the port town of Punta Arenas to be small and driven by a fishing economy. In fact, the place reminded me of Paris. The people, dressed in up-to-the-minute styles, were coolly friendly to tourists, and the streets bustled with commerce. We were eager to leave the city behind and see the endlessly horizontal Patagonian pampas and their counterpart, the astonishingly vertical Andes. We had plenty of time, there was no reason to not see everything, and so we decided to delay our visit to Lago Blanco and first drive north to visit a couple of national parks before heading down to Tierra del Fuego.

The car performed very well on the dirt roads leading to Torres del Paine, a Chilean national park in the Andes, never mind that we only took her up to about twenty-five kilometers an hour. The hours of driving were worth it: the park's trails and lakes and mountains were extraordinary. We saw a Fueguian fox, the Patagonian grey fox, the lovely and strange black-necked, white-bodied swans, giant rheas with flocks of enormous chicks, and guanacos, lots of munching guanacos.

Getting used to camping in Chile, however, was a little more challenging. The word "camping" seemed to be synonymous with the word "party." If, for example, a couple had a choice of where to erect their tent, say on the other side of a grassy meadow from ours or directly next to ours, they would choose the latter. One German couple put up their tent so that our doors were about six inches apart. If they'd left it there, we would have had to take turns getting in and out of the tents. We ended up arguing with them, making them move, and then feeling sheepish about being American bullies who are spoiled by great expanses of space and lots of privacy.

And yet, talk about space! The Andes, and the surrounding steppes, are mountains of such magnitude and glory that the word "space" loses all meaning. The peaks are stone pillars rising out of beech forests swirling in clouds. Not your ordinary puffy cumulus clouds! Ventricular clouds, elliptical and edged with eerie rings of pink and green, looking exactly like big space ships, hover over the basalt mountains. Enormous lakes rest at their bases. Lago Argentina, an exquisite aqua, the deepest imaginable aqua, reflected up on the ever present Patagonian clouds, turning them aqua as well. Over the next couple of weeks, we camped next to a Lago Grey. We drove by several Lago Azuls. The campground at Lago Verde was stunning. I began to wonder if Lago Blanco would actually be white.

Those weeks in the Andes, we hiked farther than we thought we were capable, through downpours, toward views we assumed we would never see, but then, time and again, miraculously, when we reached the cirque at the base of the peaks, the clouds swirled, gathered, swept one way, and then away altogether, revealing the stone massifs like a home of gods.

Or ghosts. Whichever, gods or ghosts, we were drawn in, enchanted even, by the howling winds, the herds of wild horses, manes flying, that would stampede through our campsite at dawn, the herd parting to flow around our tent. We were terrified of being hoofed to death, or even of the big rubbery, whiskery horse lips and hot, steamy horse nostrils that paused to nibble and sniff at our camp before galloping on. This was a power beyond the erotic, these towers, these beasts, this wind. We were drawn farther north. We wanted more mountains.

So we decided to forego Lago Blanco another week and headed for the Argentine border. Deeper and higher into the Andes.

The border was hot and dusty, as so many borders seem to be, with only another dirt road to lead the way. As we approached, checking and rechecking our car papers, hoping they didn't expressly prohibit us from entering Argentina, we had to stop for a herd of cattle getting driven across the border by gauchos on horseback. A wooden bar, nothing more, blocked the road, and so we parked in front of it and went inside the small building.

A woman and her little girl sat behind a desk. Pat charmed the woman and winked at her little girl. We showed them all kinds of papers, although she never once asked to see my passport. There are times when being two women traveling together is an advantage. In most cultures, women are perceived as less threatening than men or as being inconsequential altogether, which allows us to slip across different kinds of borders, not just international ones. This, however, was simply the line between Chile and Argentina. The woman nodded at Pat's charm, walked around to the other side of her desk, out of the building, and lifted the wooden bar. We drove through, into Argentina, and headed straight back up into the mountains.

For hours we drove with the legendary Fitzroy Massif and Cerro Torre, mountains that don't show their faces for months at a time, that day brilliant against the blue sky, beckoning us in the distance.

"What about Lago Blanco?" I asked Pat.

"Oh, we're going there."

"Eventually," I said.

"Eventually," she agreed.

I pulled out the map to look again at the lake. Far south of the Straits of Magellan and tucked under Bahia Inútil, the big lake was at the end of the last dirt road in Chile. Lago Blanco. The name was languid, sexy, a big watery spot on the map, sitting alone, miles from any town, like the heart of Tierra del Fuego.

I placed my finger on Lago Blanco and pointed out, "We *are* heading in the opposite direction."

"We have a month."

"How long do you think it'll take us to drive there?"

"To Lago Blanco?" Pat liked to say the name, too.

"Yeah."

"A day. Maybe day and a half."

I looked again at the map. Most tourists who wanted to visit the end of the world drove down the Argentine side of Tierra del Fuego to the big town of Ushuaia. There was even a paved road part of the way there. No pavement on the way to Lago Blanco, though. We'd only just started our trip, but we should have already known that ten kilometers on these Patagonian roads—which often resembled dry riverbeds—could take half a day. I didn't ask Pat if she thought the tiny tin can we were driving could even make it to Lago Blanco. That was a topic we didn't discuss the entire month in Patagonia.

As we approached the town of El Chaltén, we came upon a small tourist bus parked, if you can use that word, in the middle of the dirt road. All that was left of the bus was a charred frame. The dirt and rocks beneath the vehicle were blackened as well. The bus had obviously burst into flames, quite recently, and burned to just a husk. Where the tourists had gone to was anyone's guess.

Patagonia is haunted. You see it everywhere. In the wind, the endless space, the abandoned estancias. Wild horses tearing across the countryside. Winds that knock you over. Towers of rock. But for a couple of girls traveling on their own, this is a strange comfort, the hauntedness. I had long ago accepted that life is not as it at first presents itself, and there's relief in being in a place that starts with that premise. Traveling in the presence of mystery is so much more honest than traveling somewhere, like Texas for example, where the surface story is presented with emphatic insistence. We embraced the presence of ghosts. At least at first.

One night we'd traveled too far along a boulder-strewn, ditch-ridden dirt road to get back to the closest town before dark, and it had started to drizzle, so we began looking for a place to camp. We passed a campground, but it was full, and so was the next one. Finally, we came to a hand-painted sign with an arrow, signaling us off the road toward an estancia. The sign said, simply, "Camping."

We arrived at a lovely meadow, thick with clover, without a single human in sight. Wondering why the other two campgrounds we had passed were full and this one was deserted, we shut off the car's engine and got out. I've learned in my travels that once you enter private property, you only have to wait a moment for someone to appear.

The man's stride was extraordinary. He was walking, but his speed would be much faster than my run. He wore the Patagonian beret and spoke no English. In our best Spanish, we negotiated camping for three dollars. Then he gave us a tour.

First he pointed to a big basin he'd installed in the meadow attached by a hose to a barrel of water. A hand-painted sign nailed at an angle to an adjacent tree read, "*Agua Potable,*" the declaration itself making me doubtful. The proprietor was particularly proud of the shower. This consisted of two oil barrels, one stacked on top of the other. The top barrel was filled with water, perhaps agua potable. He'd cut a door into the side of the bottom barrel, and inside there was a pile of dry grass. The idea was to light a fire with the grasses, so that the heat in that barrel would warm the water in the upper barrel. A "showerhead" drizzled the warmed water onto your body if you were willing to stand naked in the middle of the man's meadow. The toilets, in a shack next to the shower, were the stand-up kind. Nearby was another hand-built shack, which was locked, but looking in the windows I saw a couple of tables with chairs, a wooden bar, and a sign offering roast lamb and Coca-Cola. I had no doubt that for the price of your dinner, you would get to help butcher the lamb. There was one very bright electric bulb hanging from the middle of the shack, and this he left on all night long.

That night, terrifying winds blew through the camp, and neither Pat nor I slept at all. With the absence of other campers, the eerily lit shack, the hand-painted signs, the erratic but hellacious winds, we dubbed the place "The Haunted Campground." In the morning, our host arrived again and busied himself yanking up handfuls of grass, which he tossed into the bottom barrel of the shower, encouraging us to make use of it.

We asked him about the terrific winds in the night, and he claimed that they were normal, nothing unusual at all. And yet, driving out on the road later that morning, under a now startling blue sky and Fitzroy Massif towering right above us, we came upon three places where entire swaths of the forest, trees fifty feet tall, had been knocked down. We were grateful that the trees in our campground had remained rooted to the ground.

Slowly we were learning what was possible in Patagonia. Only about a tenth of the roads were paved. Hotels were rare and grocery stores rarer still. We bought provisions where we could, ate most meals off the camp stove, and stayed most nights in our tent.

Perhaps, we thought, we'd best head south to our original destination: Lago Blanco. After all, we'd already racked up far too many days in Argentina, and our car bill was mounting correspondingly. Still, we couldn't resist driving across the continent, which, after all, was very narrow down there, to the Atlantic Coast for a quick look before heading south and back into Chile. Maybe we could actually find a hotel room in Rio Gallegas, which, judging by the size of the type on our map, might be a decent-sized town.

Rio Gallegas did indeed have a lovely hotel, where we stayed, and a well-stocked supermarket, where we bought a bag of big, glossy, green apples. After a diet of granola and noodles for the last couple of weeks, our apples were manna. We even considered staying a few nights in Rio Gallegas, because of its comfort, but were eager to push on to Lago Blanco. So we headed south to the Chilean border, which was just before the ferry crossing of the Straits of Magellan.

Pat's charm was less effective with the armed male guards at this particular border. The guns muddled my brain immediately, so that when a scrappy pair of kids, a boy and a girl, approached us and asked in good English if they might ride across the border with us, I started to say yes.

Pat pulled me aside to remind me that we were, in fact, two lesbians traveling by ourselves in a place reported to be not particularly dyke-friendly. Granted, as middle-aged women, we were quite invisible in that culture, but wanted to remain that way for the most part. Never mind that we knew nothing at all about these two kids with backpacks. I thought she was being a bit of a spoilsport. They seemed sweet, and it'd be fun to chat with them, but I agreed that our being lesbians did add an additional layer of risk that we didn't need to play with. We did not need to be taking strangers across international borders.

I told her she was right, and then I nodded at the enormous sign saying that no fresh fruit or vegetables could be taken into Chile. "What about our apples?"

"They're okay," Pat said in her don't-talk-about-it voice. Like me, she'd become addicted to *manjar*, a thick, creamy caramel that Chileans eat with most meals, and we liked it on apple slices.

"Hello?" I said to her unhearing ears. "What about two dykes traveling on our own in unfriendly Chile?" Now I nodded toward the two guys, who looked to be about twelve years old, holding rifles.

Her eyes glossed over. She really wanted those apples. I could tell I was on my own. Her lecture about being vulnerable as lesbians traveling across international borders still freshly convincing in my mind, I determined to disclose our fruit.

We shuffled into the building and began talking to different soldiers in what appeared to be a random fashion. We did as we were told, migrating from one desk to another when one of them pointed a finger, and answering the questions to the best of our abilities.

"Where are you headed?"

"Lago Blanco."

"You mean Ushuaia?"

"No, Lago Blanco."

Blank stares. No one goes to Lago Blanco. All tourists go to Ushuaia.

"Yes," I finally said. "Ushuaia."

Thamp! He stamped our papers and gestured toward the door and the border.

But he had kept our sheath of car papers, which I was sure we needed. I argued to get them back. Technically, we would not be entering Argentina again, so we probably didn't really need them. But what if we *did* want to go back into Argentina? And anyway, if I've learned anything from my travels, it's to hold onto your papers. Nevertheless, he finally convinced us that we really didn't need these particular papers anymore, and we acquiesced.

We turned to go, at last, as he thought to ask, "Any fruits or vegetables?"

You'd think this would be easy. After all, I'd already created a minor scene about the car papers. And Pat's point about us being a couple of lesbians at a very remote border crossing in South America was still quite valid. Besides, what's a bagful of green apples? But they were irresistibly big, lustrous, sour-juicy apples. We hadn't had much fresh food. And there was the issue of the unfinished tub of manjar. I had to struggle hard to tell the truth. Pat remained utterly silent and I knew that her choice would be to smuggle the apples into Chile. But my risk-taking side succumbed, after a quick skirmish with my cautious side, and I nodded a little tiny nod, as if we had only itty bitty, inconsequential apples.

The guard raised an eyebrow.

I muttered, "*Manzanas.*"

He shook his head. While Pat waited with the guard, I went out to the car and got the bag of apples, which I conspicuously handed to the couple looking for a ride across the border, who seemed surprised that I would offer the gift of big juicy apples but not a ride.

Finally, Pat and I crossed the border back into Chile.

Borders, like airports, are just not good places to experiment with challenging authority. So while we were aware of our sexual orientation at international boundaries, most other places in Patagonia we traveled quite uninhibited and without hassle. In fact, by the end of the trip we'd racked up four or five "girlfriends," women who took a particular interest in us. Granted, in this environment, it didn't take much for a woman to achieve "girlfriend" status for us. There was the woman who sent us free drinks across the restaurant. The woman who invited us to a tango show in her husband's restaurant and conspicuously kissed us both in front of all the guests. The hostel owner who spent hours helping us plan a hiking trip, which we had to cancel at the last minute, and who still kissed us both when we left her place. There were, in fact, a handful of women who recognized something in us they liked. Maybe our independence. Maybe our comfort in being different from other travelers, other Americans. I'm not sure what it was, but now and then women would offer incredibly generous help, far beyond their duties as waitress or border agent, and we called them our girlfriends.

There had been no girlfriends at the border where we lost our green apples, however, and we were eager to push on to Lago Blanco. At least that was the plan. But those apples turned out to be more important than we had thought. We had told the guards we were going to Ushuaia, which put the idea in our heads. Besides, we still had lots of time and, well, I thought it'd be great to see the Beagle Channel, about which I'd read so much, and Pat, being a sea story aficionado, couldn't resist getting as close as possible to Cape Horn. This meant, of course, crossing the border back into Argentina, racking up more daily tariffs on the car, but, we argued, when would we ever get back to Patagonia? As for Lago Blanco, we found on the map the southernmost border-crossing in Patagonia, which would take us directly over to Lago Blanco from a place not that far north of Ushuaia. We could still spend our last few days at Lago Blanco before heading back to Punta Arenas to fly home. Besides, we reasoned, in Ushuaia, we'd be able to get information about Lago Blanco, like whether there is a campground or any place at all to stay. We were learning that with the enormous distances, one best figure out the next meals and beds in advance. There was another reason Ushuaia beckoned: it was the only town south of the Straits of Magellan and there we could buy more apples, which we'd need—along with other food—if we were going to go to the un-inhabited Lago Blanco.

That night, not wanting to cross the border back into Argentina so late in the day, we stayed in San Sebastian, a few yards from the border, at the only building in the "town" other than a police out-post, a motel owned by Ernesto. The room was dank, and while there was a heater, and it was a cold, rainy night, Ernesto said he would not turn it on. Nor would there be any hot water until morn-ing. We had a couple of pisco sours in his restaurant. My steak was actually pretty good, but Pat's "pizza" was a slice of bread with cheese melted on it. We crawled into the twin beds in our room, the only occupied one in the motel, and fell asleep. Until the two women with screaming children showed up at two in the morning. With Ernesto shouting to be heard above the children, it took the group at least an hour and half to settle in and quiet down. I never did get back to sleep. An hour later, a couple of drunk guys checked into a room next to ours and continued their party until they passed out some time around five o'clock. The place was a bit spooky.

The morning's promised *agua caliente* was tepid at best, and the *inclusivo* breakfast was plastic tubes of Nescafe, more tepid water, and stale, packaged cookies. The other guests had fresh bread, butter and jam, and we could only suppose they'd somehow paid for the upgraded breakfast. We wanted to get out of the haunted motel and across the haunted border as quickly as possible, and we did indeed have an uneventful crossing.

Our campsite high on a hillside overlooking the town of Ushuaia and the Beagle Channel more than made up for the bad night at Ernesto's. In fact, it was too amazing to leave. We stayed four nights. By now we were used to party camping, and we almost enjoyed rub-bing shoulders with other campers, most of them Chilean and Ar-gentinean. The campground had a shared café where you could buy bottles of wine and use the kitchen. Each night many of the campers pooled their money to buy massive hunks of meat in town, whole animal parts, which they roasted over the kitchen's open fire. After eating our noodles early—we had trouble adjusting to the 11 p.m.

dining hour in Chile and Argentina—we sometimes drank wine in the log cabin café, looked at the view out the windows, and watched the fat drip off the shoulder or leg or side of lamb onto the flames as the other campers took turns rotating the roast. On the last night in the café, we totted up our total days in Argentina, which we realized were more than our days in Chile. Miriam, the rental car agent, would be charging us well over $600 extra.

It was time to move on to Chile, and Lago Blanco.

We did get some information in Ushuaia about our true destination. Another girlfriend, a woman who owned a tour company that sold high-priced voyages to Antarctica, among other packages, sat us down in her office and freely gave us all the information about Lago Blanco that she had. First of all, the border crossing we had planned on using required fording a river. She said she knew people who did it, depending on the season, in their four-wheel-drive vehicles, but *she* wouldn't in any kind of vehicle. What kind of car did we have, she wanted to know.

That border was as compelling to me as the apples. I wanted to try it. I knew that getting into trouble while traveling was never as bad as getting into trouble at home. There were always people ready and even enthusiastic to help you. Trouble never lasted that long.

"Let's try fording the creek!" I told Pat.

"River," she corrected.

"Only in the wet season."

"Which it is."

"We should at least go see."

"We don't have four-wheel drive," Pat said. Our girlfriend pursed her lips, clucked, and shook her head in agreement with Pat, who finished up by saying, "Have you looked at our car recently?"

I knew better than to point out how well it had done on all the crazy roads so far. I conceded Pat's point and listened to our girlfriend's suggestion, which was that we go all the way back north, cross the haunted border, and then head south from there. But she had even better information. She personally knew the man who owned a lodge at Lago Blanco! She said he was a very nice man, and if we talked to him personally, he would surely allow us to camp some-where out of sight on the lake's shore. Then she told us the town where he lived, and also served as mayor, and suggested we go find him and present our case.

Now we couldn't *not* go to Lago Blanco.

We stocked up on groceries in Ushuaia, this time harvesting from the supermarket more green apples, fresh tomatoes, and a couple of avocados. And a big, shiny red bell pepper. Driving back toward the haunted border, Pat talked about that red bell pepper as if it were gold. We would roast it over an open fire at Lago Blanco. Or, if the mayor didn't allow open fires, we'd chop it into our pasta that we cooked on the campstove. The red pepper was a fine specimen, deeply crimson and voluptuously curved.

We were, in short, obsessed with our fruit. You might even say enchanted past reason. Because we stupidly forgot about getting all that produce back into Chile. The problem was that there would be no place to buy food once we crossed, and if we were to eat at Lago Blanco, we had to smuggle in our food. There was, apparently, this lodge, but it would be some rustic affair, and who knew if it had a restaurant.

I lied to the armed guards. I did not tell the border agents who once again looked far too young to be wielding weapons about our apples, tomatoes, avocados, and glowing red pepper. I answered "No" to the question about whether or not we had any fruits in the car. The agent's face remained impassive as he stamped our papers and then accompanied us out to our car. My heart was pounding. What was the punishment for lying about fruit at the border? His eyes grazed our car and then he disappeared back into the station. We sat in the car, waiting at the wooden bar that separated Argen-tina from Chile, telling each other to look relaxed, bored even, to reveal nothing on our faces.

Another man finally sauntered out of the building. He walked to the wooden bar and raised it. We drove through. It took an hour before I was convinced that they wouldn't come after us for our red bell pepper.

Staying another night at the border's haunted motel was out of the question, but it was a day's drive to the owner of Lago Blanco's town, and another half day to the lake itself. Our flight out of Punta Arenas left in three days.

I yearned for Lago Blanco. This was our last chance. I was convinced that it was stunningly beautiful, perhaps surrounded by mountain peaks with hanging glaciers. I'd made that last part up, the map showing no geological features surrounding the lake and our guidebooks not mentioning it at all. Still, I needed to see the elusive Lago Blanco. I needed to eat our fruit on its banks.

And yet, despite these yearnings, reality began to ooze its way across the pampas into our travel-slowed brains. Several times we measured the mileage to Lago Blanco on the map, counted our days, considered the reliability of our tiny car on the boulder-strewn roads. Travel is all about calculating risk. Was this red bell pepper worth lying to a Chilean guard with a big gun? The answer to that one had been yes. But was it worth trying to get to Lago Blanco in this tin can? What would happen if it broke down? With our flight out of Punta Arenas in three days, and work obligations that couldn't be pushed back a week, we didn't have much wiggle room. With a lot of regret, we located another, much closer, lake and decided to go there instead.

But when we arrived at this alternative destination, the place looked like a bomb had been dropped there. The small motel was being used by squatters, and all the windows were busted. The lake itself was all that we could have hoped for, complete with the ring of mountains and hanging glaciers, but the feeling that a riot had just blown through made the place less than relaxing, and we drove on to a nondescript campsite down the road. That night we cut open the red pepper to find it rotted in the middle.

A couple of days later, Miriam met us at the car rental office, where we hoped we hadn't accrued any more extra charges than the $600 Argentina tariffs.

"So you had a good time?" Miriam asked in perfect English.

"*Si, si, si,*" we answered in the repetitive affirmation that everyone used.

"You went to the national parks in Chile?" she said with a small Mona Lisa smile.

"*Si, si, si!*" I replied enthusiastically, warming up to Miriam. "And to the national park in Argentina, too, and Ushuaia." The moment the words were out of my mouth, I realized that she had just offered us an opportunity. A $600 opportunity. Which I had just blown.

"Follow me," Miriam said. "I must check the car."

She walked around the car, kicking each tire with the point of her stiletto heels. I tried to tell her how wonderful the car had been, and Pat started to fill her in on the highlights of our trip, again mentioning our days in Argentina. When Miriam slid behind the wheel to check the dashboard, for what I didn't know, I pulled Pat aside. I whispered, "I think she had offered us an opportunity, and now we've both bragged about our days in Argentina."

Pat looked at me with doubt. It *did* seem impossible that a rental car company would just let go of $600 profit to two American women. Miriam had told us before we left that she'd check how many days we'd been in Argentina by looking at our passports upon our return. And anyway, why would this beautiful Chilean woman in stilettos impart favors on a couple of obvious American lesbians?

Back in the office, we sat down with the paperwork. I expected Miriam to now ask for our passports. Instead, she named the excellent price Pat had negotiated—not counting the Argentina tariffs. "*Inclusivo,*" she verified, that small smile still playing on her lips, and slid the papers to us.

"*Si, si, si,*" we agreed and signed.

We walked out, declaring Miriam our very favorite Patagonian girlfriend, marveling that there still existed a place where profit doesn't necessarily rule, where some subversive and unspoken understanding between women held power.

Soon we were in a cab on the way to the airport, enjoying our ability to understand much of the Spanish blaring on the radio, regretting that we'd probably forget it all by the time we returned to another Spanish-speaking country. We were pulling into the Departing Flights lane when I distinctly thought I heard the words "Lago Blanco" on the radio. They weren't spoken in the languorous manner in which Pat and I spoke the words; they were being punched out, ballyhooed. "Lago Blanco!" the man shouted, as if advertising a circus. "*La enchilada todo!*" At Lago Blanco, he announced, one could fly fish, eat sumptuous meals, drink fine wines, get massages, rent boats. It was the whole enchilada. Then the man rattled off a phone number and repeated the entire ad again. We were stunned. Our elusive Lago Blanco, the most remote spot in Tierra del Fuego, the mountain lake that kept slipping from our grasp, was in fact being advertised like a Club Med on the cab's radio. Lago Blanco, where you could have the whole enchilada. Thank God we never made it there!

We sat back and laughed, pleased to realize how serendipity had once again guided us through another extraordinary trip. There always has to be a pursuit, a Lago Blanco, and there always have to be obstacles, fruits at the border, but neither ever defines the trip in the end. Spaceship clouds and stunning rock towers, Rhea chicks and two-toned swans, campsites overlooking the Beagle Channel and beside *lagos verdes,* gray, and *azul,* and yes, the generosity of beautiful women—these were the true fruits of the trip, tossed from the tree as random kismet.

Following in Tim's Footsteps

PEARLIE MCNEILL

Vietnam, September 2005
Ho Chi Minh City

Ten of us are travelling in a group on an organized tour. We've stepped aboard our boat, two by two, making me think of Noah's Ark. Our guide, Dao, has a map of the country pinned to the wall. I have not done much in the way of advance reading. I want my responses to come from what I see in front of me, not from some information-driven understanding of what happened when and in what location.

I have a sense, too, that I might touch on my brother Tim's experience in Malaya. Though his war was over long before America sent combat troops to Vietnam in 1965, I suspect comparisons could be made with Malaya. Dao explains our route north and answers questions.

Our destination the next day is the Cu Chi tunnels. We've all heard about them and know how important they were to the guerrilla fighters, but the reality of looking down on those small, irregular holes makes one or two of us exclaim with shock. We are suddenly aware of the size of our bodies as compared to those of the men, women, and children who used these tunnels—like comparing the size of a wombat to that of an agile rabbit.

We are shown the entrance to a tunnel that is about one hundred yards long, one of the original tunnels from the war. This tunnel has been enlarged so that foreigners can have a more genuine understanding of what conditions underground were really like. Four women of the five in our group are willing to give it a go. The entrance is deceptive, a series of steep steps—this doesn't look too bad at all. Down we go.

Cool air is what I expected but it is so hot my glasses quickly cloud over and I can barely see. The walls close in on either side, and I need both hands to keep myself steady. Charles is in front of me. We are bent over in a crouch and can only move a few inches at a time. We head around a narrow corner, and the tunnel dips lower. Even enlarged, this tunnel is still small. It is also dark, claustrophobic, and scary.

I almost panic when a woman ahead says she can't get her leg over. Not even one Aussie snickers at the sexual innuendo; this is no theme park or thrill-ride. I try to turn around and mumble that I can't go any further, but there's a long stream of people behind me and we are packed in like the humped ridges on a squirming centipede. I tell myself to take a few deep breaths. The image of the little train puffing up a hill comes to mind. *I think I can, I think I can.*

Someone has helped the woman get her leg free. A moment later, I come to the problem step, which is surprisingly steep. Maneuvering my backside against one side of the tunnel, I lean back as far as I can and then ease one leg down at a time. Now we are turning another corner, descending even deeper. I have no idea of direction or how much further we have to go. Charles is wearing light-colored trousers. I must remember to tell him later how grateful I am he chose to wear those particular trousers today. I can do this. I *can* do this.

There is a glimmer of daylight; we are moving upward. At last we can stand up and walk out of the tunnel. Nearby, at a picnic table, women serve us green tea in tiny cups. I could drink gallons.

A few days later, we are in the Mekong Delta area. The river is wide, the current strong, the rain comes and goes. It is too hot to wear my plastic poncho. I drape it over my shoulder.

Unable to see anything much, I turn my thoughts to the era of the war. I'm here at the start of the rainy season; what must it be like in summer? How did Australian troops (as well as the Americans and all the others) cope with the hot and humid conditions?

The sun has appeared. Our boat turns onto a narrow waterway. Mangroves form an edge on both sides, and I can see a meandering path of sorts some distance away. Here and there are fish traps made of wire and held up by bamboo sticks to form a square. The greenery is dense. I hesitate to call this place a "jungle"—a word I've noted any number of times when reading of a soldier's experiences in a hot, foreign country. The word seems to suggest that the people who live in these countries are akin to animals, monkeys for example, and Vietnamese fighters were sometimes described as such in accounts of the war in Vietnam.

My attention is drawn to the right. I thought I saw something move, a snuffling pig perhaps. There is nothing to see, but I imagine men in camouflage, rifles held in front of them, bayonets in place. They are running but making no sound. Spatters of mud stain their uniforms, and their faces are so blackened it would be hard to recognize any features. It's like visiting the location of a movie, and there have been a number of those. But was it really like that in Vietnam? Was it like that for Tim in Malaya?

Before the end of the 1960s, Malaya was referred to as Malaysia. The British and Commonwealth forces were involved in a war there from 1948 to 1960. Australia first sent troops in 1955, and the conflict was referred to as "The Emergency," a term used mainly for economic reasons. Business losses in that war would not have been covered by Lloyds of London, so, to protect British industries, the word "war" was avoided for those thirteen long years.

Tim was sent to Malaysia around 1958, and he wrote to me often. He wrote about the fear of leeches—soldiers were so worried about these blood-sucking creatures that many of them wore condoms when going out on patrol. Hammocks had to be slung between palm trees when they had to stay out overnight, and even when they were exhausted sleep eluded them. What might crawl or fall on them if they dared to close their eyes?

Sitting next to me in our boat is Paul. He was conscripted for service in Vietnam but failed the medical exam. He smiles when he mentions that, but I suspect he cannot escape the idea of what might have been. As we talk, I have the impression that he, too, can see those soldier shapes making their way through the undergrowth.

Did the British and the Commonwealth forces treat the local people well? An investigation into possible war crimes was started in the UK but not a single soldier was charged, and the process was brought to an abrupt end when the newly elected government of Prime Minister Edward Heath came into power. The television age began in Australia in 1956. Perhaps if we'd had TVs in every home earlier, we might have been better informed.

Taking prisoners presents challenges for either side in any conflict. It isn't hard to imagine the dilemma involved, the danger of others coming to the rescue, what to do with the prisoners once they'd been captured, how to restrain them, get them back to camp, hold them captive, and for how long to hold them. Making sure there is no one to tell the story lessens the threat and solves all the other problems too.

Tim's background of family violence might be viewed as suitable to the development of a soldier, if they saw him as an angry young man willing to confront the enemy, stone-faced and determined. But the Tim I knew in my childhood was anything but fierce, and his temperament was sensitive rather than savage.

Almost a year after he landed in Malaysia, he came face to face with communist guerrillas. Before that, he described fruitless patrols to find an invisible enemy, boredom back at camp relieved only when the beer arrived. But on this one day, just before dusk, an Australian sergeant and his small group of soldiers had five men cornered. He promised them that if they gave themselves up right now, that minute, they would be taken prisoner and fed as soon as they made it back to camp. Two men turned and fled, one was shot down, the other got away but might have been hurt. The remaining three threw down their weapons. It was then that the sergeant ordered his men to use their bayonets.

My brother's letter spoke of how he had not been able to move at that moment but he had seen the looks on the prisoners' faces. "They could have been me," he wrote. "They could have come from families like ours; how could I run them through?"

Tim made no mention of the other Australian soldiers and how they reacted to the command or to him, an apparent coward in their midst, but his next letter brought good news. He had been thinking he'd be dishonorably discharged and sent back to Australia in disgrace, but instead, he'd been given the job of driving for a minister of religion, a man he referred to only as "the padre."

If only the story had ended there. But of course it didn't. This same brother of mine who could not use his bayonet against an unarmed guerrilla fighter returned to Australia in 1962. A year or so later, he used that same bayonet as a weapon against his former girlfriend. Why he did that, why it was even possible for him to do that, is a question that has haunted me for so many years.

Overhearing Paul and me talking about war, Dao joins us and tells us about his father. Their family is from the north, and when the war was over, veterans like Dao's father were each given a free bike. Dao smiles. He has fond memories of that bike; his father took him everywhere on it. It was a bit wobbly, and constantly needed attention, but as a means of transport and for carrying essential items, it was invaluable. Dao, conceived after the war, says that his generation, though acknowledging always the debt they owed to their parents, has a different outlook.

Dao tells us how he toured around Australia, visiting Alice Springs, Uluru, the Great Barrier Reef, and even Sydney's Opera House and the Harbour Bridge. Noting my look of astonishment, he laughs delightedly. He's been to all these places on the Discovery Channel.

Now we are heading for an island. The rain makes the path slippery. One minute we are carrying our ponchos, the next we have to put the damned things on. The day is still hot and steamy, but this is no sun shower; the rain falls as though someone is upending full buckets on our heads. We are welcomed in to see the sort of work people do—making popcorn, tofu, fish sauce, and rice paper for spring rolls. In a wooden shed close to the river, a man shows us how he makes floor and wall tiles; another man in another shed shows us how coffins are made.

On the other side of the narrow path is a big covered space, the size of an average three-bedroom house. We stand and watch a man sewing a palm leaf onto a thick bamboo stick. Each leaf has to be turned and held in just the right position. The needle is big, and the thread looks like string. Alongside him, the growing pile contains finished pieces of much the same length. He points upward, and we can see that the roof we are standing under is made of these palm leaves. Dao tells us that the average life of these roofs is three years.

Walking around that island, I realize there is no answer for me in Vietnam, no matter how closely I seek comparisons between wars. I can understand my brother up to the point he returned to Australia, but beyond that I cannot recognize a single facial feature. Odd then, to feel he is close by, walking along with me. I have tried to follow in his footsteps but I simply can't climb over the obstacles that lie between us.

He was and still is my brother, but I wish I could find someone or something to blame. My list of questions is so familiar that I can repeat the questions like a poem, emphasizing various words for greater effect. Was it the war? Did that experience turn his mind? Should we make excuses for our soldiers and the things some of them do once they are back on home soil?

It's raining again. Dao is trailing the group, waiting for me to catch up. I realize how much I like this courteous young man. He puts an arm around my shoulders and asks if I am okay. Yes, I tell him, I am okay. I smile at him and repeat my words. I am okay.

Bookstore Bound

SIMA RABINOWITZ

There is no route we have found as marvelous or mysterious as being bookstore bound. Here, inside these rooms, it is always noon. Or is it night? Always August. Or is it October? The sky is spackled stucco, or panels of plaster, or beveled tin. The ground is a parquet sea or a sidewalk of matted berber. We are reading, reading: north, south, east . . .

West

At the corner of Columbus and Broadway, the other Broadway. The magnificent Golden Gate pales by comparison. The Coit Tower seems to cower in its shadow. The incline at Pine and California, a mere slope.

We have saved this excursion for the end of the trip, wanting the last hours of the vacation to be the best, resisting the temptation to alter the plan when we realize our hotel is closer than we'd expected it to be. How is it that with any number of precise and detailed maps we have managed to misread this town so completely?

And now, finally and much too soon, it is Sunday night and we're standing in front of the grandest, brightest sight on the horizon— the City Lights bookstore. We have imagined this experience for the whole of our ten years together, the anniversary we have been celebrating these past four days, as we trailed happily up and down the legendary streets, admiring Pacific vistas through the mist, anticipating these final luminous moments, new walking shoes and worn leather jackets soaked through with the rain that began when we arrived and hasn't stopped since.

The light inside is stale and dim, as it should be, the air dry and seasonless, as it should be, ripe with the odor of packing crates, cardboard, newsprint. As it should be. It's past ten, and the place is quiet, but not deserted. The only sound, aside from the faint squeak of wet soles on damp carpet, is the small, comforting wind of pages turning.

What appears before us is stunning and overwhelming. We can't survey the whole territory in one visit. But we've got priorities — European fiction and East Asian history, small magazines, and, of course, poetry. We move slowly, maneuvering sideways in front of the stacks, fingering spines, lingering over titles, pausing to look up and take in the rows and stacks ahead and behind, and then narrowing our focus again to the volume in front of us. There is no coast, no shore, no forest, no skyline.

We lose and then find each other again, unexpectedly, hiding the treasures we've selected as surprises underneath and between what we've chosen for ourselves, the piles of paperbacks in our arms growing until we can't carry any more, and we hear the jangle of the clerk cashing out and the lock—it's closing time—turning in the door.

When we emerge from City Lights, it has stopped raining and the air is murky, but warmer. The next morning dawns gold, blue, green. The sky is nearly mistless. We can see San Francisco clearly behind us as we head to the airport.

South

Where the glare of the sun on the bay competes with the burn and scorch of our hosts' heated bickering, we take refuge between "*New York Times* bestsellers" and "Paperback nonfiction." We're downtown in the tropical midafternoon, at the corner of Main and Palm across from the harbor.

We seek the rudderless release of a good story, diversion from the tension of this long (long) weekend with my parents, who, in old age, argue with as much vigor as they did when they were younger. My lover is unused to the rancor, as tireless as the southern sun, and I've lost what tolerance I once had for it. We're exhausted.

Sarasota News & Books is a natural escape—the most comfortable scenery we know, the rows of popular novels like long-lost friends, temporary shelter from the thunderous quarreling. Given other circumstances, we'd certainly choose more challenging terrain. But, for the moment we're relieved to find ourselves in a place that is unarguably familiar. I pluck something I've read before from the shelf and happily, if only temporarily, lose all sense of space and time and of myself.

East

As the awnings on storefronts and shops flap and shiver in the bitter wind, we push forward, half-running through the coldest night on record for this date in May. The play lasted much longer than we expected, and we've only got a few minutes to reach our destination, and once there, only a few more to traverse miles and miles. We've got to head in the other direction tomorrow, so tonight's our only chance to revisit this landmark, and there's a lot of ground to cover.

We're breathless now, exhilarated as much by the view as by the pace of the walk. An endless plateau, used and new, table after table, capped with small mountains of boxes, their tops sheared off and books of all shapes and sizes jutting up and out, jagged paper peaks we know we don't have time to scale properly. The smartest strategy, we agree, is to see things we're not likely to encounter anywhere else.

But the Strand is immense, and our energy is scattered and haphazard. And even though neither of us has ever lived here, we're not really tourists—Manhattan, city of monumental stories, always feels, somehow, like home. We're not sorry to leave empty-handed; our travels will bring us back. Just having stood together in this spot again for a few minutes was oddly satisfying.

Back out on Broadway (the true Broadway), the cold is no less ferocious. We grab a cab; it's just a short ride to our small hotel in Midtown. Tonight we'll dream of the vast unread.

North

Over Minnehaha Creek and across from the cemetery, under a wide, white prairie sky, next to the bank, the new hardware store, a boarded-up bakery, is a vision as pleasing as any we might travel more than these few short blocks to see—dyke books.

Outside the flurries are fast turning into broad, fat flakes, but we don't hurry to beat the storm. After a hectic week, we're bent on escape, a route to paradise tucked under each arm. It's easy to concentrate on what's labeled "noteworthy and new." The space itself, one square, tidy plot, is small, and despite its bold presence on this understated corner of the city, the atmosphere is almost subdued.

This was the site of lonely times. In my first months in Minneapolis, I was so broke I had to choose between groceries and the steamy scenes in paperback mysteries. It took her three buses and half a day roundtrip to get here and back from her home; in those lean, love-starved years before we knew each other, the chance of sharing these passions seemed like pure fairy tale.

Now it's the site where our separate pasts and our current lusts—for language, for stories, for bookshops far and near, and for each other—bring us even closer together. Here, it is always morning. Or is it midnight? Always April. Or is it November? Here, we're in a country we've invented or one we remember. Here, we stand at the yellow dragon canyon of Huanglong or at the placid edge of Lake Balaton. We're hiking a rugged plateau or traipsing across a salt-pocked beach fourteen hundred feet below sea level. Here is the whole infinite and spectacular world, bound in every direction by ceiling, walls, and floor, a place we travel again and again, though we have never seen it before.

Contributors

LUCY JANE BLEDSOE travels to justify her writing and writes to justify her traveling. She's the author of *The Ice Cave: A Woman's Adventures from the Mojave to the Antarctic* and of several novels.

LOUISE A. BLUM is the author of the novel *Amnesty* and the memoir *You're Not from Around Here, Are You?* She was raised in a small town by a father who believed that any destination east of the Mississippi was the equivalent of Sodom and Gomorrah. A survivor of several cross-country trips westward in the back seat of the family station wagon, she reached adulthood with the firm desire to travel anywhere else. She lives in upstate New York with her partner and their daughter, Zoë, who at thirteen has already made her own pilgrimage to Mexico without either of her moms.

REBECCA CHEKOURAS is a freelance writer who lives and works in the San Francisco Bay Area. Her work has appeared in the *San Francisco Chronicle* and *Curve* magazine. Her first novel is set in Palm Springs, where she is a frequent visitor. She is at work on a second novel, about the mother-daughter relationship. She was a finalist for Astraea's Lesbian Writers Fund for fiction.

JANE CHURCHON works part-time as a nurse and full-time as a partner to her legal spouse, MK. She wishes that her name were something exotic, like "Cassandra" or "Acacia," but has learned to live with telling people that her name is "Jane, like Tarzan." One day she plans to return to Chartres to walk the labyrinth and will then learn the answers to all the eternal questions. In the meantime, she is trying to satisfy herself with knowing the names of her cats and her two children. Her work has appeared in *The Sun*, the *Berkeley Fiction Review*, *Cup of Comfort for Nurses*, and the *American River Review*.

TZIVIA GOVER, author of *Mindful Moments for Stressful Days*, lives in western Massachusetts. Her articles and essays have appeared in numerous publications, including the *New York Times*, the *Boston Globe*, *Creative Nonfiction*, the *Christian Science Monitor*, and over a dozen anthologies. Her poems have appeared in *Lilith*, *The Bark*, and the *Berkshire Review*, among others. Gover received her MFA in creative nonfiction from Columbia University. When airfare isn't in her budget, she finds that writing is a great way to travel on the wings of thought and imagination.

KATE LYNN HIBBARD is from Saint Paul, Minnesota, which is exactly like Las Vegas minus the gambling, drive-in chapels, lack of water, and desert heat. She lives with her partner, two pugs, two cats, and a fair amount of pet hair. Her first book of poems, *Sleeping Upside Down* (2006), won the Gerald Cable Book Award. Her macaroni salad could be the subject of a major motion picture.

JOURDAN IMANI KEITH lives in Seattle because it feeds her country mouse/city mouse personality. Voted Seattle Poet Populist, she is a playwright, storyteller, and educator. Her work blends the textures of political, personal, and natural landscapes to offer voices from the margins of America. She's a Hedgebrook alum and a recipient of the Office of Arts and Cultural Affairs for her play, *The Uterine Files: Episode 1, Voices Spitting Out Rainbows*. The founder of Urban Wilderness Project, Keith believes that connecting to the natural world is critical to restoring communities, reducing domestic violence, and healing historical injustices.

Whether or not GILLIAN KENDALL was moved too early, too far, and too often by her peripatetic parents is a subject of family debate. However, she has continued the trend as a grown-up. She has lived in five countries and seven states, out of thousands of cardboard boxes. She, her beloved cats, dogs, and human partner currently live on a nearly dry creek in drought-stricken Melbourne, Australia, although they plan to move to Vancouver Island for the rain. Her fiction, essays, features, and travel stories have appeared in many magazines, including *The Sun* and *Curve,* and her most recent book is *Mr. Ding's Chicken Feet.*

SANDRA GAIL LAMBERT is an all-around nature nerd who lives and kayaks in Gainesville, Florida. It took her long enough to be a writer, but there were always clues. As a child she read through whole libraries, she's always collected bookmarks—wood, leather, beaded, and tatted—and then there was that decade she spent in a feminist bookstore. She was first published in *Common Lives/Lesbian Lives.* More recently, her work has appeared in the journals *Gertrude* and *Breath and Shadow,* as well as the anthology *First Person Queer.* She blogs about her writing life at www.sandralambert.com.

PEARLIE MCNEILL, an Australian writer, spent her early adult years in and out of psychiatric hospitals. This experience became her starting point as a writer. She started with just one rule: *Write with emotion, edit with reason, but not at the same time.* Since then she has been published widely and has completed a master of creative arts; this contribution is the first chapter of her doctor of creative arts.

LESLÉA NEWMAN is the author of more than fifty books, including the short-story collection *A Letter to Harvey Milk,* the poetry collection *Nobody's Mother,* the forthcoming novel *The Reluctant Daughter,* and the children's books *A Fire Engine for Ruthie, The Best Cat in the World,* and *Heather Has Two Mommies.* Currently she is a faculty member of the Stonecoast MFA program at the University of Southern Maine and the Poet Laureate of Northampton, Massachusetts. Lesléa is happily (and legally!) married to the butch of her dreams, Mary Newman Vazquez, and devoted to their furry feline goddess, Princess Sheba Darling.

SHEILA ORTIZ TAYLOR is a California-born writer who taught fiction writing and literature at Florida State University for thirty-three years. She came out formally, though not finally, when her first novel, *Faultline,* was published in 1982. Her career as professor of literature and creative writing at Florida State University ended, appropriately enough, with the publication of *OutRageous,* the academic novel she had always promised herself she would write. Now she is retired in the Florida she learned to love and lives happily with her partner of seventeen years. Her work includes seven novels, a memoir of childhood, and a volume of poetry.

SUZANNE PARKER is usually a poet, but something about Mexico—the landscape, people, tequila—freed the prose writer in her. When not traveling, she's an assistant professor of English and codirector of the creative writing program at Brookdale Community College. Suzanne's poetry has been published in numerous journals; she's won the Alice M. Sellars Award from the Academy of American Poets and was a Poetry Fellow at the Prague Summer Seminars, where she watched *Dr. Faustus,* in Czech, in Vysehrad Castle and didn't understand a word but was still blown away.

SIMA RABINOWITZ, author of *The Jewish Fake Book* and *Murmuration,* is pretty sure she's real, even if the rest of the world seems surreal most of the time. The most interesting people, exotic places, and fascinating experiences she has known have been between the covers of a book. As she writes this, all of the independent bookstores mentioned in her story are still, happily, in business.

RUTHANN ROBSON maintains a postcard collection, a position as a professor of law and Distinguished University Professor, a writing life that tends toward the experimental, and a website at www.ruthann robson.com.

LAUREN SANDERS is the author of two novels, *With or Without You* and *Kamikaze Lust,* winner of a Lambda Literary Award. She lives in the nation of Brooklyn and in the Catskill Mountains, where she idles away the hours harvesting organic vegetables and throwing a chewed-up red Frisbee up the hill for her dog. She and her partner have recently taken up beekeeping and dream of one day owning chickens.

PATTY SMITH, originally from Massachusetts, lived in Paris and Brussels before wanderlust took her to Senegal. She finally moved to Richmond, Virginia, where she currently lives with her partner and two cats. She has been a teacher of French and now teaches American literature and creative writing to high school students in Petersburg, Virginia. Her nonfiction appears in *One Teacher in Ten: Gay and Lesbian Educators Tell Their Stories* and *Tied in Knots: Funny Stories from the Wedding Day*. Her fiction appears in *So to speak: a feminist journal of language and art* and the *Tusculum Review*.

LORI SODERLIND is the author of *Chasing Montana*, a memoir. Her essay "Sixty-six Signs That the Former Student Who Invited You to Dinner Is Trying to Seduce You" appears in the *Norton Anthology of Creative Nonfiction*. She can type about eighty words a minute without ever looking at her fingers, which gives her something to fall back on. Though she lives in Manhattan, in her heart she is a back-to-the-land, tree-hugging dirt worshipper who wishes she had more time to spend building pole barns.

HANNAH TENNANT-MOORE is a Brooklyn-based freelance writer and an MFA candidate in the Bennington Writing Seminars. She has made regular contributions to *Tricycle: The Buddhist Review* and *Babble,* and her work has appeared or is forthcoming in *The Sun, Best Buddhist Writing 2008,* the *Gay and Lesbian Review Worldwide,* and elsewhere. Hannah recently moved from Santa Barbara to New York via Amtrak train, meaning that she spent 125 hours reading Dostoyevsky and drinking Tecates with her manic Venezuelan seatmate. She's still recovering from the experience.